D1049676

THE OVERBURDENED
ECONOMY

THE OVERBURDENED ECONOMY

UNCOVERING THE CAUSES OF CHRONIC UNEMPLOYMENT, INFLATION, AND NATIONAL DECLINE

Lloyd J. Dumas

UNIVERSITY OF CALIFORNIA PRESS

Berkeley   Los Angeles   London

University of California Press
Berkeley and Los Angeles, California

University of California Press, Ltd.
London, England

Library of Congress Cataloging-in-Publication Data

Dumas, Lloyd J.
  The overburdened economy.
  Includes index.
    1. Unemployment—United States. 2. Underemployment—
United States. 3. Poor—United States. 4. United
States—Economic conditions—1981–   . I. Title.
HD5724.D775   1986   331.13'7973   85-20856
ISBN 0-520-05686-8

Printed in the United States of America

1 2 3 4 5 6 7 8 9

*To Seymour Melman, my friend and col-
league, who taught me much that
changed the pattern of my life*

*And to E. F. Schumacher, whom I did not
know, but who nevertheless taught me
that humanism and economics are not
disparate concerns*

Contents

Acknowledgments

The fabric of this work is woven from the threads of many ideas accumulated over a long period of years. Unfortunately, it is not possible to specifically mention all the creative and caring people who have helped shape the thinking here embodied. This acknowledgment must therefore be only partial.

There is little question that many directions of thought in this analysis were triggered by the insistent, impassioned, and provocative ideas of Seymour Melman. Never one to avoid controversy, Seymour's insights derive from a combination of great personal integrity and deep understanding of and commitment to the principles of free inquiry and democracy that are this nation's greatest legacy.

Many long, late-night conversations with my friend and former colleague Robert A. Karasek are clearly reflected herein. Much was gained in sharpness and clarity by the specific comments and proddings of those who read various drafts with a critical eye. My thanks especially to Kenneth Boulding, John Kenneth Galbraith, and a number of still anonymous referees. More generally, I am grateful for the support, encouragement, and faith of my parents, Edith and Marcel Dumas, and my friends, S. Brooks Morton, Randolph Riddle, and Tina Dill. I also very much appreciate the responsiveness and enthusiasm of Naomi Schneider, my editor at U.C. Press, as well as the patience and helpfulness of Dorothy Luttrell and Cynthia Keheley, who processed much of the manuscript.

Finally, it is difficult to describe all of the many ways Dana Dunn has contributed to this work. Her professional criticisms were always pointed and insightful as well as remarkably gentle. Her patience, encouragement, enthusiasm, and ability to share seemed boundless and carried me through many rough spots. And perhaps most of all, Dana gave me the rainbow that marked the end of a storm and the beginning of a brighter new day.

Preface

This is a very important book. Such a statement is not easy to justify and may take fifty years to prove, but it is my considered judgment. Lloyd Dumas has challenged one of the implicit assumptions of the Keynesian revolution and the national income statistics that embodied it: the assumption that all activity which is paid for must be productive. His questioning of this assumption may well set off a reorganization of the economic information system and point a new direction for economic research that will greatly improve our understanding of economic events. There are many indications that the time is ripe for a reorganization of economic thought, a new Kuhnian revolution, stimulated by the search for a more humanistic economics. Among these indications are the development of grants economics, the study of one-way transfers, both explicit and implicit, and the growing consensus that the simpler Keynesian model has failed in the face of the inflation-unemployment dilemma. Dumas's work is a very valuable contribution to the coming transformation of economic thought.

The development of more useful taxonomies—that is, systems for classifying, and thus simplifying, the immense complexity of the real world—is vital to the growth of human knowledge. Alchemy, for example, never got anywhere because it had the elements wrong: earth, air, fire, and water are hopelessly heterogeneous aggregates. With the development of a proper classification of the elements into oxygen, hydrogen, and so forth near the end of the eighteenth century, the science of chemistry flowered, progressing in both theory and application. The problem of taxonomy in social systems is much more difficult, simply because of the immense variety and complexity of the human race, its activities, and its artifacts. Each human being is different from every other who has ever lived—even identical twins differ significantly. The human mind, however, cannot handle this complexity. We are forced to make aggregates such as nations, classes, industries, occupations, and factors of production in order to make sense of and to act upon the complexity that confronts us so disturbingly. It is very easy, however, to get these aggregates wrong and to lump things together that are essentially different while separating things that are essentially alike. I have argued that some venerable aggregates of economic taxonomy—for instance, the factors of production land, labor, and capital—are almost as heterogeneous as earth, air, fire, and water. A much more useful set of factors of production would include know-how, a genetic factor which is limited by energy, materials, space, and time in their various manifestations.

The importance of Dumas's work lies in his revised taxonomy of rewarded economic activity, which he divides into *contributive*, *neutral*, and *distractive* sectors. Some may be uncomfortable with the terminology: although Dumas specifies that these terms are not value laden, it is hard not to prefer contributive to neutral activity and neutral to distractive activity. Others might prefer the term *economic* for *contributive*, and *noneconomic* for *distractive*, but this choice too could be seen as somewhat value laden. Taking a broader perspective, Dumas insists that economic activity is not always an ultimate good: beyond the economic there is a greater good, the quality of human life. Thus, economic activity, which produces the "necessaries and conveniences of life," is itself merely an instrumental good to be evaluated in terms of the overarching good of the quality of life. This is a view that Dumas shares with Adam Smith.

Contributive activity in Dumas's more strictly economic sense is that which increases the final product, which in turn consists of things that people want enough to be willing to pay for them. Neutral activity is that which is paid for but which does not contribute anything to the final product—featherbedding, sinecures, paperpushing, the provision of useless information, and so forth. Such activity can be considered part of what I have termed the "implicit grants economy," a redistribution of income or command over the product from those who produce it to those who do not. This edges toward Marx's concept of "surplus value" (which, however, is also a hopelessly confused taxonomic class). The question of whether interest and profit become neutral beyond a certain point is one that must be faced and on which further research is needed. The most optimistic might want to identify the distractive sector with public goods, since it includes not only the war industry, but such things as monuments, public splendor, palaces, cathedrals, and wilderness areas.

For every important classification system there are marginal cases and Dumas's is no exception. There is no doubt, however, that Dumas's classification is important and useful, particularly in identifying social pathologies. The neutral and distractive sectors are not necessarily pathological, but they have a very strong tendency to become so, simply because of the positive-feedback processes generated by such phenomena as the arms race, proliferation of bureaucracies and hierarchies, and political corruption.

Was there in the Middle Ages a "cathedral race" something like our arms race, in which each city tried to outbuild the other? There was certainly a "palace race" in the eighteenth century that culminated in Versailles, a race which probably hastened the French Revolution. Self-perpetuation may characterize even the contributive sector, causing phenomena such as the conspicuous consumption of "keeping up with the Joneses." But in the contributive sector, the disease is likely to be mild, a head cold rather than a fatal fever as it so frequently is in the distractive sector. The present-day pathologies of the distractive are so extreme that the term *fatal* is surely justified.

From time to time in the history of human thought, a new idea has emerged, perhaps in a somewhat tentative form, and then has been driven underground where it continues on its course, eventually re-emerging from its tunnel. The Dumas taxonomy can certainly be traced back to an important idea in Adam Smith's *The Wealth of Nations*: the distinction between productive and unproductive labor, there formulated rather imperfectly. The idea remained underground for almost two hundred years and has now finally emerged in Dumas's work in a purified and more significant form. Such an emergence of a new idea from below ground is usually not very well regarded by those following the mainstream, or perhaps one should say turnpike, above ground. It may take some time for this idea to gain the turnpike; however, I will be surprised if it does not. The current traffic in economic ideas must make way for new vehicles; Dumas's is among the most promising. This is why I have no hesitation in again calling it an important book.

Kenneth E. Boulding
Institute of Behavioral Science
University of Colorado, Boulder

1

The Appearance of Progress, The Reality of Decline

The Recovery That Wasn't

During the 1984 presidential campaign, there was much talk of the vigor and strength of the American economy. A powerful recovery was under way. Real gross national product (GNP) was growing at 6.8 percent in 1984, faster than at any time since the mid-1950s.[1] The consumer price index was rising at 4.3 percent, faster than the 3.2 percent rate in 1983, but slower than in any other year since the early 1970s.[2] At the same time, the civilian unemployment rate had dropped from a post-Depression record of 10.7 percent in late 1982 to 7.2 percent at the end of 1984.[3] And the U.S. dollar was showing impressive strength internationally, reaching a seven-year high against the strong Swiss franc and twelve-year highs against the German mark and Dutch guilder—and faring even better against the French franc, Italian lira, British pound, and Canadian dollar.[4]

Rapid growth, low inflation, falling unemployment, and a strong dollar: the economy was in good shape and getting better. Though there were audible grumblings, mainly about federal budget deficits and the rising national debt, most economists were optimistic. Even mildly negative signs, normally read as troubling—such as slowing growth, slightly rising unemployment, and uncertain behavior of the index of leading indicators—tended to be reinterpreted: these were actually good signs. The economy was moving to a more viable long-term growth path. America was once again an economic powerhouse.

But this was a most peculiar recovery.

Poverty and hunger.   According to the Census Bureau, during the upswing of 1983 the national poverty rate reached 15.2 percent. This was the greatest proportion of Americans living in poverty since President Johnson's antipoverty campaign began nearly two decades earlier. The poverty rate had, in fact, grown every year since the 1970s. Six million more people were living in poverty in 1983 than in 1980, nearly 900,000 of them added between 1982 and 1983.[5] While the official poverty rate did decline to 14.4 percent in 1984, the rate was still higher than it had been in any year from 1970 to 1980. For some categories of the U.S. population the 1984 poverty rate did not change, but remained at distressingly high levels: more than 46 percent of blacks under the age of eighteen continued to live in poverty. In total, more Americans were living in poverty in 1984 than in 1964—despite the retreat from the peak level reached one year earlier.[6]

Where there is poverty, hunger is usually close by. The 1985 report of the Physician Task Force on Hunger in America testifies to the severity of the problem, bearing the ominous title "Hunger in America: The Growing Epidemic." It defines the hungry as those who either periodically exhaust their food supply or are persistently unable to purchase an adequate diet; while acknowledging that "no one knows the precise number of hungry Americans," the report estimates that the number may be as high as twenty million. According to the task force report, clinics in poor areas have reported cases of diseases usually found among severely malnourished populations in less developed countries. These include kwashiorkor (a protein deficiency disease) and maramus (a condition of advanced emaciation), as well as vitamin deficiencies, lethargy, and stunting. Soup kitchens reminiscent of the days of the Great Depression have reappeared in America, and lines at these soup kitchens and food pantries have been growing—in a nation whose bountiful harvests have made it a food supplier to much of the world! The report concludes that hunger has worsened, not diminished, during the "recovery."[7]

While the ranks of the poor have swelled, a much larger segment of the U.S. population has seen its economic improvement halted. Over the first half of the 1980s, real compensation per hour in the nonfarm business sector rose only one-tenth of one percent. That is, wages and salaries (including employer contributions to social insurance and private benefit plans), adjusted for inflation, were virtually the same in 1984 as in 1979. Though improvements occurred between 1982 and 1984, they barely made up for declines in 1980 and 1981. In fact, the 1984 increase was only three-tenths percent, less than a fifth of what it had been in 1983. In 1984, the purchasing power of wages and salaries was actually less than it had been as far back as 1976.[8]

Bank failures.   Another disturbing trend of the eighties is the dramatic increase in the rate of bank failures: in the United States, 14 percent more commercial banks failed in 1983 than in 1982, and 65 percent more in 1984 than in 1983. By October 1985, the 1984 rate of commercial bank failures had already been surpassed. If the failure rate registered in the first nine months of 1985 continues through year's end, some 50 percent more commercial banks will fail in 1985 than in 1984.[9] Some have blamed the progressive deregulation of banks for the nearly three hundred failures since 1981. While deregulation may have played a significant role, the reduction of controls does not compel banks to engage in the sorts of practices that lead to their demise. A sufficiently buoyant economy would not have produced this phenomenon.

National debt.   At the end of 1974, the interest-bearing public debt of the United States stood at just under $475 billion. Only a decade later the national debt had more than tripled, reaching nearly $1560 billion by the end of 1984. As of the first quarter of 1985, the federal budget deficit projected for the 1985 fiscal year exceeded that for 1984. Even if the projected 1985 deficit were cut in half, the United States will have added as much to its national debt in the first six years of the eighties as in the preceding two centuries.[10] One of the consequences of this enormous accumulation of debt is that the federal budget has become less controllable. Interest payments on the rapidly growing debt must be met: as contractual obligations of the federal government, they are not subject to the discretion of the administration or of Congress. In an interview with the *Wall Street Journal*, the chief economist of Equitable Life Assurance pointed out that the fraction of federal spending devoted simply to paying interest on the national debt has nearly doubled during this decade and, he estimated, it could nearly double again in a recession to push the federal deficit over $300 billion.[11] The burgeoning interest payments have already offset even deep cuts in nonmilitary federal programs. As the *New York Times* reported in August 1984, "Over the last three years the *increase* in interest payments on the federal debt *exceeds all the savings . . .* achieved in health, education, welfare, and social service programs" by federal budget cuts since 1981 (emphasis added).[12] In September 1985, the president of the Federal Reserve Bank of New York estimated the interest cost of servicing the federal debt in 1985 at $130 billion—"roughly equal to total personal income tax collections from every taxpayer west of the Mississippi River."[13] He went on to project: "If the current efforts at reducing federal budget deficits are not successful, then even under fairly optimistic economic conditions, the annual cost of servicing the federal debt by 1990 will be in the neighborhood of $210 billion. That will mean that for every five dollars collected from the individual income tax, two dollars will go toward paying federal net interest liabilities."[14] None of these can be regarded as positive developments.

An even more important consequence of accelerated federal borrowing since 1980 has been its dramatic impact on the real cost of borrowing money. As the federal government entered capital markets on a grand scale to finance its rapidly growing debt, real interest rates were driven sharply higher. This is, of course, the predictable result of the government's adding greatly to the demand for loanable funds in the absence of a substantial increase in the pool of money made available by willing lenders. Real interest rates (i.e., interest rates adjusted for the rate of inflation) surged upward in 1981. For example, the prime rate charged by banks, adjusted for changes in the consumer price index, more than quadrupled in 1981, rising to 8.5 percent from the 1980 level of 1.8 percent. That 1981 rate more than doubled the previous peak rate of 3.7 percent reached in 1959. In 1982, the real rate rose still higher to 8.8 percent. It did decline somewhat during the next two years, but still stood at 7.7 percent in 1984, more than double the 1959 peak.[15]

High real interest rates seriously hamper industry's ability to finance new plant and equipment expenditures needed to modernize facilities. Similarly, high real rates make purchases of big-ticket items such as houses and automobiles more difficult for consumers. The combination of inflation and high interest rates has already put home ownership beyond the means of an ever larger proportion of the new generation of would-be home buyers, tarnishing a piece of the American dream.

Mortgage foreclosures. The dream of home ownership has become elusive even for many Americans who thought they had already achieved it. Reports in early 1985 indicated that "the rate of home mortgage foreclosures has increased to a level close to the record set in the 1974 recession, causing anguish for tens of thousands of Americans evicted from homes for which they can no longer afford monthly payments." [16] The Federal Housing and Veterans administrations (FHA and VA), the federal agencies that together guarantee about 25 percent of home mortgages (mainly for low and middle income clients), found themselves with record numbers of foreclosed homes by early 1985. The VA foreclosed 10 percent more homes in 1984 than in 1983; the FHA's inventory of foreclosed homes rose more than 40 percent from August 1983 through February 1985—during eighteen months of the "recovery." In early 1985, the executive vice president of the Mortgage Insurance Companies of America, whose members underwrite the 75 percent of American home mortgages not covered by VA or FHA, projected the industry's 1985 insurance claim payments for home foreclosures at $425 million—three times what they were in 1982. [17]

Foreign indebtedness. In addition to the huge increase in the *amount* of the national debt, there has been a change in its character: a growing fraction is now owed to foreigners. As the *Wall Street Journal* pointed out in the fall of 1984, "Government deficits . . . are soaking up savings at an alarming rate, forcing the nation to borrow heavily from abroad." [18] In 1983, some 16 percent of U.S. Treasury securities outstanding—nearly $164 billion—was owned by foreigners. [19] The increased foreign purchase of U.S. government and private securities has pumped additional money into American capital markets (while draining financial markets abroad), preventing high real interest rates in the U.S. from rising still higher. But the U.S. economy has become more dependent on these foreign sources of capital, a potentially dangerous situation. Leonard Silk, economic columnist for the *New York Times*, put it this way: "If the huge net inflow of savings from abroad were to stop, chaos would follow. The Federal Reserve would be confronted with the dilemma of whether to finance the huge deficits and risk inflation, or refuse to finance them and risk depression. It would be a no-win choice." [20]

It is difficult to predict just how long foreign sources will continue to pour huge amounts of financial capital into U.S. government and corporate securities. It could go on for a long time. On the other hand, by early 1985 the European market for U.S. corporate securities was beginning to experience serious problems. In less than two months at the beginning of 1985, American corporations had raised more than $6 billion through bond issues in the so-called Eurodollar market. This was almost one-third of the record amount they had raised in all of 1984. But international commercial and investment bankers underwriting these bond issues were having a hard time selling them. The deputy chairman of the leading underwriter of Eurodollar bonds estimated that supply was outrunning demand by five to one in that market. [21] This may represent only a temporary disturbance. But it is worth noting, as the *New York Times* reported, that "this is the first time since the Eurodollar new issue market began heating up four years ago that international investors have so firmly turned their backs on the bonds of so many of America's blue chip corporations." [22] It is not a good sign.

Net debtor status.   During the mid-1980s, in the midst of the "strong recovery," the United States rapidly approached net debtor nation status. It has been some seventy years since this country has been a net debtor internationally. Yet in 1983, total foreign holdings in the United States reached more than three-quarters of a trillion dollars—almost 90 percent as much as U.S. holdings abroad. [23] Testifying before Congress in February 1984, Paul Volcker, chair of the Federal Reserve Board, expressed serious concern at this state of affairs:

> It is ominous that the recorded net investment position of the United States overseas, built up gradually over the postwar period, will in the space of only three years—1983, 1984, 1985—be reversed. If the data at all reflect reality, the largest and richest economy in the world is on the verge of becoming a net debtor internationally and would soon be the largest. [24]

By summer 1985 the United States had already crossed the boundary to net debtor status, prompting James Robinson, chair and chief executive officer of the American Express Company, to express this concern even more strongly.

> The rapid transformation of the United States from the world's largest creditor to potentially its first trillion-dollar debtor is taking place virtually unnoticed. For the first time since World War I, our liabilities to foreigners exceed foreign liabilities to the U.S. . . . Before the next presidential election, our foreign debt could outstrip the total debt of all developing countries.[25]

This would be no mean feat, considering the astronomical heights to which the international debt of the Third World countries has recently risen.

Growing poverty, stagnating real income, a rising tide of bank failures, soaring national debt, surging real rates of interest, increasing dependency on foreign capital, and a plunge into international net debtor status: these are not the stuff of which economic recoveries are usually made. These serious problems are less disturbing, however, than another feature of our recent economic performance: the rapidly worsening international balance of trade.

The balance of trade.   In 1983, the United States imported $69.4 billion more merchandise than it exported, for a record balance of trade deficit. The trade deficit for 1984 reached $123.3 billion, nearly 78 percent higher than the record set the previous year. One might think that this trade deficit is the result of imports of high-priced oil and other costly raw materials. But the trade deficit on manufactured goods alone was $78.4 billion in 1984. In other words, if the United States had imported and exported only manufactured goods in 1984, it still would have easily broken the all-time overall trade deficit record set in 1983. In fact, if America's total exports in 1984 had remained the same, and it had imported only manufactured goods, its trade accounts would still have shown a multibillion dollar deficit.[26]

The soaring trade deficit is more than a financial matter. Its significance extends beyond imbalances in international currency flows, to a fundamental weakness of U.S. industry: its inability to compete with foreign firms both at home and abroad. If the price and quality of American goods were sufficiently attractive to foreigners, exports would be far higher; if they were attractive to Americans, we would not be awash in a flood of imported goods. The net result would be trade surpluses, not record-breaking deficits. An economy whose industries cannot compete internationally is in serious trouble—and headed for even deeper trouble over the long term.

In short, there is considerably less to this much-touted "recovery" than meets the eye. Rather than a real period of economic revitalization, it has been a temporary burst of highly distorted growth fueled by an orgy of debt. But our economic difficulties are not confined to the past few years: their roots extend back much further, into the post–World War II period. We now turn to the exploration of some of these long-term trends.

Long-Term Economic Decay

Inflation and unemployment.   In a 1960 article on anti-inflation policy, the noted economists Paul Samuelson and Robert Solow attempted to roughly estimate the much-discussed trade-off between inflation and unemployment. Looking at annual data for the period 1933–58, they estimated the cost of eliminating inflation to be about a 5 to 6 percent rate of unemployment. On the other hand, full employment (defined as about 3 percent unemployment in those days) was achievable at the cost of roughly 4 to 5 percent inflation.[27] These are very interesting numbers for comparison with actual events. In thirteen of the fifteen years since 1970, the unemployment rate in the United States met or exceeded the 5 to 6 percent level supposedly associated with zero inflation. Yet in none of those fifteen years did the annual inflation rate drop below 3 percent. On the other hand, in thirteen years of that same 1970–84 period, the rate of inflation met or exceeded the 4 to 5 percent level said to be associated with full employment (i.e., 3 percent unemployment). Yet none of those fifteen years saw full employment; in fact, the annual unemployment rate never dropped below 4.9 percent. In eleven of the fifteen years, the inflation rate was at or beyond the level that should have produced full employment, *at the same time* that the unemployment rate was at or beyond the level that should have entirely eliminated inflation.[28]

Clearly, the pattern of unemployment and inflation significantly shifted between the 1933–58 period studied and the period that began in 1970. The problems of inflation and unemployment have both become worse, and the trade-off between them more severe, since lowered inflation now seems to have a higher cost in terms of unemployment, and vice versa.

This trend can best be seen not by looking at monthly, quarterly, or even annual fluctuations, but by looking at longer-term changes. The data presented in table 1—annual rates of inflation and unemployment averaged over five- and ten-year periods for the years 1950–84—clearly illustrate these trends. For the two decades from 1950 to 1969, the five-year average annual rates of inflation were quite moderate, ranging between 1.2 and 3.4 percent. From 1970 on, the averages rose dramatically, ranging from 6.1 percent to 8.1 percent. Looked at another way, the average annual rate of inflation for the 1950–69 period was about 2.2 percent; the average annual rate since then has more than tripled, to 7.2 percent. Between 1950 and 1969, the five-year average unemployment rates ranged from a low of 3.8 percent (roughly full employment) to a high of 5.7 percent. From 1970 on, the *lowest* five-year average was 5.4 percent, nearly as high as the upper limit for 1950–69. The average annual rate of civilian unemployment from 1950 to 1969 was about 4.7 percent; since 1970, the average rate has been 6.9 percent, nearly 50 percent higher than the pre-1970 average.

The increasing severity of the inflation unemployment trade-off is also obvious. In the 1950–54 period, there was essentially full employment on the average, yet the inflation rate averaged only 2.5 percent. The five years from 1960 to 1964 saw a much higher average unemployment rate of 5.7 percent, but inflation averaged much lower—only 1.2 percent. After 1970 it was a different story. Whereas a 5.4 percent average unemployment rate accompanied inflation averaging just over 6 percent in 1970–74, by 1980–84 even an 8.3 percent average unemployment rate was insufficient to lower inflation below 7.5 percent.

Trends of rising unemployment and inflation, and a worsening trade-off between them, are signs of a deteriorating economy. But they are far from the only signs.

Productivity.   Although it is an imperfect measure, labor productivity has traditionally been used as a key indicator of the effi-

Table 1   U.S. Inflation and Unemployment Trends, 1950–84

Period	Average Annual Rate of Inflation[a]	Average Annual Rate of Unemployment[b]
Five-year Trends		
1950–54	2.5%	4.0%
1955–59	1.6	5.0
1960–64	1.2	5.7
1965–69	3.4	3.8
1970–74	6.1	5.4
1975–79	8.1	7.0
1980–84	7.5	8.3
Ten-year Trends (except 1980–84)		
1950–59	2.1	4.5
1960–69	2.3	4.8
1970–79	7.1	6.2
1980–84	7.5	8.3

Source: Calculated from data in appendix B, Economic Report of the President (February 1985), (Washington, D.C.: Government Printing Office, 1985).

[a] Averages of year-to-year changes in the consumer price index for all items, from table B–56, p. 296.

[b] Averages of unemployed as percent of civilian labor force, from table B–33, p. 271.

ciency of production. Since productivity is very much affected by temporary factors linked to the business cycle, long-term trends in labor productivity are more meaningful indicators of the true efficiency of production than are short-term fluctuations.[29] Table 2 presents data on productivity growth trends in the United States from 1950 to 1984; annual growth rates of output per labor-hour in the nonfarm business sector are averaged over five- and ten-year periods. Once again, the deterioration is quite clear. The average annual productivity growth rates for the period 1950–69 ranged from just over 2 percent to nearly 3 percent. From 1970 to 1984, the average rate was stable at about 1.4 percent. For the twenty-year period before 1970, the average annual rate of productivity growth was 2.5 percent, nearly twice as high as the average rate after 1970. With the exception of 1960–64, the five-year productivity growth averages show a fairly steady downward trend.

Table 2   U.S. Productivity Growth and Pay Trends, 1950–84

Period	Average Annual Rate of Productivity Growth		Average Annual Change in Real Compensation per Hour[c]
	Total Nonfarm Business Sector[a] (output per hour)	Manufacturing Only[b] (output per worker)	
Five-year Trends			
1950–54	2.6%	3.3%	3.2%
1955–59	2.3	4.5	2.9
1960–64	2.9	3.0	2.6
1965–69	2.1	2.6	2.3
1970–74	1.4	3.0	1.3
1975–79	1.3	1.0	0.5
1980–84[d]	1.4	0.7	0.0
Ten-year Trends (except 1980–84)			
1950–59	2.5%	3.9%	3.1%
1960–69	2.5	2.8	2.5
1970–79	1.4	2.0	0.9
1980–84[d]	1.4	0.7	0.0

Source: Calculated from data in appendix B, *Economic Report of the President (February 1985),* (Washington, D.C.: Government Printing Office, 1985).

[a] Averages of annual changes in output per hour of all persons in the nonfarm business sector; table B–41, p. 279.

[b] Averages of annual output per hour of wage and salary workers in manufacturing. Calculated by dividing the Federal Reserve Board industrial production index for total manufacturing (table B–42, p. 280) by the total number of wage and salary workers in manufacturing (table B–37, p. 275) for each year, computing annual changes, then averaging over the number of years in the indicated period. Note that these data are *not strictly comparable* to the data for productivity in the total nonfarm business sector, though each of these different measures of productivity is internally consistent and properly reflects the trends within its own area of coverage.

[c] Averages of annual changes in hourly compensation, adjusted for inflation using the consumer price index for all urban consumers (table B–41, p. 279). Hourly compensation includes wages and salaries of employees plus employers' contributions for social insurance and private benefit plans. Also includes estimate of same for self-employed persons.

[d] Preliminary figures are used for 1984. The five-year trend for total nonfarm business sector productivity is calculated using a figure for 1984 revised by the Department of Labor on 28 February 1985, as reported in "Productivity Up 2.7% in 1984" (*New York Times*, 1 Mar. 1985).

It has frequently been alleged that this decline in productivity growth rates has been caused largely by the shift to a service economy. Since productivity has historically grown more slowly in services than in manufacturing, this kind of shift would tend to slow overall productivity growth. But, as is clear from table 2, productivity growth in manufacturing alone has followed a roughly similar course. During the twenty years before 1970, manufacturing productivity grew at an average annual rate of 3.4 percent, more than twice as high as the 1.6 percent rate after 1970. For the past thirty years, manufacturing productivity has declined fairly steadily.

This decline is really quite serious. Improving the efficiency with which a nation's industries can produce is critical to improving the economic well-being of its population. It is also crucial to the success of those industries in competing effectively with industries abroad. Let us consider each of these issues.

Pay trends. Judged by the criterion of five- or ten-year average annual changes in real compensation per hour (given in table 2), growth in the economic well-being of Americans has steadily diminished for the past thirty-five years. Once more, there is a sharp difference between the pre- and post-1970 patterns: real pay per hour increased at an average rate of 2.7 percent per year during 1950–69, four times the 0.6 percent rate of increase during 1970–84. And during the eighties, gains in purchasing power earned per hour worked have been nil.

Trade deficits. The first section of this chapter described the record-shattering levels of America's international trade deficits in recent years. These deficits demonstrate the inability of domestic producers to hold markets against foreign competition—which in turn reflects the deterioration of productivity discussed earlier in this section. But since the sharp decline of productivity growth has not been confined to recent years, shouldn't the trade deficit have been a long-term problem as well?

From 1894 through 1970, the United States had a balance of trade surplus every single year. For more than three-quarters of a century, the nation exported goods and services of greater value than those it imported. But virtually every year since 1970 (1973 and 1975 being the sole exceptions), the United States has had a balance of trade deficit.[30] The reversal was sharp and dramatic, and the rapidity with which the excess of imports over exports has increased is equally striking. From 1971 to 1975, the trade deficit averaged just over $4.0 billion per year. In the next five-year period, 1976–80, the annual average deficit was nearly nine times as large, at $35.1 billion. The data through 1984 show that *every year* since 1980 the annual trade deficit has been larger still, averaging almost twice as high ($68.8 billion) as during the preceding five years.[31]

Though the competitive weakness revealed by growing trade deficits has become strikingly worse in recent years, it clearly is not just a recent phenomenon. For nearly a decade and a half, domestic producers have been losing their struggle with foreign competitors. It is particularly important to be aware of the long-term trend here because it so clearly gives the lie to commonly offered, simplistic explanations of America's balance-of-trade problems. We are told that the surprising strength of the U.S. dollar relative to foreign currencies has caused the problem: a strong dollar makes U.S. products too expensive for foreigners and foreign products all too attractive to Americans. It is, of course, true that the growing strength of the dollar has worsened the competitive position of U.S. producers. But the dollar has been gaining strength only in the past few years, since about 1980. The trade deficit was a serious and worsening problem for a decade before the dollar began this rise. Furthermore, the dollar was experiencing real weakness in the early seventies (remember, it was officially devalued in 1971); yet this is the period during which the trade balance first turned against the United States.

Another popular explanation for the trade deficit blames the Organization of Petroleum Exporting Countries (OPEC) for boosting oil prices: since the United States is a major importer of oil, the soaring oil prices have caused huge increases in import figures, leaving America's trade awash in red ink. It is certainly true that the huge increases in crude oil prices aggravated the U.S. balance of trade problem. But the OPEC actions began in late 1973, nearly three years *after* the United States began experiencing annual trade deficits. Furthermore, the last U.S. trade *surplus* year was 1975, two years *after* the OPEC actions. Finally, oil prices have been stable or declining in the past few years—yet this has been a period of record-breaking trade deficits. And as was pointed out earlier, the United States would have run a multibillion dollar trade deficit in 1984 even if it had imported no oil that year.

A third common explanation for the trade deficit is that high

American wages have raised the costs of domestic producers, rendering them noncompetitive with producers abroad. While it is still true that U.S. wages are high relative to those paid in much of the world, it has become less and less true over time. In Western European nations, for example, average wages of industrial workers rose faster than those in the United States during the 1960s and 1970s.[32] This has substantially changed the relative wage situation. As Seymour Melman has pointed out, "The idea that the United States is the highest wage country in the world is out of date. At mid-1980, the United States ranked ninth among countries in the world with respect to wages of industrial workers."[33] According to the Department of Labor, wages of production workers in manufacturing, including fringe benefits, exceeded U.S. wages in Belgium (by 31.8 percent), Sweden (by 25.1 percent), West Germany (by 22.6 percent), the Netherlands (by 21.7 percent), Luxembourg (by 18.1 percent), Norway (by 12.9 percent), Switzerland (by 11.5 percent), and Denmark (by 4.4 percent).[34] Wages in Japan have also made impressive gains. For much of the period of continuing trade surpluses, the difference between U.S. and world average wages was greater than during the last decade and a half of deficits. This could not have been the case if high wages were the crucial factor in trade deficits.

No, there is more to this trade problem than changing international exchange rates, crude oil prices, and high American wages. The problem is deeper, more structural. American industry has steadily been losing its ability to compete. But let us turn now from the international arena to a wholly domestic issue of crucial economic importance: the quality of the American infrastructure.

Infrastructure. Systems of transportation, communication, water supply, power supply, and sewage treatment form critical parts of the support structure on which both producers and consumers depend. The extent and quality of this infrastructure are so basic to the functioning of the economy and to the quality of life of the population that they have always been hallmarks of a nation's level of development. From the canals and railways of the nineteenth century to the sprawling state and interstate highway system of the twentieth, from the earliest electric power plants to the construction of massive hydroelectric dams, the expansion and improvement of infrastructure kept pace with the nation's burgeoning economy as America industrialized. What is the status of this vital support system now?

America in Ruins, a report published in 1981 by the Council of State Planning Agencies, described the decaying state of the American infrastructure:

America's public facilities are wearing out faster than they are being replaced. . . . In hundreds of communities, deteriorated public facilities threaten the continuation of basic community services such as fire protection, public transportation, water supplies, secure prisons, and flood protection. The United States is seriously underinvesting in public infrastructure.[35]

At the time of the report, nearly 20 percent of the Interstate Highway System (which handles one-fifth of the nation's highway traffic) had exceeded its designed service life and was in need of rebuilding; one of every five bridges in the country required major rehabilitation or reconstruction; and many of the nation's 43,500 dams required work to correct hazardous deficiencies. In mid-1982, the *New York Times* reported that the condition of the roadbeds and rolling stock of the nation's rail system is "so poor that some officials say there are no reliable estimates available on the cost of replacement and repair"; and that a survey of twenty-eight cities by the Urban Institute found ten of them to be losing at least 10 percent of their treated water because of deteriorated pipes (the survey did not include Boston or New York, whose water systems are famous for their leaks).[36] The problem is clearly not confined to the older cities of the Northeast and Midwest: the *Times* article noted crumbling sewer lines under the streets of Albuquerque and an estimated 1.5 million potholes in the streets of wealthy Houston. The cover story of the August 2, 1982, issue of *Newsweek*—"The Decaying of America: Our Bridges, Roads, and Water Systems Are Rapidly Falling Apart"—further documented the decline: "The decay is most acute in older industrial cities, but clogged highways and strained water systems also threaten to strangle booming Sun Belt towns." During the summer of 1982, the collapse of an eighty-year-old dam in Colorado sent a wall of water through a nearby town, and the breaking of a major aqueduct in Jersey City, New Jersey, left 300,000 residents without drinkable water for six days.[37]

It is beyond question, then, that the American infrastructure has seriously deteriorated. Roads, dams, railroads—these are expensive and long-lived systems. They do not quickly fall into a state of disrepair: this comes only after decades of neglect. Such deterioration is not only a sign of long-term economic decline but a serious and continuing barrier to economic revitalization.

America in the eighties remains the world's largest economy, one that still provides the majority of its people with a relatively high standard of living. It is nevertheless an economy that for a decade and a half has been in a protracted state of decline. Over that period, inflation and unemployment have generally worsened, and the trade-off between them has become more severe. Productivity growth has been evaporating, and growth in the purchasing power of hourly wages has evaporated along with it. Domestic producers in a wide range of industries have found it more and more difficult to compete with foreign producers, despite the relative decline of U.S. wages. Much of the nation's infrastructure has fallen into a serious state of decay. More recently, poverty rates have been setting records, hunger has become increasingly common in America, the rate of bank failures is on the rise, the national debt is reaching truly astronomic proportions, and the United States has become a net debtor nation. Yet, simply because the dollar has been doing well on international financial markets and the GNP growing briskly, this has been called a strong economy!

The False Messiahs

As the United States worked its way through the troubled times of the 1970s, there were those who began to argue that the decline of American manufacturing simply represented a natural transition to a more advanced state of economic development. Some said the older, "sunset" industries like steel-making, auto-making, and commercial shipbuilding would wither away only to be replaced by young, vital "sunrise" industries producing computers, video recorders, and advanced telecommunications equipment. These new industries were often referred to collectively as the "high-tech" industries, a vaguely defined term that reflected their generally high engineering and scientific intensity. Others argued that America's future lay in management. Other countries would have the refineries, the heavy industries, the assembly plants (which were heavy polluters anyway). The United States would make its way by contributing its know-how to the management and coordination of these far-flung operations. We would become a country of white-collar workers, running the world's business. Still others argued that the fundamental shift was from a manufacturing-based economy to one based on services. It was this tertiary sector, services, that would rescue the economy from its doldrums.

Will these panaceas, which have at various times been promoted by leading government officials, business executives, and economists, save America?

High-tech. "America's vaunted leadership in high technology, the wellspring of innovation for the entire industrial sector, is eroding rapidly in every major electronics market. The trend reflects nothing less than a crisis in U.S. high technology." So begins the cover story of the March 11, 1985, issue of *Business Week*. In 1984, after years of continuous trade surpluses in electronics products, the United States experienced a first-ever trade deficit: according to preliminary figures, electronics imports exceeded exports by $6.8 billion. The electronics trade deficit with Japan alone was about $15 billion in 1984, more than the deficit in automobiles. The American Electronics Association forecasts the 1985 trade deficit in electronics at nearly double the 1984 figure. The strong dollar cannot be blamed for the worsening deficit, since the balance of trade in crucial areas such as semiconductors has been sliding since the late seventies— before the rise of the dollar. The real problem is the inability—even in these new, up-and-coming industries—to produce efficiently enough to be competitive.[38]

Because American brand names still dominate many major electronics markets, the seriousness of the problem is nearly invisible. In fact, many of the components of these products—in some cases virtually the entire product—are manufactured by foreign workers in factories abroad. The IBM Personal Computer is an interesting example: nearly three-quarters of its manufacturing cost is accounted for by overseas production, and nearly two-thirds of that overseas production is in foreign-owned plants. "As a result, the electronics industries—one of the country's largest manufacturing employers, with a workforce of 2.6 million—are in jeopardy of being gradually transformed into a distribution business for foreign manufacturers."[39]

Management.   The increasing failure of domestically manufactured products to hold their markets here and overseas has led to what some have called the deindustrialization of America: more and more manufacturing takes place abroad, either in foreign-owned plants or in overseas plants of U.S. companies.[40] For many Americans, especially the employees thrown out of work by thousands of factory closings and the residents of directly affected communities, deindustrialization is an unmitigated disaster. But some do not find the process particularly disturbing: they see it as simply a shift in the nature of American business. Instead of a manufacturer of goods, the United States will be a generator of new ideas, a place where new industry is begun, then shifted overseas. Production will be abroad but management will remain here. In the words of Simon Ramo, a director and founder of TRW, Inc., "America goes into the financial management business rather than the production business." [41]

There is an element of fantasy in this. It is difficult to believe that firms engaged in the "financial management business" could generate the variety and quantity of jobs required to replace the jobs being lost in production. Moreover, an economy based on management may well lose control of production. If all the manufacturing is overseas, why should management stay here? And if American industry becomes little more than a financial manipulator and a distribution business for foreign manufacturers, will it not be extremely vulnerable to foreign competitors who decide to eliminate the intermediary? *Business Week* paraphrases the analysis of B. J. van der Klugt (vice-chairman of Philips, the huge Dutch electronics firm):

> That was how the U.S. consumer electronics industry played into the hands of the Japanese back in the 1950s. Japan subverted the U.S. industry by first supplying cheap parts, then subassemblies, and finally finished products with U.S. brand names. Eventually . . . key engineering and production skills in consumer electronics dried up, leaving the U.S. extremely vulnerable in all electronics markets.[42]

Finally, there is little evidence that foreign producers are in awe of American management. Quite the contrary. For example, in December 1983 General Motors and Toyota established New United Motor Manufacturing, Inc., described as a fifty-fifty joint venture. The assembly plant is a former GM operation with a work force of former GM employees; most of the machinery and tooling in the plant came from Japan. Who is managing the operation? "Under the personal direction of Tatsuro Toyoda, a member of Toyota's ruling family, a Japanese auto production system has been installed. . . . [It] is the Toyota executives, not those from GM, who are making the key decisions." [43]

In fact, if there is any significant countertrend to deindustrialization, it is the establishment of manufacturing operations in the United States by foreign firms. Honda and Nissan (automobiles), Bridgestone (tires), Sharp and Toshiba (televisions), Matsushita (electronic components), and Komatsu (construction equipment) are among the major foreign firms that have opened manufacturing plants in the United States in recent years. These Japanese companies appear to be doing well with their American plants. They do not just own them—they manage them. Even when these firms purchase existing American factories they seem to run them better than the previous American managements. For example, Bridgestone, Japan's largest tire manufacturer, bought a troubled tire-making plant from Firestone a few years ago and appears to have turned it around. What is the secret? In the words of Kazuo Ishikure, president of Bridgestone (USA), "Our management tools are total quality control and management by objective. We learned this from scholars in the U.S. many years ago, so there is nothing Oriental or mysterious about it." [44]

Services. Another view of deindustrialization is that it represents a natural stage in our economy's evolution. Economic development, which transformed the United States from an agricultural society to one based on manufacturing, is now moving us through the next transition—from a manufacturing- to a service-based economy. There had been no reason to be upset about the decline in agricultural employment during the earlier shift; there need be no great worry today about the decline in manufacturing employment. The future of the American economy lies in services.

The service sector of the U.S. economy has in fact grown relatively larger over the past decade or so. The share of the GNP contributed by value added in the service-producing industries was already considerable in 1972, at 64.6 percent; by 1983 it had risen to 68.3 percent. Services accounted for 44.1 percent of personal consumption expenditures in 1972, compared with 47.1 percent in 1983. And services were responsible for 74.0 percent of all employment in 1983, up from 67.9 percent in 1972. During that period, service-sector jobs increased by nearly 17 million, while the goods-producing industries lost more than a quarter of a million employees.[45] Given that service industries *have* become a larger part of the American economy, two questions arise: Has this been a positive (or even neutral) trend for the employees shifted? Has it been a positive development for the American population as a whole, one that could possibly steer the economy toward a better future?

It is true that the shift of workers from farms to factories in the mid-nineteenth to mid-twentieth centuries occurred at a time when demand for farm labor was decreasing, owing to rapid improvements in agricultural productivity. But workers were not so much driven off the farm as lured by job opportunities in the growing industrial sector and by the promise of life in the bright lights of the rapidly growing cities. It was much more an era of "How're you gonna keep 'em down on the farm?" than of "How are we going to employ all the farmers crowding the cities?" In contrast, the vast majority of workers who have more recently left manufacturing for the service sector have not done so voluntarily: they left manufacturing because their jobs were eliminated and entered services because those were the only jobs available. Although it is undoubtedly true that the relocated workers are better off working in services than unemployed, the forced nature of the shift indicates that it has not been a positive change for the workers.

Looking at this shift purely in terms of money income, it is not difficult to see why it has been mainly involuntary. In mid-1984, average hourly earnings in manufacturing were $9.13; in wholesale trade, $8.86; in finance, insurance, and real estate, $7.53; in business and health services, $7.53; and in retail trade, $5.88.[46] In other words, in mid-1984 a manufacturing worker earning the average hourly wage would take an hourly pay *cut* of 3 percent by moving into wholesale trade, more than 21 percent moving into finance, insurance, and real estate or into business and health services, and more than 55 percent moving into retail trade. Of the jobs created in the service sector between July 1981 (the previous business cycle peak) and May 1984 (during the ostensible recovery), nearly 30 percent were in retail trade, the lowest paying category; about half of these were in eating and drinking places. Nearly 60 percent of the new service-sector jobs were in the second-lowest paying category, business and health services. Less than 4 percent were in the relatively high-paying wholesale trade category.[47]

It thus does not seem that this shift to services has been a boon to the employees involved. But what of its value to the economy as a whole? To answer this question we must examine the reasons for the shift. When the economy changed from one based on agriculture to one based on manufacturing, it was not because agriculture was becoming progressively less efficient. On the contrary, advances in agricultural productivity made it possible for fewer and fewer workers to supply more than enough to satisfy the nation's agricultural needs. A rapidly growing manufacturing sector, itself becoming increasingly efficient, was able to absorb more and more of those who had previously worked on the farms. The shift could legitimately be seen as a highly beneficial one which promised to greatly improve the standard of living of the mass of the population. And, of course, much of that promise was fulfilled.

The shift to services, however, is occurring under completely different circumstances. It is not that manufacturing is becoming so productive that the nation's need for manufactured goods can be satisfied with fewer employees. Quite the opposite: a long-term slide in manufacturing productivity growth has taken place. Jobs in the goods-producing sector are disappearing because domestic producers have become less and less able to compete with foreign firms. It is the loss of markets that has driven people out of the factories, not reduced labor needs brought about by spectacular increases in efficiency. Nor have America's need and desire for manufactured goods been reduced: they are just being satisfied by goods produced elsewhere. Services have become a refuge for workers displaced by this decline in domestic manufacturing.

Still, the fact that services have become an employer of last resort for many does not explain why these service-sector jobs exist. They are not the conscious result of a public jobs program. Why do they exist? Although this complex question cannot be thoroughly analyzed here, a partial explanation can be found in the Commerce Department's *1985 U.S. Industrial Outlook*, which includes a special report titled "The Growing Role of the Service Sector in the U.S. Economy." As the report argues,

> the growth in service sector employment is as much a result of the changing composition of the labor force as it is of the general increase in the demand for services. . . . One factor stimulating the growth of employment in services in the past two decades has been the increasing number of women and youths seeking employment. Because

many of them were unable to find jobs in the goods-producing sector, a large labor force of *low cost* workers became available for service sector employment [emphasis added]. Also, as more women entered the labor force, especially wives and mothers, demand for consumer and social services such as day care and family counselling increased. This trend was augmented by the affluent young who, often without families, are more prone to life-style type expenditures such as recreational services.[48]

In other words, a large number of workers ready to work for relatively low pay have become available on the supply side, while on the demand side, services traditionally provided in the home are less available there because the former providers are working for pay instead. These services, or substitutes for them, therefore must be purchased in the marketplace. Fast food and day care have become symbols of the 1980s. And why have so many women and young people entered the labor market to supply this low-cost labor? The demographics of the baby boom clearly has had something to do with the flood of youths into the labor market. But women—and to a lesser extent young people—have increasingly entered the labor force in an effort to maintain the level of material well-being their families have come to expect. Without two or more family members working, it has become more and more difficult for families today to achieve the standard of living that single wage earners were able to provide in better economic times.

It is important to separate this phenomenon from the very different one of women entering the labor force in response to the lowering of sex discrimination barriers. The entry of large numbers of women into the labor force has not been accompanied by the exit of large numbers of men; this exit would be occurring if women were becoming as likely as men to be the single wage earner (in families where both male and female adults are present). Nor is the standard of living for families with multiple wage earners dramatically better than what it previously was for families with a single wage earner. This would have been the case if sex roles were changing in a steadily improving economy. It thus seems likely that the addition of large numbers of women and young people to the work force has been the result of attempts by families to make ends meet. To the extent that it is fueled by these attempts, the supply-side stimulation of the service sector cannot be seen as a good sign. And the demand-side stimulation—to the extent that it is attributable to people's need to purchase in the market services previously supplied at home—represents an economic treadmill effect rather than a real net gain. As such, it is hardly a cause for optimism.

There is nothing inherently wrong with the idea of an economy based on services. If agriculture and manufacturing had become so productive that they required little labor to supply the needs and wants of the population, if new jobs in the service sector represented improved economic opportunities that lured workers from manufacturing, and if the services provided yielded net improvements in the population's standard of living, the shift to services would be a truly positive development. But given the reality of failing manufacturing productivity, lower pay, and treadmill effects, this shift must be seen as merely another symptom of an economy in protracted decline. The analysis presented here, though far from comprehensive, strongly suggests that there is little reason for either optimism or complacency. It seems highly unlikely that high-tech, management, or the service economy will save America. Under present conditions, they do not provide a solid foundation on which to build a brighter economic future. They are neither turning points nor starting points—only false hopes.

Reversing Economic Decay

There is nothing natural or inevitable about the long-term decay that grips the American economy. It is neither the result of the maturation and decline of an advanced economy nor some sort of terminal crisis of capitalism. Quite the contrary—it is the very unnatural and unnecessary product of policies the United States has doggedly pursued for decades. Ongoing national policies, together with dysfunctional personal incentive systems in public and private institutions, have needlessly handicapped the American economy. For the vast majority of Americans, the unintended but very real result has been an economy less and less able to provide a high and improving standard of living. It is worth emphasizing that this attack on the American economy—this clear and present danger to our nation's power and security—did not come from outside our borders. Although it may have been unintentional, it has been self-inflicted. And it is therefore wholly within our power to reverse.

Present theories of how economies as a whole operate, ranging from the still-dominant Keynesian approach to the models of the monetarists and the new supply-siders, have generated a series of macroeconomic policies which have been applied by a range of administrations. These policies have each affected unemployment, inflation, GNP growth, the international value of the dollar, and the like in different ways, but they all have one thing in common: none of them has lifted the American economy out of its long-term decline. Although the various policies have caused the symptoms of decay to shift from one form to another, and have even temporarily created the appearance of progress (as in the post-1982 "recovery"), they have not produced the thoroughgoing revitalization required for a real recovery. A real recovery is not GNP growth pumped up by huge amounts of debt, kept alive by financial manipulation, and bailed out by record flows of foreign capital. It is instead based on the solid foundation of efficient domestic production, generating goods and services highly competitive in price and quality with those produced anywhere in the world. It is rising wages and salaries with stable prices, and thus enhanced economic well-being spread throughout the population. It is, in short, the kind of progress that made the American economy so vital for so much of its history. This real progress none of these policies has even begun to achieve.

To create real recovery, to generate policies that will reverse the long-term process of economic decay, requires a substantial reorientation of our macroeconomic thinking. There is, of course, quite a bit of disagreement among the various schools of macroeconomic thought today; the debate is both interesting and important. Yet the crux of the problem lies not in the points of disagreement between different theories but in what they all neglect. Current macroeconomic theory is not so much incorrect as incomplete. The purpose of this book is to point out the power of what has been left out, and thus to begin the process of reorientation. I will explain how even a vital and healthy economy can be unintentionally undermined, and why this process can be invisible when seen through the eyes of conventional macroeconomic theory. More important, this understanding will serve as a basis for recommending policy that should prove effective in putting things right.

The main thrust of the book is the development and elaboration of what I have called the theory of resource diversion, intended to supply a missing piece of macroeconomic theory. But surrounding this core are ideas intended to encourage an even broader reorientation of our economic thinking. Some basic concepts are reexamined. The tendency to confuse means with goals, the false pragmatism of quantification, the narrowness of focus that leads to counterproductive policy, the entrapment resulting from lack of attention to economic transitions, the importance of "noneconomic" mechanisms to economic life—these are among the issues that surround the development of the core theory. Though these ideas lie in the periphery of the present work, they are not peripheral in the sense of being less important. They are central to the reorganized approach to economics that I believe can help make our economic thinking at once more productive, more pragmatic, and more human.

It should be noted that this is not intended to be an empirical work: though some empirical analysis is presented, the main emphasis is on ideas and conceptual frameworks. It is also important to emphasize that the discussion, while clearly applicable to the American economy, is not restricted to that case. The general principles presented here evolved through years of trying to understand the American economic situation, but they *are* general principles, and as such have wide applicability.

To properly develop this body of ideas, it is necessary to proceed carefully and systematically; this requires some time and patience as the building blocks are laid out and assembled, then the resulting construct applied. Not all the ideas developed are tightly tied to resource diversion theory per se. But this core theory and its related concepts together constitute a body of thought consistent with and necessary to the reorientation that is the purpose of this book. Chapter 2 places my analysis in the context of present schools of macroeconomic theory. It argues that conventional theory has defined the macroeconomic problem too narrowly, looking primarily at the issue of short-term "economic coordination." My analysis addresses the other half of the problem, focusing on the long-term effects of the pattern of "resource deployment." Chapters 3 to 5 provide the concepts needed to reorient macroeconomic thinking so that the missing theoretical piece may be supplied. Two taxonomies are introduced— one a set of subcategories of labor and capital defined by function, the other a set of categories of economic activity defined by degree of economic contribution.

Chapters 6 and 7 assemble some of these building blocks, analyzing the connection between long-term patterns of resource use and such central macroeconomic concerns as persistent unemployment and inflation. Chapter 8 discusses the problem of economic transition, of central importance in implementing substantial rearrangements in the pattern of resource use. Such rearrangements may be necessary to repair the kind of economic damage that can be caused by prolonged heavy emphasis on noneconomic activity. Elements of the earlier analysis are brought together in chapter 9 to systematically present the core theory of resource diversion. Chapter 10, which summarizes the analysis and discusses a variety of its implications, is a bit technical and is aimed chiefly at readers with some technical economics background. It is intended to sharpen the analysis, but can be skipped without confusion. In chapters 11 and 12 the conceptual analysis is applied. Chapter 11 discusses in detail some applications to the present situation in the United States and suggests applications to planned (as well as market) economies, and to less developed nations. Chapter 12 uses the insights of the analysis to develop strategies for the revitalization of economies experiencing this sort of long-term economic decay. Finally, there is a brief epilogue.

2

The Macroeconomic Problem

The difficulty lies, not in the new ideas, but in escaping from the old ones.
—John Maynard Keynes, *The General Theory of Employment, Interest, and Money* (1935)

When the disaster of the Great Depression struck in the 1930s, the United States experienced the irony of a society whose standard of living had been crippled, while its capacity for the needed production lay undiminished but idle. The very same workers who stood in breadlines were ready and willing—even eager—to get to work producing the goods and services they so desperately needed. But the economic machine had faltered, and it resisted attempts at revival. If the depression taught us anything, it was the importance of effectively coordinating total demand and full-employment supply. Whether by direct intervention or by indirect, impersonal means, total spending had to be maintained at a high enough level to keep unemployment low. Previous downturns in the business cycle had highlighted the problems that could result from the failure to mesh economic needs and wants with the activation of the existing productive capability to satisfy them. But because of the sharpness and severity of the Great Depression, the importance of this kind of economic coordination was etched deeply in the public consciousness.

It was during this period of nearly fatal economic collapse that John Maynard Keynes's *General Theory of Employment, Interest, and Money* was published, in 1936. Keynes's greatest contribution was the development of a policy-oriented theoretical framework for achieving a greater degree of coordination—and hence stability—in the economy. The classical economists had been convinced that the economy tended automatically toward full employment and that intervention was harmful (or at best unnecessary). Rejecting this view, Keynes argued eloquently for the systematic intervention of government policymakers, in prescribed ways and under prescribed conditions, to keep the economy on a steady, progressive path. Coordination was the problem he faced, and coordination was the problem he attempted to solve. Keynes's *General Theory* focused on unemployment rather than inflation; considering the historical context in which it was written, that is not at all surprising. But the theoretical system Keynes constructed applied to inflationary as well as deflationary periods, as he himself argued in *How to Pay for the War* (1940). Certainly, the Keynesians trained in the following decades saw the system as providing a framework for powerful discretionary policy in fighting both unemployment and inflation.

Although the inflation and unemployment problems troubling the American economy today resemble those with which Keynes and his followers wrestled, these problems have not responded to the Keynesian medicine the way they once did. The reason is quite straightforward: though the symptoms are similar, the disease is not. It is not faulty coordination that is threatening our present well-being and future development. The avoidance or mitigation of inflation and unemployment, and more centrally the achievement of a sustained stable or improving state of economic well-being, require more than effective coordination. That is only half the macroeconomic problem.

Ultimately, the economic well-being of any society depends on the way it deploys its productive resources—its labor, its machinery and equipment, its natural resources, its land. The way in which these resources are put to work and the nature of the goods and services they produce are vital to the society's present and future standard of living. It is this simple yet fundamental matter of resource deployment that constitutes the other half of the macroeconomic problem. And it is this half of the problem on which we are presently caught. To enjoy the highest standard of living that its endowment of productive resources can generate, a society must coordinate its needs and wants with its productive capacity. But the goods and services produced from these resources must also be the kind that serve to enhance that standard of living. For the roots of persistent inflation and/or unemployment lie not only in faulty coordination but also in the nature of resource deployment. To ignore *either* of these two parts of the macroeconomic problem is to jeopardize the present and future economic well-being of the society.

Economic Coordination

According to Keynesian theory, the crucial problem is the manipulation of total demand (i.e., of total spending by consumers, business, and government), so as to keep the volume of that demand in line with the total value of goods and services the economy is capable of producing with full employment of all resources. Since the full-employment supply is seen as essentially fixed, the attention of policymakers is directed to the demand side. If total demand exceeds full-employment supply, inflation will be generated: to counteract that inflation, demand must be damped by such policies as reducing government spending, discouraging business investment, and lowering consumer disposable income through increased taxation. If demand is too low, unemployment will result. Hence the road to full employment lies in pumping up demand through means such as increased government spending, stimulation of investment, and lowering of taxes. Only if total demand and full employment supply are kept in line with each other is it possible for full employment to be achieved without generating inflation. There is the further implication that if these aggregate values are kept equal, the possibility will be realized and there will in fact be full employment without inflation.

Manipulation of the money supply is important in the Keynesian system primarily because of its indirect effects (through its influence on the interest rate) on the components of total demand—especially business investment. If the money supply is restricted, interest rates will be driven up, with the consequence of reduced investment spending and hence lessened total demand. By driving down interest rates, monetary expansion encourages investment and thus can be used to stimulate total demand. Discretionary monetary policy is *one* of the available tools for stabilizing total spending to keep it in line with full employment supply, thus combating both inflation and unemployment.

Monetarism is the other main, established school of macro-economic thought. In counterpoint to Keynesians, monetarists hold that the money supply is not of indirect and secondary importance—it is central. This is particularly true in the short run, where money supply is seen as the dominant factor in setting the levels of prices, employment, and output. In the long run, money supply is viewed as the most important determinant of price levels, but as of little importance in determining output. Over the long period, the economy is believed to be essentially self-stabilizing, following a long-run growth path and exhibiting a "natural rate of unemployment" that is independent of monetary policy.[1] In further contrast to Keynesians, monetarists generally believe that discretionary policy is not an effective means of economic stabilization.

Relatively recently, a version of monetarist theory called the "new classical economics" has gained considerable attention. More extreme than mainstream monetarism, this approach argues that the unemployment rate is completely insensitive to demand-management policies even in the short run. The only systematic factor that affects the present unemployment rate is the past pattern of the rate; activist antirecession policy achieves nothing. Manipulations of monetary or fiscal policy will affect only prices, not output or employment. Anti-inflation policies, monetary or fiscal, therefore impose no social cost in terms of lost output or employment.

At the core of the new classical economics is the so-called rational expectations hypothesis: the public so well understands the consequences of government monetary and fiscal policies that it will rationally develop accurate expectations of their impact as soon as the policies are implemented—and act on these expectations immediately. This will offset the policies completely, rendering them useless. For example, suppose the government attempts to lower unemployment by increasing the money supply. The public will immediately understand that this policy is inherently inflationary: prices will leap upward as businesses and workers try to maintain their real incomes in the face of the inflation they "know" is coming, leaving output and employment unchanged.[2] I must admit that I find it more than a little puzzling that the public should be credited with fully and immediately understanding economic policy consequences about which there is so much disagreement among economists.

These are, of course, vast simplifications of much more sophisticated theories. Yet they will suffice for the present purpose. It is not my intention to enter into the lengthy and somewhat complex theoretical and empirical debate over the relative merits of these approaches. Rather, it is what they have in common—or perhaps more to the point, what they lack—that is of concern here. For all their differences, Keynesian and monetarist analysis have some striking similarities. They are both essentially theories of economic coordination. They both focus attention on the size of a total money aggregate as being the crucial factor: total spending by government, business, and consumers in the case of Keynesian theory, and money supply in the monetarist case. That is, neither theory assigns importance to the way productive resources are used or to the nature of the goods and services the resources ultimately produce. These matters are simply not viewed as critical to the macroeconomic problems of unemployment, inflation, or general economic stability. Even for Keynes, who divides total spending into such categories as government, investment, and consumer expenditures, this division is useful only in elaborating the different factors that determine the volume of spending in each category. As long as total demand comes out equal to full-employment supply, it makes not the slightest difference what kinds of goods and services are bought.

For the monetarists, the case is even clearer. While Keynesian theory is explicitly short-term in focus, monetarist theory is a bit more eclectic. Mainstream monetarists view fluctuations in the money supply as critical in the short run, dominating other factors. Yet at least one important school of monetarism does not support discretionary monetary policy as a tool for offsetting short-run economic fluctuations, but advocates a "simple rule," such as constant slow expansion of the money supply; following this rule will allow for long-term growth without worsening short-term fluctuations.[3] These monetarist positions seem inconsistent: if money supply is so important in the short run, why not manipulate it to offset short-term fluctuations? The positions also seem to indicate a focus on the long run. But both of these perceptions are misleading.

Monetarist advocates of the simple rule do not claim that short-term discretionary monetary policy is necessarily harmful, but believe that at our present state of knowledge there is too great a chance that our timing will be poor and hence that discretionary policy will make matters worse. As Milton Friedman, the leading advocate of the simple rule, puts it:

> There is little to be said in theory for the rule that the money supply should grow at a constant rate. The case for it is entirely that it would work in practice. There are persuasive theoretical grounds for desiring to vary the rate of growth to offset other factors. The difficulty is that, in practice, we do not know when to do so and by how much. In practice, therefore, deviations from the simple rule have to be destabilizing rather than the reverse. I should like to emphasize that I do not regard steady growth in the money stock as the be-all and end-all of monetary policy for all time. It is a rule that has much to recommend it in the present state of our knowledge. But I should hope that . . . we would . . . learn to understand more fully the workings of the monetary mechanism. As we did so, we could perhaps devise still better rules for controlling the stock of money.[4]

The impression that monetarists take a long-term view is correct in one sense. Their view, as earlier mentioned, is that the economy is self-stabilizing over the long run, so that a stable simple rule will not be incompatible with long-term requirements. But since no real theory of long-term processes is put forth, monetarists are actually dealing with short-term processes only—which, they argue, should not be purposefully manipulated, given our present state of knowledge. Keynes's famous prescription, "In the long run we are all dead," has truly taken root among macroeconomists: the short-term focus has become routine. But this glorification of ideological myopia is inherently unwise. It is worth briefly directing separate attention to this matter.

The Long Run and the Short Run

It is, of course, correct to say that the long run is made up of a series of short runs strung together. So it would appear that careful analysis of each of the short terms, followed by development and implementation of policies directed at each of them separately, is an effective way of producing the best possible results over the long term. But that is not so. What is lacking in such an approach is the capability for effectively analyzing the interactions between the successive short terms. For if behind the most striking short-term phenomena there is a slowly changing long-term current, its effects may be too small to be noticed short term by short term, given the "noise" of simultaneous, multidimensional changes. Yet this current may be profoundly altering the context within which the short-term processes are operating. In applied science, for example in engineering design, it is generally true that optimizing the performance of each subcomponent of a system does not necessarily lead to the best system performance. Because of interactions between components, virtually all systems of interactive components are greater than the sums of their parts. If this is true for systems whose components are clearly distinct and sharply defined, it is all the more likely to be true for systems as fuzzy as are the short-term components of long-term economic life.

Furthermore, there are many examples of processes in which behavior that seems rational or even optimal when viewed in the short term is seen to be not only suboptimal but actually irrational when viewed in the long term.[5] For example, firms focusing narrowly on the short term may well adopt policies that enhance short-term profitability at the expense of long-term profitability or even of continued economic viability—for example, neglecting research and development (R&D) expenditures or new capital investment. This phenomenon is not confined to economic affairs: the post-1945 nuclear arms race provides a good example. Each step in the arms race, taken separately, might appear to be a rational step toward maintaining or increasing national security. Yet in the long term, the result of all this short-term rationality has been massively irrational—that is, security-decreasing. The likelihood of mutual destruction in the event of nuclear war between the United States and the Soviet Union has not only failed to be reduced by the arms race, it has greatly increased. To put it graphically, in the long run we *may* all be dead if we continue to think only in short-run terms.

Not that long- and short-term considerations are necessarily antithetical to each other: that is certainly not true. It is more accurate to say that long-term processes often provide a context for short-term phenomena—a context which, if not properly understood, can lead to misinterpretation of those short-term phenomena. The gradual, continued operation of long-term processes can produce what appear to be dramatic and inexplicable shifts in the short-term situation. Indeed, these shifts *are* inexplicable when viewed from a strictly short-term perspective. The proverbial straw that broke the camel's back is one such case. Clearly it was not the short-run addition of a straw that caused disaster. It is inconceivable that such a small weight could produce such striking results. It was instead the long-run process of adding more and more weight that ultimately stressed the animal's spine beyond endurance, producing a dramatic change that cannot be understood in terms of the short run.

This is not to denigrate the importance of the short run; after all, it is necessary to live through the short term in order to get to the long term. A business formed to exploit a new technological development may have extraordinary long-term profit potential, but it still needs sufficient cash flow to pay its bills in the short term or it will be forced out of existence before it can ever tap that potential. But policies based solely on short-run analyses run a considerable risk of becoming ineffective or even counterproductive when long-term changes occur.

Pre-Keynesian analysts believed, on the basis of logical and internally consistent theory, that the economy would inevitably tend toward full employment equilibrium. Even if such a tendency existed, it would not preclude the possibility of the economy becoming stuck on its path toward equilibrium as a result of short-term considerations. Nor would it take into account the pain and suffering that might be felt during the transition period. For that matter, as long as the equilibrium shifts occasionally and there is sufficient system inertia, the system may rarely, if ever, actually be in equilibrium.

The Other Half

Keynesian and monetarist theory thus have two main similarities: focusing on money aggregates and ignoring the nature of the products created. Neither approach includes a theory of long-term processes. Inflation and unemployment (at least beyond a "natural rate") are seen as transient, short-term problems resulting from temporary maladjustments in the economy. In the monetarist view, these maladjustments will eventually be ironed out in the absence of perverse and persistent discretionary policy. In the view of the Keynesians, they are curable through the purposeful application of appropriate short-term discretionary policy.

It is not unreasonable for theories of macroeconomic coordination to be aggregative in nature, or for that matter to focus on the relatively short term, as long as they are recognized simply as theories of short-run coordination. But these characteristics render them incomplete, and therefore highly misleading when applied as overall theories of inflation, unemployment, and other issues of macroeconomy.

What is needed, then, is an integration of short-term and long-term analysis. Keynesian theory has taken us too far into the world of the short term and consequently has made our macroeconomic policy insensitive to one of the most fundamental economic issues—the uses to which productive resources are put and the implications of those uses for the functioning of the macroeconomy. These are long-term considerations, and they are, I believe, vital to understanding how our current economic problems arose. Even more importantly, they are crucial to developing the policies needed to put things right.

3

Rethinking
Basic Economic
Concepts

A reexamination of some fundamental economic concepts and their underlying assumptions is the first step in sweeping away much of the confusion that today surrounds the field of macroeconomics. "Unemployment," "inflation," "income," "money," "value," "the standard of living": it is not only the individual meanings of these terms, but also their connections to other concepts and to each other that are crucial. For example, it is not really possible to understand "unemployment" without first understanding "work." It is also important to ask questions like: How is "income" related to the "standard of living"? What is the connection between "money" and "value"? And perhaps the most basic question of all: What is an economy supposed to do?

This all sounds deceptively simple; but the purpose of this chapter is neither to restate the obvious nor to cater to the uninitiated. It is to try to inject a greater measure of realism into our understanding of some of our most commonly used concepts. These are, after all, not merely abstract academic issues—they affect the well-being of society and touch the daily lives of each one of us. By re-thinking these basic concepts, we can begin to build a theoretical framework capable of once again yielding fruitful, effective policy.

Work and Unemployment

"Work," as it is typically used in economics, refers to an activity in which time and effort are exchanged for money. Ordinarily, it is implied that work is an unpleasant activity that would not be undertaken in the absence of a sufficient rate of pay. Working is, in short, purely an economic exchange. To be sure, it is sometimes allowed that work may generate "psychic income" as well as the more commonplace money variety. But this sidesteps rather than confronts the narrowness of the view of work as economic exchange. It also implies that the more pleasant jobs should involve a lower rate of pay, all other things being equal. Yet this doesn't generally seem to be true—though admittedly it is very difficult in this case to keep all other things equal. While it may be common for more dangerous jobs to pay a kind of risk bonus in the form of higher pay, it is on the whole the most interesting, most pleasant, most creative, and generally most nonmonetarily desirable jobs that pay the highest wages.

Work is actually much more than a simple economic exchange. It is a complex activity, the physical, psychological, and social relational aspects of which greatly influence the life, behavior, and general well-being of the worker. The impact of work environment on job performance has been studied for some time. The incentive to do so has been strong because of the potential for improving productivity by manipulating the nature of work and of the environment in which it takes place. Only recently, however, has serious attention been paid to the work environment's impact on life outside the job.[1] Given the amount of time that employees spend at work, it is no surprise that those hours should have a considerable effect on their broader lives. It is more surprising that it has taken so long to get around to studying that effect.

The disutility attached to a particular type of work may arise from purely physical strain: heavy muscular exercise, assaults on the senses (eyestrain, exposure to excessive noise), discomfort due to postural problems (prolonged periods of standing or sitting in one position). The strain may also be mental or emotional, as with boredom caused by performing extremely simple or repetitive tasks. But other work characteristics are positive and desirable: work can be creative, challenging, educational. Not only the output of work activity but also the work process itself can be fulfilling and rewarding.[2]

Work can also convey a sense of purpose and direction, a feeling of belonging. It is typically a social activity, involving a variety of human interactions of which at least some are likely to be positive.

It is usually tacitly assumed that workers are more or less indifferent to what they are producing. Even those analysts who recognize that work is more than a mere money-labor exchange tend to focus more on the characteristics of the immediate work environment than on the type of output that is produced. Yet it is unlikely that people always ignore or are unaffected by the end product of their labors. In fact, it may be impossible for them to avoid being affected even if they try. There seems to be a human need to believe we are contributing to society in some positive way. And when, for reasons of the moment—for narrow economic interest or expediency—we try to suppress that need and participate in activities about whose value we have deep internal doubts, we are inevitably damaged over the long run. That need, it seems to me, is one of the most important assets of humankind. We would be wise if we spent less time and effort trying to override it, and learned to cherish and strengthen it instead.

The character of volunteer work provides some evidence that the nature of output is meaningful to workers. Where there is no element of economic or other compulsion or coercion, work is typically altruistic or other-directed. Such work tends to be performed at hospitals, nursing homes, schools, and other care facilities. It is also commonly associated with organizations supporting medical research and with religious charities. Finally, much volunteer work is performed in political campaigns and for "cause"-oriented organizations, such as environmental and peace groups. It is not so much that these organizations have no funds or paid positions (though they are rarely overwhelmed with either). Many small businesses (and occasionally even large ones) find themselves in severe financial straits without attracting volunteers. Nor is this kind of work always exciting and creative—often it is dull and routine. Rather the important common characteristic of these organizations is that they produce outputs that volunteer workers consider beneficial.

Work and Pay

Work has obvious importance as a means of acquiring money with which to buy goods and services. But in a society as materialistic as ours, a paying job is in itself a source of personal worth. Though it is certainly not a strict relationship, the amount of money earned is correlated, in this materialistic calculus, with the magnitude of personal worth. To be unemployed is therefore not only to be without an income but also to be judged worthless as a member of society, particularly as the period of unemployment lengthens. Money transfers such as unemployment compensation may help cope with the income problem, but not with the feeling or label of worthlessness. In fact, being on the public dole—and thus returned to the status of dependent child in the eyes of both the individual and the wider society—may accentuate feelings of worthlessness.

Having argued that work (and hence unemployment) is not simply a matter of income-labor exchange (or of income loss), it is of value to distinguish work-like activities that involve payment in money or in kind from those that do not. The importance of doing so lies in fundamental differences of implication and organization. Where pay is involved, someone other than the worker is bearing a cost in order to get the work performed. If it is assumed that those who bear the cost are both rational and in control of the employment decision, it follows that they must view the output of the work as having a positive value at least as great as its cost. This is true independent of any utility or disutility the work may have for the worker. This is not to say that only paid work is viewed as having positive value by individuals other than the worker, but rather that if control and rationality are assumed, the existence of pay demonstrates that someone other than the worker thinks the work is valuable.

The assumption that control is exercised by the cost bearers is nontrivial, and in some cases unrealistic. For instance, taxpayers bear the cost of the salaries of government employees. Yet, though rational, taxpayers are not necessarily in control of government personnel decisions. Hence it is quite possible that individuals will be hired whose salaries exceed the value of their work output in the eyes of the taxpayers. In the opinion of the government administrators doing the hiring, the value of the salaries may far exceed the opportunity cost of that use of budgeted funds. But the administrators are not paying the salaries—the taxpayers are. This situation is not peculiar to government. Managers of private corporations, for example, may engage in bureaucratic empire-building and hire people whose work output is less valuable than its cost, in the eyes of the stockholders and/or customers who share the salary costs. It is thus the judgment of the decision makers that holds sway when the decision makers and the cost bearers are different individuals. More will be said about this later.

Because remunerated work requires that people willing and able to perform a task work together with other people willing to pay for its fruits, organizing such activity is more complicated than, for example, volunteer work. Paid work also provides its performers with the means to obtain material goods and services for their present or future consumption. To the extent that such goods and services are considered necessary or desirable—but only to that extent—there is a degree of compulsion associated with remunerated work that does not necessarily accompany similar or even identical nonpaying activities.[3]

It is therefore not the job as such that is necessary or desirable, but rather the positive aspects of its three subcomponents: psychological (creativity, satisfaction); sociological (interpersonal contact, a sense of belonging, status); and narrowly economic (the means for satisfying material needs or wants). While economists can ordinarily be faulted for taking an unduly narrow and unrealistic view of work as a pure wage-labor exchange, others—including labor leaders—often take the overly broad and equally unrealistic view of jobs as indivisible packages. The latter approach causes union leaders to feel compelled to fight to maintain jobs that may be physically draining, unhealthy, and unsafe, in order to preserve the necessary flow of income to union members. Historically, much (though certainly not all) of the opposition to mechanization of work has come from this quarter. If instead the goal were perceived as one of maintaining or increasing income, achieving healthy and safe work environments, *and* having the right to share in the meaningful and useful work of society, the struggle would take quite a different form—one that in my view would be much more to the point. There is, then, some value in distinguishing paid from unpaid work—that is, in separating the pay associated with work from other work characteristics.

Any activity requiring labor time and effort with the goal of producing or assisting in the production of a good or service will herein be defined as *work*. It may be paid or unpaid, pleasant or unpleasant. If there is compensation attached, it may be in any of a variety of forms: wages, salaries, commissions—even profits earned from the sale of goods or services produced by individual entrepreneurs, such as artists' profits from sales of their paintings. Uncompensated work may be purely voluntary, such as work performed by members of a volunteer fire department, or it may be coerced—such as unpaid prison labor.

It may seem odd to refer to unpaid activity as work, especially if that activity is enjoyable. Yet defining work as any activity involved in production, independent of pay or pleasure, liberates our thinking. Work is important, pay is important, but the two do not always have to be tightly connected. Rather there are two separate problems: providing people with the means to satisfy their material needs and wants, and providing them with the positive psychological and sociological benefits of work. These problems may be solved jointly through paid work, but they don't have to be.

Furthermore, at least some of the opposition to making work more enjoyable (or less oppressive) by changing the workplace stems from a conviction that work is supposed to be unpleasant: if it's pleasant, it isn't really work. Yet even from a conventional economic standpoint, it is the characteristics of the product, not the sweat and strain of the work force, that make a good or service valuable; the good or service makes the same economic contribution whether or not the workers enjoyed the act of producing it.[4] The economic purpose of work is to produce, not to punish.

Unpaid work, even if pleasant, is not the same as leisure. However, some components of what is commonly regarded as leisure activity do fall into this category. A hobbyist carpenter building furniture for his or her own use or as a gift for someone else is performing unpaid work, as is a home gardener growing vegetables in the backyard. But there are many leisure activities that are clearly not work; playing recreational sports for exercise and amusement, listening to music, and lying in the sun are examples.

Money and Value

Anything that functions as an accepted medium of exchange is *money*. That acceptability is its essential defining characteristic. That money may also function as a store of *value* (i.e., a form in which value may be accumulated) follows directly from its exchange acceptability. It is important to understand that money has no inherent value or significance—only that which is assigned to it by mutual agreement. It is thus a wholly artificial social construct. Money is not the only asset whose value is nearly completely artificial. Stocks and bonds, for example, have the same characteristic. They are legal claims to money, other assets, or ownership. By what definition of value may the value of such assets be seen as artificial and not inherent?

Something will herein be considered to have inherent economic value if, in and of itself, it either contributes directly to the standard of living or can be used to produce goods and services that contribute directly to the standard of living. *Consumer goods* will be defined as those goods and services that contribute directly to the standard of living, while *producer goods*, or *productive resources*, will be defined as those goods and services that *can* be used to produce consumer goods or other producer goods. These definitions coincide with the common understanding that food, clothing, and haircutting services are consumer goods while sheet steel, machine tools, and labor are productive resources or producer goods. However, it is clear that money and other forms of financial assets are neither consumer nor producer goods, and so by definition are lacking in inherent economic value.

Because money is a medium of exchange, everything bought and sold must have an associated money value. Hence, money value can be used as a unit of measurement or a unit of account. Doing so is both convenient and efficient—but it is also dangerous. The danger arises because there is not necessarily a correlation between money value and inherent economic value. When everything is valued in money terms, the critical distinction between things of differing inherent economic value is lost. Activities and goods that are not at all comparable in terms of economic value appear to be so. For example, suppose a worker is paid $10 per hour to dig holes in the ground and then immediately fill them up again. Over the course of a forty-hour work week, $400 worth of hole-digging and refilling services have been produced. Suppose that same individual is paid the same wage to repair roadways. Over the course of a forty-hour week, $400 worth of road repair services have been produced. It is obvious that the hole digging has produced nothing of inherent value (i.e., no contribution to the standard of living), while the repair of roads has made travel safer and more comfortable, thereby improving the standard of living. Yet in money terms, the output values are identical. To the extent that money values are used as measures of economic value, a major distortion of reality occurs.

The question naturally arises: Why would workers be paid identical salaries to provide services of such radically different inherent economic value? In fact, why would economically valueless output be associated with a nonzero money value? Excluding irrationality, there are three main answers to these questions. First, an output having no inherent economic value may have other forms of value. The cathedrals of Renaissance Europe were built not for economic reasons, but in the belief that there was spiritual value in their construction and use—just as in an earlier age the great pyramids of Egypt had been constructed for their spiritual and political value.

Second, there may be a discrepancy between the value of an activity or output to the decision maker who authorizes its purchase and its value to those who actually pay the price. The Tammany Hall political machine operating in New York City during the nineteenth and early twentieth centuries was famous for creating well-paid, do-nothing jobs as political patronage. The politicians who created such jobs gained political benefits (reelection support) and personal financial benefits (the continuation of their own salaries, as well as kickbacks). Those who actually paid for the activity (the taxpayers) gained no benefits. These jobs clearly generated no inherent economic value, yet they bore a money value considerably greater than zero.

Third, given incomplete information and uncertainty, there is a real possibility that mistakes will be made. That is, a good or service may be produced in the belief that it has inherent economic value when it actually does not. During the early 1980s, the pesticide EDB (ethylene dibromide) was withdrawn from agricultural use in the United States as a result of evidence that it was carcinogenic. In light of the new information, EDB came to be seen as contaminating, rather than enhancing, the nation's food supply, and its earlier use was thus seen as a mistake.

Ordinarily, the existence of a money price at which a good or service is actually purchased is by itself taken as proof that the good or service has economic value. Yet, if we define economic value functionally, it is clear that this is not true. The mere fact of a money price in no way establishes the existence, let alone the magnitude, of economic value. Rather, such value is a property of the activity, good, or service, and the use to which it may be put. Empirical constructs like gross national product are subject to this confusion of money value with economic value, and therefore require caution in their use—caution that has often been neglected. A high or rising GNP per capita (even one that equals potential GNP) says nothing unambiguous about the condition of the standard of living, and hence the presence of real economic prosperity. Similarly, focusing attention on the behavior of money value aggregates, such as total demand and money supply, obscures the nature of resource use and the composition of output. This is, as I argued earlier, one of the key reasons why neither Keynesian nor monetarist macrotheory has offered much useful guidance in coping with the persistent economic difficulties from which the United States has suffered since 1970.

Inflation and the Distribution of Income

While any rise in the general level of prices is considered *inflation*, price increases that outrun increases in money income are clearly the most troublesome. The level of general prices, as opposed to the structure of relative prices, is of course meaningful only in relation to the level of money income and wealth. To the extent that command over goods and services is achieved by money exchange, it is this price-income relationship that determines purchasing power. Since the levels of prices, money income, and wealth are average or aggregate values—and nothing is so rare as an average individual— any given rate of inflation can be associated with a nearly infinite variety of distributional effects on individual purchasing power. These distributional effects are ordinarily thought of as having a negative impact on social equity. But there is no conceptual reason why this should be true. Even if the money incomes of wealthier people were rising faster than those of poorer people, it is conceivable that prices of luxuries and other goods found mainly in the market baskets of the wealthy would be rising much faster than prices of necessities; the poor would then gain purchasing power in relative terms while the rich were losing it. Though this is possible, there are at least two reasons why it is highly unlikely to occur more than fleetingly.

For one thing, wealthier individuals tend to have far more flexibility in coping with inflation. They have many more alternative asset forms available in which to hold wealth (or forms in which to earn income) and hence can shift to assets (or income forms) that maintain value more effectively for the particular shape of the inflation that is occurring. This flexibility is augmented by the fact that the wealthy spend relatively less of their income or assets in acquiring the necessities and basic comforts of life, and so have a greater margin for error—a fact which renders the possible consequences less dire and, ceteris paribus, makes the wealthy more willing to take any risks incurred in such asset or income shifting. A second reason involves the structure of social and political power relations. The ability to influence governmental policy, through a wide variety of avenues, tends to be roughly correlated with wealth. So does the ability to influence private-sector markets. Wealthier individuals are thus in a better position to affect the character of inflation so as to ensure that it will not put them at a relative disadvantage. It is therefore no surprise that the negative effects of inflation fall most heavily on those least able to cope—the poor.

The effect of inflation on income distribution, however, should not be viewed in purely relative terms. People's subjective assessments of their material well-being may be based to a significant degree on how their stocks of goods and services compare with those of other people. This is particularly true at higher levels of income, where "status" consumption may loom larger. But, more objectively assessed, standard of living depends primarily on the absolute level of an individual's command over goods and services. And a minimal, decent standard of living can also be at least roughly defined in absolute terms. Thus, even when the poor lose relatively less purchasing power during periods of inflation than the more affluent, they are far more seriously affected because there is so much less distance separating them from this decent minimum.

Casting the evaluation of individual material well-being in the usual terms of subjective and unmeasurable pleasure, satisfaction, or utility is another in the long string of techniques economists employ to sidestep the issue. In these purely subjective utility terms, nearly anything can happen. Theoretically, it is perfectly possible for an individual at the near-minimum standard of living to suffer a smaller loss in utility from a 10 percent diminution of purchasing power than a very wealthy individual who has experienced a 1 percent drop in purchasing power. But there is clearly an unreality here that is detrimental to the making of equitable social policy. Even if we knew this utility differential existed, it would be hard to accept its implication for the maximization of social welfare: the justification of policies that enrich the wealthy and impoverish the poor. A more reasonable and realistic approach might be to redistribute some purchasing power to the poor individual and send the rich one to a psychologist.[5]

The Standard of Living and the Quality of Life

The fundamental conceptual measure of an individual's material well-being is the extent of his or her command over consumer goods and services. That is, it is the quantity and quality of goods and services to which an individual has access and the degree to which he or she can use them as desired that is the defining characteristic of standard of living. Utility derives not so much from a stock of goods and services itself as from the flow of services the consumer can extract from that stock. Ownership is irrelevant. So is income, whether measured in flows of money or flows of goods.

That income is beside the point can easily be illustrated. Suppose automobiles were made to last twenty-five years instead of five years, and suppose these more durable cars were sold for $20,000 each rather than the $10,000 that the less durable cars now cost. An individual's income could now be reduced by the price of three present-day cars ($30,000) over a twenty-five-year period without any effect on his or her standard of living. (For simplicity, assume no increase of car prices over time.) That is, even though the price of cars has doubled, buying one car (at a cost of $20,000) now provides automobile transportation over a period that would have previously required the purchase of a series of five cars (at a cost of $50,000). A savings equal to the price of three cars has occurred. Thus, removing income equivalent to this savings leaves the individual neither better nor worse off than before; it is clearly neither money income nor the flow of new goods that counts. This is true whether the savings are thought of in terms of money ($30,000) or goods (three cars). The individual has access to twenty-five years of automobile use in either case, so the standard of living is unaffected. It is even more obvious that ownership is irrelevant. For example, if a company-owned car is made available to a corporate executive for business or private use, operationally speaking it is that executive's car. As long as the car is available when needed, it doesn't matter who owns it. Furthermore, if a car is not available because a relative is always borrowing it or because it breaks down frequently, ownership does not alter the fact that it is not available for use when the owner wants it.

Increased durability of goods is often looked upon with disfavor on the grounds that it would reduce replacement demand. Income would then be reduced because less production, and therefore less labor, would be needed to satisfy the lowered demand. Thus, a series of strategies from planned obsolescence to poor-quality manufacture is considered to be rational, even necessary for maintaining jobs and income. In view of the concept of standard of living just defined, this is patent nonsense. For although reduced demand for labor would result in less money income, less money income would be needed, since goods would require replacement less often. There is no reason why the standard of living should be negatively affected.

It is important to differentiate between the standard of living and the broader concept "quality of life." *Standard of living* will be used to connote well-being in terms of access to the "things" of life: consumer goods and services. *Quality of life*, however, measures economic, social, psychological, and even spiritual well-being. In fact, quality of life is the ultimate measure of well-being. The material standard of living is relevant only to the extent that it enhances the quality of life. That last point is hard to sell in a materialistic, object-oriented culture such as that of the United States. Discussions of quality of life are often seen as vague, dewy-eyed idealism counterposed with the hard-nosed pragmatism of material production. Ever greater growth in the standard of living is seen as an end in itself. This is a species of what sociologist C. Wright Mills once called "crackpot realism"—the tendency of people to become "so rigidly focused on the next step that they become creatures of whatever the main drift . . . brings."[6] Of what value are continued increments to the standard of living if they do not make a net positive contribution to the quality of life?

This should not be seen as a nihilistic, anti-materialist argument. Material well-being *is* an important component of the quality of life. It is hard to feel happy and fulfilled when you are starving, sick, or worried about meeting the incoming bills. However, it is also true— and perhaps is most obvious in a fairly affluent country like the United States—that fancy cars, superstereos, and expensive clothes, while they may provide a kind of narcotic rush, bear no necessary relation to lasting happiness or deep feelings of personal fulfillment.[7] When increments to the standard of living are pursued singlemind-edly, reductions in the quality of life may well result. In the name of industrial efficiency we create depersonalized, deskilled, excessively routinized, and rigid jobs that produce feelings of alienation and anomie. Too many of us may come to feel like "cogs in something turning." We destroy natural amenities and introduce virulent, long-lasting poisons into the environment. It is not necessary to be a back-to-nature purist or a radical anti-technologist to understand that not all changes that increase the standard of living necessarily add to the quality of life. Yet what legitimacy can improvements in material well-being have other than as contributions to the quality of life?

If it seems strange for an economist to focus on such "noneco-nomic" considerations, it is only because economists have strayed so far from basic principles as to lose sight of underlying goals. It is to this matter that we now turn.

Goals of the Economy

Economic activity is centered on producing and consuming the material component of human well-being. Yet ultimately, an economic system or a particular economic policy should be judged by its contribution to the quality of life, not just to the material standard of living. As vague and difficult to quantify as it may be, this is the foundation on which all rational economic activity must rest. Without this broader perspective, it is easy to fall into the trap of evaluating policy or efficiency according to intermediate objectives that come to be looked upon as ends in themselves. Too often the result of this narrow and myopic view is to degrade rather than to increase well-being. For example, it was long ago discovered that specialization of labor tends to increase labor productivity, measured in conventional terms such as physical output per worker.[8] This basic insight inspired a long process of simplifying and routinizing work tasks. This process was successful in terms of increasing the physical output from a plant for a given labor force.[9] But at the same time, many have argued that these alterations have had dulling, alienating, and stifling effects on the work force.

It is not important to establish the correctness of these latter arguments. The point is, these changes in the workplace would have been made even if they were known to have major negative effects on the nature of work and thus on the workers involved. They were judged only on their helpfulness in rolling more output per worker off the production line—which they did quite effectively. It is easy to see that the cumulative effect of many such changes could be a massive deterioration in the quality of life. The gains in well-being that result from a greater output could well be too small to balance the negative effects on the workers.

This leads to a related point concerning the measurement of output. It seems reasonable to define the *output* of a system to be all the things that happen as a result of operating that system—not merely the direct effects but the indirect effects or "externalities" as well. Given this definition, the output of a firm is not only the volume of goods and services produced, but also the pollution it generates, the technical knowledge and other skills it disseminates, the impacts (positive and negative) that working in a firm has on all its employees, and so on. If this more complete concept of output, which we might call *full output*, were used to measure productivity, it is quite possible that a very different picture of the impact of various policies would emerge. If negative impacts on the work force or on the environment were considered, certain policies now seen as increasing productivity might very well be seen instead as reducing it.[10]

It should be understood that paying serious attention to workplace design, environmental pollution, and other positive and negative externalities is not light-headed, unserious, or impractical. Of course, there is work to be done, and a workplace must be designed so that work can be carried out efficiently. It is not a matter of turning factories and offices into country clubs. Nor is the total elimination of environmental pollution likely to be feasible or even desirable. But there is no reason why people should have to spend most of the waking hours of their economically active lives doing boring, dehumanizing, or dangerous work, or why they should sicken themselves and their fellow human beings, tear at the intricate web of life, and perhaps even poison future generations in mindless pursuit of ever larger quantities of increasingly marginal things.

This view is completely consistent with the fundamental principles of the neoclassical microeconomic theory of the consumer. According to that theory, behavior is driven by the desire to maximize utility (i.e., satisfaction, pleasure, well-being). Goods and services are purchased not for themselves but for the utility they yield; they are thus ends rather than means. And how are these goods obtained? They are obtained by the expenditure of wealth, of income. And how is the wealth or income obtained? For most individuals, and certainly for society as a whole, it is obtained in exchange for some form of labor. If one then pierces the veil of intermediaries, what is really happening here is that people are exchanging time and effort for utility (i.e., they are using their labor to raise their level of satisfaction, pleasure, well-being). The ultimate purpose of work is to produce utility. What sense does it make then to perform work in a way that generates high levels of direct negative utility so that a slightly higher level of positive utility can be obtained indirectly, through exchange? Put more affirmatively, if the purpose of work is to generate utility, does it not make sense to pay at least as much attention to those things which affect the utility of work directly as to those things which affect it indirectly?

In a society scratching out the bare necessities of life, it may well be that the value of things—of material goods and services—is so high that it makes sense to trade even quite unpleasant labor for these things. Furthermore, in such a society the available pool of productive resources and technology is likely to be so small that it may not even be possible to reduce the unpleasantness of labor by much. But surely as a society develops, this ultimately ceases to be true. If there is diminishing marginal utility for "things" as a whole, at some point the utility reduction caused by work simplification (and by other processes intended to make workers more "efficient" in producing physical output) will outweigh the utility gain caused by greater availability of goods. As that point is reached, continued concentration on the sorts of work design that have negative impacts on the work force becomes counterproductive. (A similar argument can be made with respect to negative environmental impacts associated with greater physical output.) If we cannot see that most of the economically developed societies in the present-day world have long since reached that point, I think we need to do some serious soul-searching.[11]

There is a tendency to regard the preceding arguments as impractical, partly because of an uneasy feeling that they are diversions from the hard-nosed realities of production. After all, workplace and environmental effects are much more difficult to measure than volume of production. But the fact that something is hard to measure does not have anything to do with how important it is. It goes without saying that most of the very important things in life—happiness, talent, love—defy measurement. And the pragmatism that focuses solely on increasing the stock of things without asking why—without understanding that this is not a goal in itself but a means to a larger goal—is not pragmatism at all but foolishness. Like René Magritte's *Castle of the Pyrenees*, it is built of the most formidable and solid stone but floats unsupported in the air.

All economic and political systems must ultimately be evaluated by social criteria, and the ultimate social criterion is the contribution the systems make to the quality of life. It is therefore very important when choosing shorter-term or narrower goals to choose only those that are compatible with this overriding criterion. There are a whole series of goals that society may impose on an economic system: equality of income distribution, full employment, equality of opportunity, reward of effort or achievement. The commonly expressed objection that economic systems cannot be expected to meet whatever social goals may be arbitrarily established, while certainly true, is also exactly backwards. No matter how arbitrary the social goals may be, if they are in fact the goals of that given society, it is completely appropriate that the economic system be judged by them. It is the economic system that needs to be tailored to the social goals and not the reverse.

4

Contributive, Neutral, and Distractive Activity: The Fundamentals of Resource Use

In the short term, the full employment of productive resources, particularly labor, and the efficiency of their use, are of paramount macroeconomic importance. The use to which the resources are put seems to be less significant than the fact that they are functioning in some sort of activity generating money value. But though it may make little difference in the short run, it is the pattern of use of a society's productive resources—and not the mere fact of their employment or their cost-minimizing application—that is crucial for long-term economic health. If improvement in the quality of life is the only legitimate goal of economic activity, the achievement of that goal *must* depend on both what is produced and how it is produced. In addition to the full employment of resources, the nature, quality, and quantity of goods and services generated determine the material standard of living (setting aside questions of distribution). Similarly, the techniques of production determine those aspects of the quality of life related to the characteristics of the work environment and to the externalities generated.

Economic Activity and Economic Value

Independent of any money value it might have, an activity is of inherent economic value to the extent that it contributes to increasing either the present or future material standard of living—that is, to the extent that it adds to the stock of consumer or producer goods. Such an activity will be called *contributive*. For an activity to be considered economically contributive it must meet two tests: (1) Is it part of a process that results in the production of a good or service that has inherent economic value? and (2) Does it perform a function necessary to the efficient operation of that process? A negative answer to either question disqualifies the activity from being considered contributive. If the end product of a process has no inherent economic value (the first test), the activities that make up that process clearly cannot be contributing to the enhancement of the standard of living. The second test is necessary because even if the process results in an addition to the standard of living, redundant or unnecessary activities within that process do not contribute to that addition. Eliminating those activities will not lessen the effectiveness of the process in maintaining or increasing the level of material well-being.[1] In the economic development literature, for example, there is reference to the problem of "disguised" or "hidden" unemployment. It is argued that in the agricultural sector of a less developed country there may, for reasons of culture or tradition, be enough excess labor on farms to have driven the marginal product of labor to zero.[2] Therefore, even without further mechanization, significant quantities of labor could be shifted out of the agricultural sector with no significant effect on agricultural output. The work that constitutes such "hidden" unemployment is clearly noncontributive, even though it is part of a production process (agriculture) that is highly contributive. Such activities, which pass the first test of contributiveness but fail the second, will be called *neutral*. The process of which they are a part is contributive, but their part in that process is unnecessary.

Finally, activities that fail to pass even the first test of contributiveness will be called *distractive*. They are part of a process whose end product does not enhance the material standard of living. Resources engaged in such activities have been distracted, or turned away from the main object of the economy and toward other purposes. *Distractive* is used here as a value-neutral term. It does not imply that the purposes toward which these resources have been turned have no value to society or even that they have less value than contributive activities. Classifying an activity as distractive only means that it is part of a process resulting in a good or service that has no inherent *economic* value.

It is worth emphasizing that the term *noncontributive* and its sub-categories *neutral* and *distractive* are not pejorative. Categorizing activities as contributive or noncontributive therefore is *not* equivalent to classifying them as "worthwhile" or "worthless," "good" or "bad." It is simply a statement about whether or not they add goods and services of inherent *economic* value to the pool of such goods and services on which the population draws. While they do not contribute to the quality of life by adding to the material standard of living—they might contribute to it in other ways. After all, economic values are not the only human values. Contributing to other values can add to the quality of life without increasing material well-being.

Regardless of how efficiently the resources employed in distractive processes are used, they are wasted from the point of view of the economy. The process as a whole fails to generate inherent economic value. Both the unnecessary, inefficient use of resources in a basically contributive process and the use of resources in processes that themselves do not generate inherent economic value deprive the economy of the higher standard of living that efficient use of these resources in contributive activities would allow. In other words, both types of noncontributive resource use have serious opportunity costs. It is nevertheless useful to distinguish between them. Freeing resources from neutral activities is simply a matter of an efficiency adjustment within an economically focused process; freeing resources from a distractive process requires terminating the process itself and rechanneling all resources involved to contributive activities. Furthermore, the political difficulty of terminating distractive processes tends to be much greater than that of eliminating inefficient resource use within contributive processes.

Since distractive processes generate no inherent economic value, they must be carried on for fundamentally noneconomic reasons or because of a misconception that they are somehow contributive. But once resources are locked into such processes, the elimination of the activity is often opposed by those with vested interests. So the distractive processes continue either because the noneconomic reasons that caused them to be initiated continue or because vested interests strongly resist the conclusion that the process is not contributive after all. In either case, the processes usually lock up more kinds of resources, in greater quantities, for longer periods than do neutral processes, and their negative economic effects tend to be stronger and more difficult to overturn. Thus, the more compelling term *distractive* is used for them. However, the distinction between neutral and distractive activities or resource uses, while useful and informative, is far from crucial to the analysis presented here. The separation of contributive activities or resource uses from noncontributive, on the other hand, is of central importance.

Perhaps it is useful to illustrate the kinds of activities that fall into the categories *contributive*, *neutral*, and *distractive*, for further clarification. There are two kinds of goods whose production involves contributive activity: consumer goods and producer (or investment) goods. Ordinary consumer goods such as furniture, television sets, food, haircutting services, and housecleaning services obviously contribute to the present standard of living. In fact, the quality and quantity of consumer goods available *is* the present material standard of living. Producer goods like machine tools, industrial trucks, warehouses, and consulting services contribute to the living standard in a less direct way: their production adds to the economy's capacity to produce, increasing the *future* living standard an economy is able to provide. Producer goods are tools, valued not for what they are themselves but for what they can produce when put to constructive use. This is fairly straightforward, and consistent with traditional thinking.

The practice of "featherbedding," that is, maintaining jobs that have become obsolete (typically as a result of union pressure), is an example of neutral activity—assuming, of course, that the featherbedding takes place within a basically contributive process. For example, "firemen" responsible for shoveling coal into the boilers of steam-powered locomotives were maintained aboard locomotives after diesel, electric, and diesel-electric designs had entirely eliminated their main function. The activity was unnecessary but the process itself—the transport of passengers and cargo—was basically contributive.

Digging holes and then immediately filling them—the classic example of economically useless make-work—falls under the category of distractive activity. Neither that activity itself, nor any process in which it is embedded, makes more available any good or service that contributes to the present or future material standard of living. The

iency with which the holes are dug is of strictly secondary im-
tance since the end product of the process as a whole (no pun intended) has no inherent economic value. The only reason internal
efficiency is not entirely irrelevant to distractive processes is that, for
a given level of output, lower internal efficiency implies that more
productive resources are locked into the distractive activity, and
therefore that more resources are being diverted from potential use in
contributive activities. The opportunity cost of the inefficient distractive activity is accordingly greater.

In today's world, military-oriented activity is undoubtedly the preeminent example of distractive resource use. Both military forces
per se and the entire apparatus of support systems—most notably
military-related industry—absorb huge amounts of virtually all categories of productive resources. Military expenditures are one indicator of the magnitude of this activity. From 1960 to 1982, worldwide
military expenditures totaled more than six trillion dollars; military
spending in 1982 alone amounted to nearly two-thirds of a trillion
dollars.[3] As the principal antagonists in the post–World War II arms
race, the United States and the Soviet Union have together accounted
for half to two-thirds of worldwide military spending in recent
years.[4] Of course, it is not the number of dollars that is of real moment, but rather the enormous quantities of productive resources diverted from potentially contributive economic activity, which the
dollars represent.

Clearly, the carrying out of military action (either by government
or subnational forces) is distractive. Wars—whether revolutionary or
international, traditional or guerilla, conventional or nuclear—are
highly damaging and have over the span of history destroyed an enormous amount of consumer and producer goods—not to mention their
sickeningly heavy toll in human suffering and death. Resources used
in the fighting of wars are quite obviously employed in distractive
activity. But what of the resources used in preparation for wars, or
perhaps in the attempt to prevent war through the threat of force? Are
they being used distractively as well?

The answer is, quite straightforwardly, yes. The products of military industry, and the military itself, add to neither the stock of consumer goods nor the stock of producer goods. A fighter bomber, a
nuclear warhead, a missile submarine, are not consumer goods—
they therefore do not add to the present material standard of living.
They also do not enhance the economy's capacity to produce and so

do not augment the future standard of living. Since they fail the 1 test, they are by definition distractive. To repeat, it is important to understand that this does not imply that military goods, or the existence of military forces, have no value. Classifying an activity as distractive does not eliminate the possibility that the activity has noneconomic value. Indeed, it was argued above that the existence of noneconomic value is one of the chief reasons why rational people may choose freely to divert productive resources to distractive activity.

The preeminent contemporary example of neutral activity is undoubtedly the untoward expansion of administration relative to production. Over the course of the twentieth century, there has been a steady and striking secular rise in the amount of administrative and managerial activity relative to direct production work both in the manufacture and supply of goods and in the provision of services; the process may actually have accelerated in recent decades. There is no inherent reason why this rise in administrative activity should be considered neutral. It was, after all, largely carried out under the assumption that the greater extent and intensity of administrative control would contribute to improved coordination within productive processes and thereby contribute greatly to productive efficiency. If this were true, the additional administrative activity could hardly be called neutral. However, by now there is considerable empirical evidence that, contrary to theoretical predictions, this trend of rising administrative intensity has not been associated with rising productivity.[5] If that is the case, the theoretical justification for increased relative scope and intensity of administration is eliminated, and the use of resources for this unnecessary control activity should be considered neutral. In the conventional wisdom, the phenomenon of excessive administration is most strongly associated with government. However, it appears that this type of neutral activity may be prevalent in organizations of the nonprofit and private sectors as well; more will be said about this shortly.

Distractive Activity: A Closer Look

The idea that certain classes of activity absorb economic resources without contributing to the production of economic value is not a new one. For example, Adam Smith, the father of capitalism, made this distinction in his landmark work *The Wealth of Nations*, published in 1776:

> There is one sort of labour which adds to the value of the subject upon which it is bestowed: there is another which has no such effect. The former, as it produces a value may be called productive; the latter unproductive labour.[6]

Smith goes on to discuss the economic implications of such unproductive work, particularly when it is maintained at high levels:

> Both productive and unproductive labourers, and those who do not labour at all, are all equally maintained by the annual produce of the land and labour of the country. This produce, how great soever, can never be infinite, but must have certain limits. According, therefore, as a smaller or greater proportion of it is in any one year employed in maintaining unproductive hands, the more in the one case and the less in the other will remain for the productive, and the next year's produce will be greater or smaller accordingly.[7]

> Such people [i.e., unproductive workers] as they themselves produce nothing, are all maintained by the produce of other men's labour. When multiplied therefore, to an unnecessary number . . . unproductive hands, who should be maintained by a part only of the spare revenue of the people, may consume so great a share of their whole revenue . . . that all frugality and good conduct of individuals may not be able to compensate the waste and degradation of produce occasioned by this violent and forced encroachment.[8]

Furthermore, Smith includes the military in his category of unproductive labor: "The whole army and navy, are unproductive labourers. . . . [G]reat fleets and armies . . . in time of war acquire nothing which can compensate the expense of maintaining them, even while the war lasts." But for Smith, the essential distinction between productive and unproductive labor is that the latter "does not fix or realize itself in any particular subject or vendible commodity," while the former does. And so Smith also includes "churchmen, lawyers, physicians, men of letters of all kinds; players, buffoons, musicians," as well as "the sovereign, with . . . the people who compose a numerous and splendid court" in his category of unproductive labor.[9]

It would appear that the tangibility of the output, rather than the use to which the product is put, differentiates between Smith's categories of productive and unproductive. Because this is obviously very different from the distinction I have drawn between contributive, neutral, and distractive activity, my list of "unproductive" activities would be quite different. But the purpose of this section is not to defend the categorization of activity that underlies the theory of resource diversion, or to compare this taxonomy with others that have gone before it. Rather, it is to attempt to clarify this crucial concept of distractive activity, and to add some degree of specificity to the activities included in that category. Military-oriented activity, both direct activity of the armed forces and, more important, indirect activity of the supporting network of research and industrial production, has been cited here as the primary present-day example of distractive activity. But what other sorts of activities would be considered distractive? And are all distractive activities indistinguishable in their economic effects?

The societal activity most closely analogous to that of the military is police activity. Police forces do not create economic well-being—they are not intended to do so. Instead they are intended to enforce that portion of a society's rules and regulations that has been incorporated into the criminal code of its legal system. The police thus stand as a societal force opposed to another societal force, the lawbreakers. It is in the area of crimes against property (e.g., burglary, embezzlement) that the police most directly and least controversially interact with the economic system. Here the crimes are economic in nature, as opposed to crimes against persons (e.g., murder, rape), which are basically noneconomic. But while people committing theft of various sorts are clearly not creating economic wealth, neither are they destroying it. Rather, they are engaged in redistribution. From the standpoint of aggregate economic well-being, it matters little whether you have your television or a thief does (though it may be very important to you). In either case the television set exists and is adding to someone's standard of living. Hence the activity of police in preventing such redistribution, while it may be considered to have great social value, does not constitute an addition to the general material standard of living. Of course, police also interface with economic activity by engaging in the enforcement of societal rules that prohibit the production or sale of certain goods and services, such as heroin or prostitution. Even if such goods and services are considered detrimental to moral well-being, as well as lacking in economic value, the role of the police in opposing them still does not add to the availability of contributive goods. If illegal goods are considered desirable consumer goods—as was liquor during Prohibition, for example—then it is obvious that police enforcement of the laws actually hampers contributive activity.

The part of police activity that involves thwarting crimes such as murder and arson, however, has a different flavor. If more people or property would be destroyed in the absence of such police activity than in its presence, such activity amounts to maintaining the population and the stock of contributive goods against everyday societal forces. It is in a sense much like the activity of servicing an industrial machine to maintain it against the normal forces of wear and tear involved in its everyday use. How then should such activity be classified?

Because maintenance activities mitigate ordinary, ongoing processes of depreciation and destruction, a smaller stock of contributive goods and services would be available in their absence. They therefore result in a higher standard of living than would otherwise exist, and so seem to be contributive. But they are contributive only in a limited sense. On the whole, contributive activities are those that create *new* goods and services that add to the material standard of living. All other things being equal (particularly the ways in which production is carried out), the more contributive goods and services produced, the higher the level of material well-being. Maintenance activities clearly create nothing new. They are contributive only insofar as they are effective in reducing normal processes of wear and destruction operating on the stock of contributive goods, including productive resources. Beyond that point they cease to be contributive and become neutral. Hence the maintenance of contributive goods and services is a considerably more limited form of contributive activity than their production.

Thus, while the vast majority of police activity is distractive, the part of police activity that specifically "maintains" people and contributive property is contributive. This illustrates the fact that the classifications *contributive*, *neutral*, and *distractive* apply to activities, not necessarily to whole occupations—and certainly not to people or institutions.

Generally, the local governmental activity most closely associated in people's minds with that of the police is fire fighting. How would this activity be classified? Whereas preventing the damage or destruction of people and property is one of many activities performed by police, it is the central function of fire fighters. Their work is mainly concerned with "maintaining" people and keeping the stock of contributive goods at a higher level than what it would otherwise be. Such maintenance activity, as I argued earlier, is contributive so long as it is actually effective, and becomes neutral only if carried too far. In any case, the ordinary activity of fire fighters would not be classified as distractive.

Much of the activity of organized religion, on the other hand, is clearly distractive. Neither the construction of religious buildings nor most of the activities carried on inside them contribute to the material standard of living of the society. They are not intended to do so, but rather are focused primarily on spiritual guidance and other nonmaterial needs of human beings. In fact, one could argue that one of the central purposes of religious institutions is precisely to be distractive—to divert people's attention from the materialistic world of economic activity toward matters of a presumably higher order. However, religious institutions do also operate hospitals, soup kitchens, day-care facilities, and schools that provide a great deal of secular education. All of these activities are obviously contributive. This once again emphasizes the importance of understanding that the labels *contributive*, *neutral*, and *distractive* are appropriately applied to activities, not to institutions or occupations.

It is worth explaining in a bit more detail here why the production of military-oriented goods and services has been given as the prime example of distractive activity in the world today. To begin with, military personnel, and the weapons and other tools they work with, are peculiarly oriented to the effective destruction of goods and services and the killing or injuring of people. Military forces are designed as means to the violent settlement of disputes: soldiers are not trained as negotiators or mediators, but as killers; weapons are not designed to persuade or restrain, but to destroy. Accordingly, when militaries are put into action for the central purpose for which they were designed, the destruction of contributive goods and services (as well as people) is a virtual certainty, whether that destruction is the primary objective of the employment of the force or its collateral effect. Thus the direct use of military forces not only fails to add to the stock of contributive goods and services, but invariably reduces it. This has become more true as warfare has become more modern. At one time, warfare may have consisted of two combatant forces slugging it out in the middle of a field, with minimal damage to the surrounding population and their goods. But if that kind of warfare was ever really conceivable, it is certainly not conceivable today. As military technology has become more advanced, civilian populations have increasingly found themselves and everything they own in the midst of the battle.

But (it might be argued) could not the existence of military forces (and in some cases even their use) be thought of as preventing the destruction of people and contributive goods that would occur in their absence? And if so, does that not make their activity somewhat akin to "maintenance"—earlier classified as a limited form of contributive activity? The central purpose of military forces, even when they function purely as deterrents to actual use, is not to prevent destruction but to prevent (or promote) political domination, or redistribution of contributive goods and services. "Better dead than Red," we are told by radical anticommunists among the supporters of a continuing military buildup in the United States—a slogan that clearly implies that the purpose of the buildup they support is to prevent political domination of the United States even at the expense of considerable destruction (or risk thereof). The ferocious defense of the Soviets against the Nazi invasion of their country during World War II provides an even more striking twentieth century example. The Soviets burned their own crops and destroyed their own property in order to deny sustenance to the Nazi invaders and prevent them from gaining control of the USSR. Prevention of political domination—not prevention of destruction—was the primary objective. The U.S. military in Vietnam and, more recently, the Soviet military in Afghanistan, similarly destroyed people and contributive property to oppose shifts in political control.

Nearly all wars are fought to prevent (or promote) control or to redistribute economic goods, not simply to destroy. Consequently, though the absence of a defending military might well make it easier for an external invader to dominate a society or redistribute its goods, it would generally not result in greater destruction should such an invasion occur.[10] On the contrary, in nearly all cases it is highly likely that there would be far less destruction in the absence of a defending force. The presence of a defending military would thus not reduce destruction, though it could well frustrate external attempts at domination or forced redistribution. In other words, in the absence of a defending military, an external invader might more easily succeed but would not generally destroy. What would be the point? Successful conquest would bring the conquered people and their goods under the control of the invader; destroying them would only lessen the degree of the conqueror's success. Hence, even though military forces may *deter* such invasions, they do not "maintain" the stock of contributive goods and services at a higher level than that at which it would be in the absence of those forces. So the activity of military forces does not qualify as a contributive form of maintenance.

As I have argued in the case of the police, preventing undesired redistribution does not add to the aggregate standard of living, and therefore is distractive—though it may well be a valuable function. Preventing political domination is more obviously noneconomic and distractive. Thus, whether activated or used as a threat system, military forces are clearly engaged in other than economic activity. Having said all this, it is worth emphasizing that the prevention of political domination or of forced redistribution is an extremely important function. To the extent that military forces are effective in performing those functions, but only to that extent, their activity is of real value to society. Nevertheless, that activity does not lead to the production of goods or services that contribute to the material standard of living, and so is distractive.

While it is true that military activity and much police and church activity fall into the *distractive* classification, there are of course many significant differences among them. One particularly interesting difference lies in the fact that the buildup of military forces frequently, if not always, indirectly worsens the threat it is intended to protect against. It is hard to imagine circumstances under which having a larger police force would actually increase criminal activity or having more churches would increase spiritual waywardness. But there is massive evidence that the buildup of military forces to counter a threat posed by an opponent's military forces typically results in a further expansion of the opponent's forces and hence an escalation of the threat. It is a commonplace that arms races are partially, if not primarily, driven by such action-reaction phenomena. And since historically the vast majority of arms races have resulted in war, there is clearly a counterproductive element to this form of distractive activity which is absent in most, if not all, other forms.[11]

Although various activities other than the three discussed here are properly classified as distractive, there is little to be gained at this point by attempting to compile a comprehensive list. And, as in any taxonomy of human activity, there are bound to be borderline cases. But that is of no great importance: in order to be useful, any theory must be simpler than the reality it models; and any model simpler than reality must be less than complete.

The concepts of noncontributive activity in general, and distractive activity in particular, are useful in understanding why even macroeconomics that appear to be doing things right, short term by short term, can be so resistant to conventional macroeconomic policy in the short run and can experience such severely degraded performance over the long run. These concepts, which constitute a critical part of the analysis developed in subsequent chapters, are set aside for now while the phenomenon of neutral activity is explored further.

Neutral Activity: How Does It Happen?

Neutral activity is unproductive in the most straightforward sense—it is unnecessary to the contributive process in which it is imbedded. That process would produce no less contributive output in terms of either quality or quantity if the neutral activity were eliminated. "Featherbedding" is a neutral activity of production labor; maintenance of excessive capacity and redundant equipment (beyond backup systems needed for a reasonable safety margin) is a neutral capital use; and maintaining an overlarge bureaucracy is the neutral use of management and administration. At present, the last form of neutral activity seems to be both the most widespread and the most economically important. How did this come about?

For reasons of status, power, and salary, managers and administrators generally seek to expand the bureaucratic structures they control, whether in the public or private sector.[12] When all is said and done, managers of larger organizations are simply better paid and more important in the community of managers. That constitutes a powerful incentive toward expansion, especially since individuals attracted to management as an occupation tend to be particularly interested in high pay and prestige. But it would of course be very difficult to justify expansionist strategies on those grounds to those who might need to be persuaded to go along—stockholders or taxpayers, for example. It might even be difficult to justify them to oneself on those grounds. What is needed is a legitimating theory.

The essence of the theory that has filled this need can be stated in two simple propositions: (1) more control is better control; (2) better control means more efficient operations. Hence continual increase in the scope and intensity of management is fully justified by its contribution to productivity improvement and thus to reduced unit cost of the good or service the organization is supplying.[13] The cost savings allegedly more than offset the increased costs associated with enlarged management and administration, so net gains are achieved.

Now, there is no inherent reason why this should be the case. It is perfectly possible that more control is *not* better control, and that tighter control not only does not contribute to increased efficiency but actually inhibits it. How might this occur? In practice, increases in the scope and intensity of management break down into such mundane acts as filling out more forms, sending more memos, and producing more frequent accounting and other progress and status reports. In addition to becoming more frequent, these reports often proliferate in kind, as increasingly detailed information is sought. This deluge of paperwork is far from costless; the materials and equipment alone can be quite expensive. But the time and effort expended by management, administrative, and production employees in executing the paperwork is perhaps the greatest cost. Many workers, especially production workers and production managers, are irritated by such a distraction from what they consider to be their real work. Some react by rushing through it—filling in seat-of-the-pants estimates when more precise figures or analyses are, in their view, unduly time-consuming or difficult to obtain. This, of course, introduces a potentially serious and virtually inestimable degree of error into the information flow.

Once the information is collected, and particularly after it is entered into a computer, it is typically treated as though it was solid and precise. Ironically, the more reports and memos a particular figure or analysis is incorporated into, the more accepted and relied upon it tends to become; as it is aggregated with other similarly provided data, the original data disappears and is rarely retrieved and reevaluated. What was originally no more than an estimate becomes gospel. That such phenomena occur in all large organizations is virtually certain. The degree to which this distorts the information on which decisions are based is extremely difficult to ascertain without empirical investigation far beyond the scope of this analysis. But that such distortion occurs is unquestionable.

After expending considerable time, effort, and materials in preparing the forms and reports, workers transmit them to other individuals who must expend time and effort to read and evaluate them. But the escalation of the quantity and frequency of these reports makes it impossible for managers to absorb the information and still have sufficient time and energy remaining to actually manage. This leads to a perceived need to hire more submanagers and administrators, who, of course, produce more reports and memos. They add to each other's workloads and produce more pressure to hire more submanagers. So the process continues. It is this phenomenon that caught the eye of C. Northcote Parkinson a quarter of a century ago and led to his now famous laws.[14] The end result is that all the managers and administrators and their subordinates are working very hard, but it is difficult to determine by observing this beehive of activity how much of the work is necessary to the efficient functioning of the organization and how much constitutes making work for each other.

The expansion of managerial and administrative activity is restrained by the need to earn a sufficient rate of profit to keep the stockholders quiet (in the case of a private business) or by the need to stay within politically acceptable budgets to keep the taxpayers quiet (in the case of government organizations). As long as managers stay within those bounds, the cost to them of expanding the bureaucratic control apparatus is low, while the value to them of such expansion may well be substantially higher. (In standard economic terminology, to the managers the marginal cost of expansion will tend to be less than its marginal utility.) The managers have the relevant decision-making power: they are in operational control of hiring and purchasing decisions. Therefore, as long as the value of expansion exceeds its costs from *their* perspective, they will continue to expand the bureaucracy.

As the bureaucracy is expanded, the cost to the managers of further expansion is likely to stay roughly constant (or perhaps to rise only slowly) until the point at which net profit has been driven down to the minimum level required or the politically acceptable budgetary limit has been reached. At that point, or perhaps as that point is neared, the cost to the managers of further expansion begins to rise sharply. (That is, the marginal cost curve is horizontal or slopes only mildly upward until it approaches the point of "capacity," the point at which the minimum profit or budgetary constraint is binding; the marginal cost curve then increases at a strongly increasing rate.) If the value to the managers of further bureaucratic expansion tends to diminish as the bureaucracy is expanded, the managers may stop pressing for further expansion before the budgetary or minimum profit constraint is reached: the constant or slowly rising costs of more expansion may come to exceed the falling value of that expansion before the minimum profit or budgetary limit is reached. (Diminishing marginal utility of bureaucratic expansion can result in an optimum prior to the point at which the relevant constraint is binding.) Assuming the managers are pursuing their own interests and are rational, they will not want to press expansion to the point where its cost to *them* exceeds its value to *them*.

However, it is quite plausible that rather than diminishing, the value of bureaucratic expansion to the managers will *increase* as the expansion proceeds. It may be, for example, that as top managers acquire more subordinates they become increasingly enamored of the idea of having more subordinates. If this is true (i.e., if there is increasing marginal utility), it is very likely that the value of further expansion will continue to exceed its costs and expansion will be pursued until the budgetary or minimum profit limit is reached. (The increasing marginal utility curve will not intersect the essentially horizontal marginal cost curve anywhere, and so the minimum profit or budgetary constraint will be binding.) Accordingly, there will be continuing pressure to expand, held in check only by the solidity of the constraint. Even if the value of bureaucratic expansion to the managers does increase, it is possible that bureaucratic expansion will cease before the minimum profit or budgetary limit is reached, if managers also perceive the *costs* of further expansion as rising before that limit is closely approached. (That is, a rising marginal cost curve may also intersect the marginal utility curve prior to the point at which the constraint becomes tight.) This may happen if, for example, managers feel that beyond some point, hiring more subordinates diverts too much money from their own salary or perquisites.

From the perspective of the stockholders, consumers, or taxpayers, the situation looks very different. The cost of managerial expansion is far higher and is likely to be rising well before the budgetary or minimum profit limit is approached. In a managerial organization that is already of a substantial size, it is virtually certain that most, if not all, of the efficiency gains from increased managerial specialization will have long since been achieved. So, although it is possible that the cost of further expansion will be relatively constant, it is more likely that it will rise. More important, the *benefits* of further managerial expansion will be subject to sharply diminishing returns, dropping to zero at some point most likely well within the range of present managerial bureaucracies. Further, the benefits are likely to be negative (i.e., to turn into penalties) beyond this point, owing to the interference and irritation effects discussed earlier.

Because the cost impact and benefits of managerial expansion differ from the standpoint of the managers on the one hand and that of the stockholders, taxpayers, and consumers on the other, the desired size of a managerial organization will tend to be much greater for the (utility-maximizing) managers than for the (profit- or utility-maximizing) stockholders, taxpayers, and consumers. But since the managers control the decision-making process within wide bounds, the actual situation will be closer to what they desire than to what is seen as best by the taxpayers, stockholders, or consumers. At the point where the benefit of increasing the size of management becomes zero in societal terms or in terms of organizational efficiency, any additional personnel hired for managerial-administrative positions will be engaged in neutral activity.

The question of whether greater control leads to gains in productive efficiency that more than offset increased managerial costs is not theoretical but empirical. There is by now a significant body of empirical analysis that tends to show that in fact the dramatic increases over most of the twentieth century in the number of nonproduction personnel relative to production workers are *not* correlated with increased productivity of production workers. The seminal work by Melman, and later analyses by Dogramaci, Boucher, Fraiman, and others, suggest that much of the swelling in the ranks of nonproduction personnel is due to their engagement in what appears to be neutral activity.[15] The mental and physical skills of all the workers so engaged have been diverted from contributive labor. This is a very serious matter indeed.

This question is far from closed, and further empirical investigation would certainly be worthwhile. For example, the results of the analyses performed for manufacturing enterprises would surely be replicated in studies of the service sector and of government. However, an empirical test of this hypothesis awaits the development of effective measures of the contributive output of such organizations. For certain limited services, such as haircutting, output is not difficult to measure; but for most (e.g. teaching or medical care), output measurement is quite a problem. In fact, it is precisely the difficulty of measuring service output that creates a fog sufficient to make the excessive expansion of managerial and administrative activity possible in the first place. If the real effect of this activity could easily be determined, it would be far more difficult to justify expanding bureaucracy into the zone of zero or negative marginal returns. It is because all the managers and administrators are working hard and generating all sorts of output that it is so difficult to see whether this furious activity actually has anything to do with the coordination that is required for efficient production.

At any rate, it is clear that neutral activity does not contribute to the maintenance, much less the improvement, of the capability for efficient production, even though the basic process of which it is part may in fact contribute importantly to that capability. A society with superabundant productive resources would not have to concern itself with this issue, since there would still be a sufficient quantity and quality of resources available for contributive purposes. But a society with superabundant resources need not particularly concern itself with economics either, since the essence of the economic problem is the allocation of *limited* resources among competing objectives. For all existing real world societies, superabundance is not the problem.

The Myth of Beneficent Waste

The idea that economic systems, especially capitalist economic systems, not only produce waste and wasteful activity but thrive on them is a widespread and tenacious socioeconomic myth. Much of the multibillion-dollar business of advertising, especially advertising of durable goods, is aimed at convincing consumers to get rid of perfectly serviceable products they have bought and buy the newest, up-to-date version. Yet this is legitimized on the grounds that it is good for the economy. A popular introductory sociology text, for example, expresses this common view: "Although some advertising offers useful information to consumers, much of it is devoted to creating artificial demands for various products. Without such advertising, demand for many goods or services might shrink to insignificance, and entire industries could face economic ruin." [16] Planned obsolescence, rapid style changes, and throw-away products are also legitimized in this way. This wasteful activity is thought to keep people working, to keep the wheels of industry turning: it is supposedly vital to full employment and continued economic growth. In the words of a former chairman of General Motors, "planned obsolescence, in my view, is another word for progress." [17]

The reality is quite different. Economic systems can tolerate some level of waste; under some restricted circumstances in the very short run, some fleeting benefit may be derived. However, the idea that waste is beneficial, or even required for the proper functioning of the economic system, is simply incorrect—and the falsity of such a notion is important to the analysis being developed here. Considerable emphasis will be placed on the impact of distractive and neutral activities on the functioning of the economy, and both these categories of activities are clearly wasteful from an economic point of view.

The origin of the myth of beneficent waste clearly lies in the idea of demand maintenance and expansion. Since, in a market-oriented system, investment in enterprise depends on the voluntary action of private individuals, profit levels need to be maintained or increased in order to attract investment. Both the willingness to own and/or operate an enterprise and the willingness to provide funds to others to do the same are assumed to depend at least in part on the profitability of that enterprise. Attraction of investment is in turn critical to maintenance of employment and economic growth. But profit levels can only be maintained or increased in the long run if markets are maintained or expanded—if product demand is renewed or enhanced. Waste, in the form of both planned obsolescence and pure inefficiency in the use of productive resources, guarantees renewed and expanded demand. If products wear out quickly or rapidly go out of style, that is good because they must quickly be repurchased. If fuels and materials are squandered (within reasonable bounds) that is also good, because more must be purchased. Waste thus oils the gears of the economy and keeps it running smoothly and well.

It is important to note that this view of the benefits of waste to a capitalist economy is as widely held by the proponents of capitalism as by its critics. The captains of capitalist industry and the harshest left-wing opponents of capitalism appear to be in agreement on this basic point. Marxist critics push the analysis one step farther, arguing that over the long term, capitalism results in the concentration of control and wealth in the hands of a smaller and smaller elite. As the masses become increasingly impoverished, Marxists contend, markets tend to decline, requiring both imperialistic expansion and what I have called noncontributive activity to absorb the overproduction, i.e., to maintain and expand market demand.

The net conclusion of this line of reasoning is that economic activity cannot flourish, nor can employment be maintained, without waste in general—and neutral and distractive activity (such as military expenditures and adventurism) in particular. But this is utter nonsense. Perhaps the clearest way to see this is to hypothetically construct a purely wasteless economy and then analyze whether or not it can operate effectively in both the long and short term. A series of assumptions is necessary to construct the wasteless economy: (1) no waste or scrap of any kind is produced in the manufacture of any good or service; (2) there is no planned obsolescence; (3) nothing ever physically wears out; and (4) there are no neutral or distractive activities of any kind. If this hypothetical economy can function well without any waste or inefficiency, it should be obvious that waste cannot be necessary to the effective functioning of any real economy.

Consider this situation first from the viewpoint of the entrepreneur. The decision to establish a firm to produce any nondurable good or service will proceed in pretty much the same manner as it does in ordinary real-world economies. The demand for the product is naturally renewable, since the good or service is used up as it is consumed. Greater efficiency in the production process (owing to lack of waste) will simply result in lowered cost of manufacture. This savings may be passed along to consumers to a greater or lesser extent (depending on the relative market elasticities of supply and demand, and including market power considerations). But greater productive efficiency in itself cannot conceivably lower the firm's profitability—most likely it will significantly increase it. So there is no real problem here.

But what of a firm producing one of the everlasting goods? Would profit-seeking entrepreneurs willingly invest in an enterprise established to produce a good that need never be replaced by anyone who had acquired it? Yes—provided there is sufficient profitability available from the production and sale of the good to the point of market saturation. There is no need for a profitable opportunity to be eternal in order for its exploitation to be attractive. If this were not true, no one owning a fixed resource, such as an oil field, would develop it. Extracting and selling the resource necessarily depletes it, and ultimately eliminates that source of profit. No entrepreneur would finance the production of any fad item, from Davy Crockett hats to hula hoops to Star Wars toys, for it is clear to everyone that the fad will ultimately (often quickly) run its course and the demand for the product evaporate. In the real world, such markets are often viewed as extraordinarily attractive because of their high levels of profitability, and are characterized by a massive crush of entrepreneurs eager to invest.

Let us suppose that a new good called "television" is invented, and that consumers consider it a highly appealing product. Since no one yet has TVs, a large potential market awaits a firm organized for the purpose of producing and selling them. Such a firm is created, TVs are made and sold, and profits roll in. But after a time the market becomes saturated and demand begins to slacken. What is the firm to do now? For one thing, technological innovation, whether produced by the firm's own research and development activity or externally generated, may result in a truly improved version of the product, say color TV. If the new product version is considered desirable by consumers, a new spurt of demand will be produced and the firm can turn to the production of color TVs. Profits will thus continue to roll in. But, it might be objected, does not this new technologically induced demand imply waste, since the old TVs are junked? Is the spirit, if not the letter, of the wasteless society assumption being violated?

Assuming a society to be wasteless is not the same as assuming it to be stagnant. Real technological progress, as opposed to purely marketing modifications ("new and improved" products that are essentially the same as the products they replace), has been and continues to be a key element in the long-term rise of the material well-being of humankind. Permitting such technological progress may seem to compromise the wastelessness of our hypothetical economy, since it implies scrapping technologically obsolete products. But to eliminate any suggestion of real waste, we need only assume that the older versions are kept in use or are broken down and recycled. However, even if we wish to assume away entirely the existence of technological progress, this causes no real problem. The firm has other options.

Given the saturation of TV demand, the firm may turn to the production and sale of a good complementary in demand and substitutable in production, for which the availability of TVs has created a market. For example, production may be shifted to videocassette recorders (VCRs). Without TVs there will be no demand for VCRs, but with them, demand can be extensive. Furthermore, the labor skills and capital required for the production of TVs are similar to those required for the production of VCRs, so that this shift will represent no great difficulties. Rather, VCR production can be phased in as TV production is being phased out. There may be other products, such as home video games, that can replace VCR production and sale as that market too becomes saturated. Thus, the life of the profitable opportunities available to the firm producing this type of product can be substantially extended.

But what will the firm do when, sooner or later, the markets for the whole range of suitably related goods are saturated? There are still three options available. It can turn to the production of a new, wholly different durable good, and repeat the process. Or it can choose to produce a nondurable good or service, with a naturally renewable demand. Finally, it is also possible for this firm to disband, releasing its labor and capital resources to other uses in various sectors of the economy.

The last point raises an important issue. The closing down of all or part of any activity using productive resources (whether it is contributive, neutral, or distractive in character) creates a serious transitional problem of redirecting those resources into other activities. In our enthusiasm, particularly when resources are being removed from neutral or distractive employment, we often speak of "freeing up" these inputs for more productive use. But this process does not seem much like liberation to those people who are "freed up"; to them it means losing paid work, and that is a very serious and unpleasant matter. Nor does the economist's tendency to speak blithely of the reabsorption of those resources offer much comfort. Even if reemployment does eventually occur, it is still necessary to keep body and soul together during the period between jobs. And reemployment is rarely guaranteed.

Economists have generally focused on equilibrium states, either static or dynamic. Far too little attention has been paid to the problem of handling transitions between different economic states of the world smoothly and efficiently—not in some abstract, formalized mathematical manner, but in a detailed real world sense. Yet this is a vitally important question, particularly in human terms. There is a great need for a field of economics devoted to the analysis of such problems. An economics of transition could go a long way toward breaking the bonds that often trap societies in clearly inferior positions for extended periods of time. This will be discussed at much greater length subsequently.

The functioning of the wasteless society has so far been considered only through the eyes of the firm. It must now be viewed from the vantage point of the workers. Assuming the availability of sufficient "unpaid work" positions, the only reason for people to be concerned with the availability of paying jobs is their need for income. It is not difficult to arrange for the availability of sufficient volunteer work, though that is not as trivial a problem as it may seem. Unpaid work often does have significant capital and other resource requirements, and somebody must be willing to provide these. For example, even if all the medical, administrative, and support staff of a hospital were volunteers, someone must provide the building, the equipment, and the supplies.

This problem would not be eliminated even if one conceived of a society where no workers received money in exchange for their labors. For the difference between paid and unpaid work is not the existence of a money wage as such, but the existence of remuneration, broadly construed. That is, paid work involves trading labor for claims against goods and services, whereas unpaid work does not. Therefore, if any members of society have any material needs not provided directly by the goods or services that they produce or to which they have already achieved use rights, some remuneration will be necessary. Only the forgoing of all exchange would eliminate the need for paid work in this broad sense. But eliminating exchange would require that everyone be self-sufficient. Even if this were possible, it would mean forfeiting all of the considerable advantages of specialization and organization, which have played a vital role in achieving the huge increases in material living standard accomplished since the beginnings of organized and differentiated human activity. This is clearly not a reasonable option. Therefore, paid work will be required. And as long as there is some paid work, providing the collateral resources needed by volunteers will not be a trivial problem. However, the difficulties involved in setting up unpaid work opportunities should not be overemphasized. Unpaid work is certainly much less difficult to provide than paid work. And it is quite easy to conceive of many volunteer activities (particularly in providing services) whose capital and other resource requirements are minimal. So the assumption of sufficient unpaid work opportunities is, on balance, quite realistic. It is the paid work problem to which primary attention should be directed.

A society that does not generate waste in the form of planned obsolescence, or neutral or distractive activities, cannot, it is commonly argued, generate sufficient paid work opportunities to keep the labor force fully employed. The key here lies in the word "sufficient." To be sufficient the paid work opportunities need only supply enough income to satisfy the material needs and wants of the population, given the availability of goods and services for which no income is necessary. In the hypothetical purely wasteless economy, that means the workers must earn only enough income to supply them with the nondurable goods and services for which they must pay, plus any required or desired increase in their stock of durable goods. But once they have obtained access to a durable good, whether by purchase, gift, or inheritance, they need only enough income to cover the costs of its operation and maintenance. They do *not* require income for the purpose of eventually replacing that durable good, since it never wears out. So although there is less paid work *available* because durable goods are not built to become artificially obsolete or to fall apart, for exactly the same reason there is also less paid work *needed* by workers in order to achieve a given material standard of living. Accordingly, the permanence of durable goods may reduce the volume of paid activity, but it does not reduce the material well-being of the work force. Nor does it necessarily produce any psychological or sociological loss that otherwise might accompany work deprivation, since we are allowing for the provision of sufficient unpaid work opportunities to accommodate the need to work for nonmonetary reasons.

The elimination of sheer wastefulness and of neutral and distractive activity thus poses no serious disadvantages either to producers or to the work force. But what about consumers? Again, for nondurable goods and services the situation is pretty much the same as in real-world societies. The lack of waste in the production processes for these goods can only be an advantage. It will reduce pressure on supplies of nonrenewable resources, such as petroleum products, for which the consuming public also has direct demand. Availability of these nonrenewable products to the consuming public will thus be greater, and their prices lower (particularly over the long run), since the competition between intermediate and final demand uses will be less intense. Furthermore, because inefficient use of such resources (e.g., inefficient burning of fossil fuels) is a major source of environmental pollution, wasteless use of materials and energy resources by industry will slow resource depletion and vastly reduce the ecological problems generated by industry. This must be counted as highly beneficial to the general public.

The effect of infinitely durable goods on consumers is also highly beneficial. For if goods are built well enough to last indefinitely, the consumer will have access to them more continuously than if they frequently break down as they get older. Furthermore, the process of searching for and acquiring a replacement involves time and effort, in addition to monetary costs.[18] Thus, everlasting goods convey significant benefits in reduced shopping costs as well. Suppose the everlasting goods are substantially more expensive to purchase than ordinary durable goods. Will this not cause considerable problems for the consumer? The answer is no, provided that time purchase agreements are available. In other words, this is primarily a problem of financing, and with proper credit arrangements period payments can be arranged to cover the initial purchase price. In fact, since the goods are infinitely durable, their use value—and thus their resale value—will not be reduced over time. Therefore, liens against these assets will be that much more valuable and loans using these goods as collateral that much less risky. Thus, financing should be more readily available and cheaper than for ordinary durable goods.

It is clear then that producers, workers, and consumers do not suffer as a result of the elimination of wastefulness—they actually experience substantial gains. There are no incentive problems for producers even in a profit-based economy. There are no standard-of-living or job-fulfillment problems for workers. Consumers spend less of their money and time shopping for and repairing durable goods. Society as a whole gains from lowered rates of resource depletion and environmental pollution. And the substantial opportunity costs of pure waste and of neutral and distractive employment of resources do not have to be borne.

The point is not that a purely waste-free society should be our goal, for such a society is clearly not achievable. The point is rather that the reduction of waste in real-world societies need not produce any economic problems. On the contrary, it would create great potential benefits. Some waste may be tolerable in an economy or in a society. But waste is never beneficial.

5

Breaking Down Capital and Labor

In order to fully understand the macroeconomic impact of diverting productive resources to noncontributive activity, it is necessary to go beyond the usual labor-capital dichotomy. Since different types of labor and capital serve different purposes, it is logical that their diversion should have different effects on the economy. For example, redirecting machinists from contributive to noncontributive activity is not likely to have the same economic effect as redirecting financial managers or mechanical engineers. Likewise, the impact of diverting office furniture to noncontributive use is virtually certain to be different from that of diverting blast furnaces or electron microscopes. A finer subdivision of resources is clearly required. To be most useful, this system of subcategories should reflect differences in the economic functions that different types of labor and capital perform. And since there are hundreds of types of labor and thousands of different machines, structures, and other forms of capital, the system must strike a balance between specificity on the one hand and useful generality on the other. In other words, there must be some further breakdown of labor and capital so the major differences in economic function will not be lost; but if there are too many categories the system will be too complex to be useful.

Most macroeconomists currently work mainly with the broad labor-capital dichotomy. If subcategories are discussed at all, they tend to be relatively simple dichotomies such as fixed vs. working capital, physical vs. financial capital, production vs. nonproduction workers, or owners vs. employees. Although there is nothing wrong with any of these category systems in the abstract, they do not fully capture the differences in economic purpose that are most relevant to the present analysis.

In view of this, I propose a fairly simple system of subcategories which I believe better reflects the economic purposes served by the broad groups of labor and capital it encompasses. This taxonomy should therefore make it easier to distinguish the differing economic impacts caused by the diversion of these different types of labor and capital. Labor is subdivided into five categories: managers, administrators, technologists, highly skilled production workers, and less skilled production workers. Capital has six categories: control capital, production capital, research and development capital, infrastructure capital, raw materials, and fuels. The economic role of each of these eleven classes of resources is considered in turn.

Labor

Managers.   Managers are distinguished from administrators in this classification by virtue of their decision-making power. Managers not only make policy and strategic decisions but also set the operational boundaries within which administrators must function. They clearly wield the primary power in directing an organization, be it governmental, nonprofit, or commercial. There are three broad categories of management: internal, interface, and external. Internal management is concerned with the inner workings of the organization, particularly the operation of the production system and the services that directly support it. The primary responsibilities of internal managers are keeping the firm operating as efficiently as possible (cost minimization) and maintaining or improving product quality. Interface management concerns itself with the firm's direct interactions with the external world. On the one hand, interface managers deal with the acquisition of required inputs (purchasing, financing, hiring personnel), and on the other with the marketing and sale of output. The goal of interface management on the purchasing end is to minimize costs while acquiring a sufficient quantity and quality of resources on a timely basis. On the marketing and sales end, the goal is to maximize the flow of revenue while achieving profit targets. Finally, external management concerns itself with those elements of the political, economic, and legal environment that affect the firm (other than those encountered in the normal buying of inputs and selling of output). For example, external managers may monitor and attempt to influence legislation or the operation of regulatory commissions. They may attempt to counter the effects of publicity and political actions by citizen groups opposed to some aspects of the firm's operations. One example of this has been the reaction of the nuclear industries to the efforts of antinuclear activists.

There has long been considerable controversy concerning the appropriate boundaries of external management. Debate over the actions of external management has primarily centered on the extent to which such actions are a legitimate part of conducting business within the context of a democratic society, and the extent to which they are corrupting and antidemocratic actions of powerful vested interests. However, external management is being neither condoned nor condemned here—merely recognized as part of present-day management activity.

It is important to note that a single individual may be involved in more than one type of management. For example, personnel managers may be involved in hiring, a function of interface management, while at the same time being responsible for designing and operating employee motivation schemes, a function of internal management. Nevertheless, these three categories of management activity should be distinguished because they have such different microeconomic and macroeconomic implications. For instance, the influence of internal management on the efficiency of the firm's production system is profound and very different from the effects of external management on the political and legal environment. This is true in terms of both private costs and costs to the wider society.

We are accustomed to dealing with hierarchical management structures, in which decision power is layered. As lower levels of management are reached, decision power becomes increasingly circumscribed. There may not be a sharp demarcation below which it is clear that individuals, although they may have managerial titles, are primarily executors of decisions rather than decision makers. Nevertheless, the conceptual distinction is very important, and for most individuals it will be fairly clear whether they are making substantive decisions or mainly reacting to the decisions of others.

As a result of their microtheoretical abstractions, economists tend to take a mechanistic "black box" view of the firm. The firm responds to changing external conditions as though it were a computer programmed with some appropriate optimizing algorithm; it is not a social organization of living, breathing human beings. If this were the case, managers would not play nearly as critical a role as they do. But the decision-making and policy-setting process is not that mechanistic. The judgment and intuition of human beings play a very large part in the operation of any enterprise. The degree to which the potential prosperity of any firm is realized depends to a great extent on the decisions of the particular human beings who are its managers. Attempts to shield organizations from the individual characteristics of their managers are both dehumanizing and foolish. They are dehumanizing because they seek to turn people into executors of automatic, predetermined responses to particular situations, deskilling and routinizing management much as the time and motion study experts earlier in the twentieth century "successfully" deskilled and routinized production work. Such attempts are also foolish because they seek to remove some of the most fulfilling and challenging aspects of managerial work, and are therefore self-defeating. They are even more foolish for squandering the greatest asset of human beings as managers: their ability to inject judgment, intuition, creativity, and humanity into the managerial function.

To place the economic impact of the decision-making role into proper perspective, it is important to recognize the part that is played by chance here. In the real world, very little decision making takes place under conditions of certainty. Most decisions are made under conditions of risk (where all possible outcomes and their probabilities are known) or uncertainty (where at least some of the probabilities attached to outcomes, and perhaps some outcomes as well, are unknown). Therefore, there is a difference between a good decision and a decision that works out well. A good decision is one that takes into account all relevant information available at reasonable cost, applies intelligent decision criteria and educated or experienced judgment, and makes a choice. Because of chance, lack of information, and the general messiness of the real world, there is no guarantee that a good decision will work out well in all circumstances. Nor is there any guarantee that a random decision or even a bad decision will not work out better than a good decision in any given situation. However, good decisions are so named because they produce better outcomes in the vast majority of circumstances.

It is worth keeping this in mind to avoid overromanticizing the role of managers or overstating their degree of control. Nevertheless, the fact remains that organizations do what they do, for better or for worse, because they are directed to do so by their managers. And what happens in the collection of firms commonly referred to as the supply side of the economy depends on the combined effects of the actions each firm is directed to take by the individuals who manage it. Of course, the nature of the institutions people manage and the institutional objectives they pursue strongly affect their decisions and actions. But the institutions and their objectives do not *dictate* those decisions and actions. Within basic institutional constraints there is considerable flexibility, especially at higher levels of management. Whether or not people in managerial positions are willing to employ that flexibility is a different matter; it is in fact available. And this does not apply only to firms. Managers in government organizations operate under a similar mix of institutional constraint and managerial flexibility. They may be more obligated legally and morally to follow explicitly stated institutional goals, but they are not—or should not be—straitjacketed. This is not to say, though, that they should not be held strictly accountable for their actions and directives: they most certainly should. Governmental managers are public trustees, and as such should be subject to the highest standards of public scrutiny and accountability.

Managers, both public and private, thus play a role of great economic importance. Their decisions direct the application of productive resources and strongly influence the conditions under which those resources are employed. Since it is the flow of productive resources and the nature of the output (and not the flow of money) that is vital to the functioning of the economy, the economic significance of managerial activity is apparent.

Administrators.   The main task of an administrator is to execute, or supervise the execution of, decisions made by managers.

Not that administrators are robot-like implementers of directives; they may have significant discretion in performing their jobs. But they do not have the formal authority to alter the main policy or strategic decisions (or tactical decisions, in some cases) of the managers. Note that what they lack is the formal authority, not necessarily the physical ability. Administrators can, and often do—either intentionally or accidentally—alter managerial decisions by their effects on implementation.

There is a certain amount of overlap between managerial and administrative activities: the same individual may do both. The difference between managers and administrators is sharp in the hierarchical managerial-administrative structures we normally deal with. But such functions do not, of course, have to be performed within a hierarchical structure. It is quite possible to set up organizations in which the same individuals who are the technologists and the production workers are also the managers *and* the administrators. The terms *worker management* and *worker control* are frequently used in the significant and growing literature on nonhierarchical decision making.[1] The possibility of such structures raises important and interesting questions concerning, for example, their scale-efficiency properties and their effects on the nature of work; these questions are, however, beyond the scope of our discussion here.

The economic significance of administrators lies in the link between decision making and implementation. The supervision of implementation involves a vital feedback process. Administrators not only see that managers' decisions are carried out, but also monitor performance and results. The information they provide should be a key input to the policy evaluation process—which is, in turn, a crucial part of effective decision making in a dynamic and uncertain world.[2] The transmission of valid and reliable information throughout the managerial-administrative structure is not a simple matter of mechanical message transfer. Serious problems can and do arise as information is edited at each stage of transmission.

Editing is necessary, especially in a hierarchical decision-making structure. It is not possible, nor would it be useful, to transmit all information received. At the upper levels of the hierarchy the deluge of information would be completely overwhelming. Yet ensuring that decision makers receive both valid and reliable information is very difficult. Subordinates are often reluctant to transmit information calling attention to errors they or their superiors have made. They may report only information supporting their own views and the views they believe to be held by their superiors—a phenomenon that could be called the "good news syndrome." Personal beliefs, rigid world views, and concepts of loyalty have been shown to inhibit the generation and communication of valid information to upper levels.[3] The result may be an accumulation of misinformation at the top that can lead to a false concept of reality, at best, and at worst a loss of control. For example, Arthur Schlesinger, Jr., has pointed out the necessity of what he calls "passports to reality" in upper levels of government, particularly the presidency, precisely because superiors are often encapsulated in an unreal world.[4] Contrary to what one might expect (or at least hope), these information transmission problems tend to get worse, not better, as the decisions involved become more important.[5] And organizational barriers to communication do not operate in only one direction: the downward flow of directives can also be distorted, diverted, or ignored.

Although these problems occur in management as well as administration, they are highlighted here in order to emphasize that administrators do not behave in a robot-like manner. Instead, they are a critical part of the organizational control structure.

Technologists.   Technology is simply knowledge concerning the laws of nature (biological, chemical, and physical) and their application. Technologists are individuals who participate in developing new technical knowledge or in applying such knowledge to new uses. Engineers and scientists are the primary technologists, though technicians are also included.[6] Note that place of employment and formal title are not among the criteria for inclusion in this category. One does not have to be classified as an engineer or scientist, or employed at a government, industrial, or university research and development facility to be a technologist. Many of the most important inventions of the twentieth century were largely, if not exclusively, the products of single inventors, often working at home or in small university laboratories. Such inventions include FM radio (E. H. Armstrong), air conditioning (W. H. Carrier), penicillin (A. Fleming), ballpoint pen ink (F. Seech), the autogyro, predecessor of the helicopter (J. de la Cierva), and electrostatic copying (C. Carlson).[7] The inventors were not always formally classified as engineers or scientists—the best-known inventor of the twentieth century, Thomas Edison, had no formal training in science or engineering.

On the other hand, in the course of an ordinary career path many engineers and scientists who are successful in their roles as technologists are promoted to management status. In many cases, the move to management eventually cuts them off from the process of technological development; their technological skills then tend to obsolesce—sometimes quite rapidly. Thus, though they still may possess even advanced degrees in science or engineering, operationally they have ceased to be technologists. The sole defining characteristic of a technologist, then, is participation in the process of development and adaptation of technology.

In order to properly understand the importance of technologists to the functioning of the economy, what they can and cannot do, it is first necessary to understand the nature of the technological development process. Although the improvement of technology is often surrounded by a kind of mystique, there is in reality nothing mystical about it. Technology is developed when people with scientific and engineering expertise are provided with access to the necessary equipment and facilities and set to work solving particular problems. The nature of the problem being studied influences, though it does not always determine, the nature of the equipment and facilities needed. These may range from the simple and inexpensive—a hand calculator, pencil, and paper—to the very complex and expensive—a major astronomical observatory. More important, the nature of both the problem being addressed and the solutions being sought very strongly conditions the type of new technology developed. This is true of basic research (conceptualization), applied research (embodiment or laboratory prototype), and development (practicalization or commercialization). There is some transferability of technology, often referred to as *spinoff* or *spillover*. Working to develop or apply technology in one area sometimes does uncover knowledge applicable to other areas of technological concern. The magnitude of spinoff is an important issue that will later be discussed in some detail. For now suffice it to say that this transferability has often been overstated. The primary applicability of technology is generally to the range of problems addressed in the course of developing that technology.

That this is so significantly affects the interaction between technology and society. In much of the literature, technological progress seems to be viewed as a unidirectional path. According to this view, society has a certain degree of control over the speed at which this path is traveled, but technology itself largely determines the direction—a direction to which society must then adapt. But this is simply not the case: technology is actually more like a network of roads running off in many directions into the unknown. Although there are spaces between the roads—and some dead ends—many, many directions are possible. Furthermore, the choice of which roads to follow, and at what speed, is a social, not a scientific one— an extremely important distinction. Scientists and engineers are better able than the lay public to explain technical trade-offs and assess technical feasibility. They are also clearly better able to perform the actual research and development work. But their technical skill does not make them any more competent than the public to decide the direction and speed of technological development and application. For that choice is not scientifically determinate; it is a matter of societal preferences and judgment.

The engineering design of any product begins with a central design objective and a list of explicit or implicit design criteria. The central design objective is the effective performance of the primary function for which the product is being created. The design criteria relate to the product characteristics relevant to its use, implying a set of subobjectives. For example, the central design objective for a sound reproduction system, say a stereo, is obviously to reproduce recorded sound. The design criteria will include quality of the sound reproduction; portability; initial cost; flexibility in reproducing sound recorded on different media; appearance; operating cost; reliability; maintainability; safety of operation; and ease of operation. Since no single design can optimize all these criteria simultaneously, each feasible design will involve numerous trade-offs. For instance, it may be possible to achieve an extraordinarily high sound fidelity only at the expense of complex operation and high initial cost. It is thus obvious that whoever sets the priorities attached to the various design criteria plays a critical, in fact controlling role in determining the nature of the final product.

There are two major ways in which design criteria priorities can be established by social choice. The first is through government action on behalf of society. By promulgating and enforcing regulations, governments can seek to compel or coerce producing enterprises to offer products designed with particular criteria priorities; antipollution and safety regulations for automobiles are one example. The second way is through marketability—i.e., what sells determines the nature of what is produced. For example, if home buyers emphasize low initial cost in their purchasing decisions rather than energy efficiency, the result (in the absence of superordinate intervention) will be cheaper, energy-wasting houses. If consumers are more concerned with the appearance and power of automobiles than with safety, auto makers trying to sell safe but awkward-looking or low-powered vehicles will be at a disadvantage.

These means of social control over the application of technology both operate in market and in state-controlled economies, though certainly in controlled economies the role of government is greater and the role of marketability less.

The same forces operate through similar processes to guide the development of wholly new technology. Which paths of technological R&D are pursued also depends on the priorities set by the government acting on behalf of the society and by the marketability of the product or process being researched and developed. For example, the strong bias during the second half of this century toward the development of nuclear energy technology rather than solar or other alternative technologies was clearly not decreed by any law of nature: it was the straightforward result of very heavy government subsidies.[8] Similarly, the relative lack of attention to development of the technology of low-polluting automobile engines accurately reflected the lack of interest shown by new car buyers in car pollution characteristics.

A final point regarding the path of technology: if society does not intervene in the decision-making process to direct technology in what are considered socially appropriate directions, then the power to make such decisions will fall by default to a far smaller group of individuals in more direct contact with the R&D process. If those individuals make such decisions in accordance with their vested interests or private priorities, there may well be considerable divergence between the flow of technology that develops and that which would have been socially chosen. Because of the enormous impact of technology on society, the ability to make technological choices carries with it, in the aggregate, awesome power. Yet these decisions will be made. If they are not to be left in the hands of a very small group, society (that is, you and I) must conscientiously assert its inherent power to choose.

The purpose of this apparent digression on the social control of technology is to point out, in the strongest possible terms, that technologists acting as technologists do not have the power or special knowledge to determine the avenues of technology that are followed. Thus, the economic impacts of the technological pathways chosen are not legitimately attributable to technologists in their role as technologists. Rather, the essence of the positive economic contribution of technologists lies in their ability to develop better products and production techniques. These two aspects of contributive technological development are, of course, closely related, since the better products of producer goods industries become part of the improved production techniques of customer industries.

In any case, the advance of technology has been a key driving force behind the increased productivity of human labor, which has made possible the vast improvement in material well-being achieved over the course of human history. And, in fact, the pattern of productivity growth, or the lack of growth, has great relevance to both inflation and unemployment; much more will be said about this later.

Production workers.   The actual making of the goods and services produced by an economy is carried out not by its managers, administrators, or technologists, but by its production workers: they are the core of the production system. Managers, administrators, and technologists, insofar as they are economic actors, exist mainly to service the functions being performed directly by production workers. The relatively low status usually accorded to production work in our society is therefore wholly unjustifiable.

A production worker is anyone directly engaged in the manufacture of a good or the provision of a service. The meaning of this term differs from the point of view of a producing organization and from that of the wider society. To the firm, any individual who directly produces the firm's product is a production worker. In a management consulting firm, then, the employees who actually do the consulting are the production workers. Yet if they were performing precisely the same function *within* the firm that hired them as outside consultants, society would consider them managers, not production workers. Any definition of a functional category of work which makes sense from a societal point of view cannot depend on the organizational structure within which the work is performed, but must instead depend on the nature of the work itself and how it fits into the societal production system. Thus, from the viewpoint of the economy those management consultants are managers, not production workers.

The division of production workers into highly and less skilled categories is intended not to differentiate roles—as with the categories of managers, administrators, and technologists—but to establish categories such that job transfers within each category are more easily accomplished than transfers between categories. The capabilities that define a production worker as highly skilled often require lengthy training periods. The location of the training, whether in school or on the job, is of much less importance than the length and difficulty of the training period.

Of course, transferability of job skills within the category of highly skilled production work varies greatly, depending on the subcategories in question. Neurosurgeons and professors of economics are both highly skilled production workers, but their skills are hardly transferable. Nor is the fact that they operate in different types of production organizations the reason for the lack of transferability. Professors of economics and professors of art history are hardly interchangeable; nor are neurosurgeons and obstetricians. Yet it is probably true that the transferability of highly skilled workers functioning in similar organizations is somewhat greater than that of workers in vastly different organizations. It is probably easier to transfer medical doctors among specialties (with appropriate retraining, of course) than it is to turn an economics professor into a competent surgeon.

A related question of considerable importance is whether skills acquired are of general use or are specific to the particular institution in which the individual is now at work. The distinction between general and specific training is a particularly important consideration in redirecting productive resources from noncontributive to contributive activity—as shall become obvious further along in this analysis. For since noncontributive activity typically exists for primarily noneconomic reasons, the milieu of organizations focused on noncontributive activity is often quite different from that of organizations engaged in contributive activity. The standards of performance applied, the ways in which defined goals are achieved, the bounds of normal and abnormal behavior, the production characteristics that are emphasized or de-emphasized—the entire orientation of the organization and its work force—will likely differ.

This distinction is not confined to the category of production workers: the transferability of managers and technologists is also greatly affected by the specificity of their training. But because the problem is potentially greater the higher the skill level involved, among production workers it tends to loom larger for those classified as highly skilled. Less skilled production workers are generally more transferable within that broad category of work.

Capital

The term *capital* is often used to refer to both nonhuman physical productive assets (machines, buildings) and to financial assets (money). Since my intention is to focus on real physical capital, not artificial financial constructs, I will use *capital* only for the former purpose. Money and other financial assets will be referred to as *financial capital*.

The disaggregation of the capital resource is particularly important. Investment plays a central role in both macroeconomic theory and the theory of economic growth. But the economic effects of augmenting the capital stock—in other words, of investing—are markedly different depending on which kind of capital is involved. Adding to the stock of, say, control capital has very different effects than adding to the stock of production capital or R&D capital. For example, investing in the stock of control capital may not be all that useful as a means of generating growth in productivity. Such investment is likely to be subject to sharply diminishing, perhaps even negative marginal returns beyond a relatively low level. Investment in the stock of production capital, however, will tend to be more effective in yielding present productivity improvements. And potential productivity increases from investment in R&D capital are very small in the short run, but quite substantial over the long haul.

Control capital. The machinery, equipment, and structures that function in the service of control—of coordination and organization—are referred to as *control capital*. This is the capital of management and administration. By this definition, for example, all of the paraphernalia of the standard office—typewriters, word processors, filing cabinets, desks, calculators, the office building itself—is control capital.

Production capital. The production process, of course, directly involves considerable capital. Much of what fills the modern factory—machine tools, furnaces, chemical vats—is readily and unambiguously recognizable as *production capital.* But the building itself, the lighting, the ventilating systems, are also included in this category. They may be differentiated as "overhead" in the accounting sense. However, since they function directly in the service of production, they are still considered production capital. Production capital is thus the capital that highly and less skilled production workers require to do their work.

R&D capital. Facilities and equipment devoted to carrying out any phase of research and development, from basic research to final commercialization, are designated *R&D capital.* R&D capital may be as simple and inexpensive as pencil and paper or as complex and costly as a particle accelerator. It is the capital of technological development, which directly services neither production nor control, but rather advances the process of innovating and inventing new products and developing more efficient production techniques. Investment in R&D capital thus seeks to stretch the technological constraints that limit the firm's, and perhaps the society's, set of possible product types and production techniques. Therefore, the use of a society's resources to build up the stock of R&D capital is in a very real sense an investment in an investment.

Infrastructure capital. The capital component of the systems of transportation (e.g., roads), communication (microwave towers), water supply (pipes), waste treatment (sewage plants), power supply (generators), education (school buildings), and health care (X-ray machines) is *infrastructure capital.* These systems *indirectly* service production, control, R&D, and, for that matter, consumption. They are clearly a critical element in the functioning of any economy, and more critical the higher the level of that economy's overall development.

Raw materials and fuels. *Raw materials* are separated from *fuels* as a class of capital because the former are more directly embodied in the product. Fuels are desired not for themselves, but as sources of energy. Alternate sources of the appropriate form of energy (e.g., heat, electricity), in the proper quantity at the proper time, are interchangeable. For example, a television set or an electric furnace can be operated as well with electricity produced by the burning of oil, coal, or gas as with that produced from sunlight or by nuclear fission. The TV does not, so to speak, know or care which fuels were used to produce the electricity that energizes it. The same cannot be said of raw materials.

Of course, fuels are not *instantaneously* interchangeable—a present-day automobile cannot be fueled by loading lumps of coal into the fuel tank. Energy-using systems are often designed to use energy derived from specific fuels. But the possibilities of interchangeability of fuel sources among numerous energy uses are clearly greater than those for the interchangeability of raw materials. For example, the primary use of energy in the United States is heating, and heating can be effectively carried out (given the proper equipment) by virtually every known fuel or energy source.

Some final notes.   Most machinery, equipment, and (to a lesser extent) structures are specialized to one of the first four categories of capital. There are, however, some interesting exceptions, the transferability of computers being a case in point. As a general category, there are of course computer applications in the service of control (e.g., accounting, financial analysis), production (optimization of combustion processes, numerical control of machining operations), and R&D (experimental simulation, statistical analysis)—as well as in the provision of infrastructure services (switching of communications, medical diagnosis). It therefore seems that computers are readily transferable capital. The real question, however, is not whether something called a computer can perform each of these varying functions, but whether a particular machine can be moved among these characteristic uses. That degree of flexibility exists in some cases but not in others. There is a huge variety of equipment within the category "computers," and that equipment is not universally interchangeable.

Having discussed the basic characteristics and economic roles of the various human and nonhuman productive resources, we can now consider the micro- and macroeconomic implications of the diversion of these resources to neutral or distractive activity.

6

The Impact of Noncontributive Activity on Productive Competence

The main business of any economy is contributive activity. Only contributive activity provides the goods and services that enhance the material standard of living of the population. Since a great variety of goods and services fall into this category, a great many types of production are consistent with contributive resource use. Some of these goods and services may fit better than others any given individual's particular set of preferences and concept of what is best from a social welfare point of view. Nevertheless, all such activity is contributive and therefore an economically positive use of resources. This would be true even if there were an extraordinary concentration of all of the economy's productive resources in one very narrow area of contributive activity. In that case there would be a serious imbalance in the economy, leading to neglect and deterioration in other sectors. While this kind of concentration is not particularly wise, with fairly free international trade a highly unbalanced contributive economy might still be macroeconomically workable. The world stock of standard-of-living goods and services would still be enlarged.

As previously argued, the use of productive resources in contributive activity increases material well-being by directly adding to the stock of consumer goods (quantitatively or qualitatively), and so enhancing the present standard of living; by adding to the economy's capability for producing standard-of-living goods and services in the future; or by a combination of the two. The role of consumer goods production in promoting material well-being seems obvious, and will not be discussed further. The second aspect of contributive activity, an issue of central importance to the operation of the economy, does require further attention.

Productive Competence

Productive competence—the capability for efficient production—is primarily the result of three things: an appropriately skilled and motivated work force; a sufficient quantity and quality of capital, particularly production and infrastructure capital; and an up-to-date process and product technology. Without conscious and ongoing efforts to maintain it, productive competence will erode. The maintenance or improvement of productive competence requires a flow of resources adequate to preserve and strengthen these three pillars. But how is this achieved?

The skill level of the labor force is maintained through education and experience both in formal school settings and on the job. Therefore, maintaining the skill of the labor force requires continuing investment in educational infrastructure: a sufficient fraction of a nation's labor and capital must be directed to its educational institutions. However, the importance of on-the-job experience and training for maintaining and increasing the skill levels of *all* types of labor should not be underestimated. Whether or not there is a formal program for on-the-job training, some skill, physical or mental, is acquired as a result of working, except perhaps at the simplest and most boring of jobs. This implies that the enrichment of jobs so as to enhance creativity, variety, and other skill-augmenting characteristics is not only a useful means of improving immediate job performance through increased interest and motivation, but also a solid educational investment. Therefore, the nature of jobs, as well as their quantity, is an important concern of sound economic policy. Another consequence of the educational character of work is that maintaining high levels of employment (in paid or unpaid work, or both) should in itself be part of a strategy for maintaining the skill

level of labor. Thus, full employment (in this broad sense of employment) is not only a social goal but also a means to that goal.

Maintaining or improving the quantity and quality of capital
requires direct investment in the capital *and* investment in technological development. Physical depreciation of the stock of production and infrastructure capital will cause the deterioration of a
nation's productive competence over time; preventing this requires
devoting an adequate portion of a society's capital and labor resources to the maintenance, repair, and eventual replacement of
existing capital. However, this physical deterioration process has
often been outpaced by the far more rapid process of technological
obsolescence. A sufficient flow of investment in the development of
technology that will produce more efficient production capital is vital
to overcoming this technological depreciation. Technology does not
advance automatically: the needed rate of technological progress can
only be achieved by devoting a large enough part of a society's labor
and capital resources to the development of the type of technology
that enhances productive capabilities.

Is there not something circular here? After all, it is the rate of
technological progress that causes technological obsolescence. How
then can the rate of technological depreciation be overcome by investing in technological development? The answer lies in the distinction
between *absolute* and *relative* productive competence. The *absolute*
level of productive competence can be maintained without technological progress. In fact, appropriate technological development
tends to *increase* absolute productive competence, not maintain it.
But *relative* productive competence is an entirely different matter.
Any enhancement in the competence of a competitor's production
system reduces a producer's own *relative* productive competence,
clearly placing the producer at a competitive disadvantage. The competitor's rate of technological progress renders the producer's own
stock of production and infrastructure capital technologically obsolescent compared with the competitor's capital. Hence, the producer can maintain *relative* productive competence only by out-
pacing the competitor-imposed rate of technological obsolescence
with a sufficiently high rate of its own technological advancement.
This is true whether we are considering micro-level interfirm rivalry
or macro-level competition between the production systems of different societies.

The final pillar of productive competence—the level of product and process technology—has already been discussed, in part. However, the questions of "disembodied technology" and consumer product technology still remain. Disembodied technology, because it has not been incorporated into the design of a piece of capital, can be applied without having to purchase new and better machines. Examples include new techniques for scheduling work in a factory so the work flow is smoother and more efficient, and improvements in chemical processes that change the mix of chemicals, reducing the cost of manufacture while using the same production equipment. Even disembodied technology may require additional capital investment, however, for it is possible that a different mix of types of existing capital may be required to fully implement the new technology within a given production system. For example, perhaps the disembodied technology is a refining process requiring more heat than the existing process. Additional furnaces of the type already in use will have to be installed to make use of it. But on the whole, the key economic difference between embodied and disembodied technology is clear: the former causes the existing capital stock to obsolesce, the latter does not.

Nevertheless, there are no critical differences between the development processes for embodied and disembodied technologies. Nor are these processes essentially different from consumer product technology improvement. Both cases involve the application of engineering and scientific talent, with access to appropriate R&D capital, to the solution of product and process improvement problems. In the struggle to maintain an ongoing rate of technological progress, there is no effective substitute for the consistent efforts of scientists and engineers. This is not to disparage the role of the single inventor, the prolific inventive genius (such as Edison), or the flash of insight.[1] Even in this era of sophisticated technology, it is simply not true that technology is advanced only by the efforts of large flocks of scientists and engineers working in research and design teams. However, in order to be economically (as opposed to scientifically) significant, new technology must pass successfully through the entire development process—from the initial stage of understanding the fundamental concepts involved, through the laboratory or prototype stage, and then through the process of commercialization, which establishes economic viability. Though the scientific status and importance of the commercialization stage is often downgraded, it is from both an economic and a broader societal view a crucial part of the process. It is what transmutes an interesting possibility into a widely applied reality—with all of the attendant social and economic impacts about which so much has been written. And if the entire process of technological progress is considered over the whole range of contributive technologies, it is clear that the efforts of many individuals are needed to move it along quickly enough to maintain a society's relative productive competence.

Given that the ultimate purpose of economic activity is the improvement of human well-being, the production of consumer products is not an end in itself, but a means to this overarching goal. But if consumer products are valued for their contribution to the material well-being of the population, making products of higher *quality* can increase real output just as much as making them in greater *quantity*. Thus, for a given use of inputs, a production system that produces higher-quality, technologically improved consumer products is more efficient than one that produces the same quantity of lower-quality products. This is true even if relative productive competence is viewed more narrowly, in terms of its implications for competitive advantage in the sale of products: in that case, quality competition is clearly as significant a factor as price competition. The empirical difficulty of the concept of quality (a result of great measurement problems) may explain why economists have traditionally been loath to incorporate it in a meaningful way into the theory of competition. But the fact that quality competition has become a neglected theoretical stepchild does not diminish in the slightest its importance in the real world of economic activity. The real improvement of consumer product technology (as opposed to the "new, improved" hucksterism of marketing) can thus legitimately be considered an increase in productive competence.

Resource Diversion and the Decline of Productive Competence

If, as has been argued, the maintenance of productive competence requires a continuing flow of productive resources into contributive activity, it then follows that diverting significant amounts of resources permits, perhaps even fosters, an erosion of productive competence. The channeling of productive resources into noncontributive activity reduces the availability of those resources to the contributive economy. From the viewpoint of the real business of the economy, it is as though some resources had been destroyed, leaving the economy poorer. This effect can be made worse if the diverted resources are used in such a way as to interfere with the effective use of some of the resources that have not been diverted.

Short-term effects. Of course, it is not only productive competence that is threatened by resource diversion: there may also be a more immediate effect on the standard of living. Which of these effects dominates clearly depends on the contributive uses from which the resources have been diverted. To the extent that they have been diverted from the kinds of investment activities that are necessary to maintain and improve productive competence, the former effect will be dominant; to the extent that they have been directed away from consumer goods production, the latter effect will occur. The focus here remains on the issue of productive competence.

Shrinking the resource base of the contributive economy has a serious opportunity cost, measured by the degree to which the population has forgone additions to the present or future standard of living—additions that could have been generated by contributive use of those resources. Furthermore, that opportunity cost may grow at an increasing rate as the resource diversion expands, depriving the contributive economy of increasingly scarce and thus increasingly important types of capital and labor resources. Considerations of opportunity cost are conventionally expressed by the "production possibilities" or "transformation" curve. It is this type of analysis that gives rise to the famous "guns vs. butter" representation of the short-term trade-off between military and civilian goods. This analysis could be interpreted as implying that military and civilian goods (or more broadly, distractive and contributive goods) are economically comparable categories of products. But they are not. It would be more appropriate to use the production possibilities curve only for illustrating resource trade-offs between production of different types of contributive goods, and to represent resource diversion as tending to move the curve inward over time. To do so would in effect be to recognize that ongoing resource diversion does indeed secularly shrink the contributive resource base.[2]

Long-term effects. In the long term, a large, continuing

resource drain into noncontributive activity can so diminish productive competence as to cripple the ability of the contributive economy to function effectively, much as a parasite growing for too long can cripple its host. This is, of course, ultimately deadly to the parasite as well as to the host. While it is certainly true that the contributive economy can stand alone—can in fact function better without neutral activity or the distractive economy—the converse is not true. Neither neutral nor distractive activities can survive without the support of the contributive economy, which is their lifeblood.

In the short term, resources diverted from the contributive economy do not appear to cause a problem. They are employed, not idle; the workers involved have paid work and thus have income. They are not adding to what society ordinarily regards as the welfare burden of unemployed labor, or worse yet of "loafers" and "no-accounts." Yet they are, in economic terms, in precisely the same position, creating a demand for present standard-of-living (i.e., consumer) goods without contributing to either the present or future supply of such goods. Because they may be working hard, it might be argued that in work-ethic terms distractive-sector workers are more deserving than the unemployed of the goods and services they drain from the contributive economy. But ultimately their activity does not result in one iota more economic value than does the inactivity of the unemployed. It is therefore legitimate to consider them part of society's welfare burden.

Similarly, the capital resources diverted are wrapped up in the furious activity of the neutral and distractive economies and do not appear to be standing idle. Yet for at least some of these resources, for example nonrenewable energy sources such as oil and coal, society would be economically better off if the resources were standing idle rather than being used up in the service of noncontributive activity. The fact that their use also seriously contributes to the generation of societal "bads" like environmental pollution strengthens this argument.

If working conditions in noncontributive activities are good, and pay rates are higher than for contributive activities (as is in fact often the case), the existence of such opportunities for paid work creates greater societal problems than does unemployment. For virtually by definition, no one in the labor force *chooses* to be unemployed (except perhaps very temporarily). But many people not only choose but actively seek employment in neutral and distractive work when higher pay and other incentives are offered. In other words, the existence of unemployment does not serve as a magnet to draw resources away from the contributive sector. Quite the opposite—the larger the pool of unemployed workers, the more tenaciously those with jobs hold on to them. However, neutral and distractive paid work opportunities may actively draw people away from contributive activity.

In the long term, the effects of distractive activity on productive competence can be very severe. Whereas neutral activities are essentially redundancies within the organizations of contributive industries, distractive activities may themselves be complete industries. That is, to the extent that the final product of an industry lacks inherent economic value, the industry itself may be described as distractive. The resources most critical to maintaining and improving productive competence are not as likely to be drawn into neutral use as into distractive industry. In the long term, productive competence depends most heavily on technological advance (and hence on R&D capital and labor), on investment in production capital, and on a skilled and motivated production work force. None of these resources—engineers and scientists, R&D equipment, production capital, or skilled production labor—are very likely to be heavily engaged in neutral activity. But they are certainly likely to be a part of every distractive industry. What makes an industry distractive, after all, is not its internal structure or efficiency but rather the nature of its output. A firm engaged in distractive activity looks pretty much like a contributive firm does. It will have a personnel department, a sales force, a production work force, an R&D operation, maintenance crews, a shipping department, warehouses, and so forth. It will therefore need all the resources those activities require.

To the extent that distractive industry serves as a sink for technologists and investment capital, it has particularly strong effects on productive competence in the long term. This is perhaps even more true for the technologists than for the capital. For more than any other factor, the advance of production-oriented contributive technology has been responsible for the vast improvements in productivity achieved by modern economies.[3] But, as earlier noted, the kind of technology developed is conditioned very strongly by the kinds of problems being studied and the kinds of solutions being sought. Therefore, applying engineering and scientific talent (and associated

R&D capital) to the purposes of distractive industry may very well result in a large, ongoing stream of innovation, very important to the functioning of the distractive sector. But that innovation may not be all that useful to the contributive economy.

Technological Resource Diversion

When technological resources are diverted to noncontributive activity, a kind of internal "brain drain" is set up that is bound to slow down the kind of technological progress most applicable to the contributive sector. In particular, the part of the stream of technology directed at improving the efficiency of production will be curtailed, with negative effects on productive competence in the long term. In the short term, these effects may be practically invisible, even when the diversion is on a large scale. Why should this be? In the first place, there are natural time lags throughout the process of technological development. The gestation period between the theories and discoveries of basic research and the emergence of prototypical application may be lengthy. There are a variety of reasons for this, including the need for development of complementary technologies. For example, the concept of wave-front reconstruction photography, more commonly known as holography, considerably predated the development of a sufficiently pure monochromatic coherent light source—the laser—to make the concept workable.[4] In addition, the careful experimentation and verification procedures of serious science take time, as do the thorough design evaluations and prototype production of serious engineering. Furthermore, a significant amount of time is required for the dissemination of information concerning the discoveries of basic research and the successful achievements of applied research. Generally, different individuals—even different institutions—are involved in basic and applied research and in commercialization. Therefore, time is required for dissemination of the information and for its absorption and integration into the thought processes of its recipients. Because of these various time lags, the effects of significant (but not total) diversion of technological resources are not immediately observable on the factory floor. The passage of time eventually makes the diversion's drag effects on productive competence painfully obvious. But in the short term, the process of applying new technology already in the pipeline may continue, strengthening the illusion that the diversion has had little effect.

The second reason why technological resource diversion may go undetected in the short run also relates to time lags. The dynamic nature of technological progress implies that even an economy with a substantial technological lead either must continue to at least match the rate of contributive technological development of its foreign competitors or must see that lead eroded over time. Foreign contributive economies not burdened by heavy resource diversion may begin closing the *productive competence* gap immediately, but it will take some time before that change in relative productive competence is translated into a significant change in relative *competitive position*. In other words, other economies subject to little or no distractive-sector brain drain will require some time to close enough of the technological gap between themselves and a technological leader to gain a competitive advantage over the original leader's industries. Until that point is reached, the decline in relative productive competence of the diverting economy may literally not be noticed. If noticed, it still may be intentionally ignored, even by the leaders of the contributive industries whose competence is eroding. It will not affect their sales (or even their orders) in a serious way prior to the actual loss of their competitive edge. For that matter, because of customer habits and time lags (in setting up distribution networks and disseminating product information to customers), sales of the former leader's contributive industries may not be significantly threatened for some time *after* its competitive edge has in fact disappeared. Again, technological resource diversion is not seen as having caused any real problem in the short run.

Threshold effects.   The enlargement of the noncontributive sectors may appear to produce a kind of "threshold" or "switching" effect. The decline in productive competence it produces seems to have little effect until it proceeds to the point at which relative competitiveness has significantly shifted. Then real impacts on sales begin to be felt. There may be another threshold effect, however, more relevant to the immediate analysis. It is possible that until the amount of resource diversion reaches a certain threshold, its effects on relative productive competence are minimal; beyond that threshold, growing diversion produces an increasingly severe effect. Even more ominous is the possibility of a critical threshold of diversion beyond which the negative effects on productive competence may become extremely difficult to reverse. If such a threshold exists, it is more likely to depend on both the size and duration of the diversion than on the size alone. Neither a large, short-lived diversion of resources nor a very small, long-lived one is likely to have any lasting effect on productive competence.[5]

Technological progress is not a sharply defined process—not only because of the risks involved but because of a whole range of uncertainties. And it is not a smooth process converting technological inputs of known quantity and quality into new technical knowledge of corresponding value. Some of the output of technological processes develops smoothly, but there is also a component that develops by fits and starts. Given these characteristics, it is possible that the impact of small diversions of technologists will, in effect, fall within the statistical noise of the process and will have virtually no definable impact on contributive technology.

For similar reasons, once the diversion becomes sufficiently great, there may be a point at which the rate of technological development begins to deteriorate very rapidly. After all, contributive technology is not a single, unified field. The technologists available to the contributive sector are spread over a great many separable areas of contributive technology. At a high level of diversion, there may not be enough engineers and scientists left working within each of these areas to generate technology efficiently. With too few colleagues working on related projects, progress may be slowed by the lack of interaction. Furthermore, the technical capacity within each area of contributive technology may well be too small to support very many research and development projects. Considering the many risks and uncertainties involved in R&D activity under the best of conditions, the inability to spread risk over many projects may make investment in R&D look unattractive. (In other words, the inability to undertake a variety of R&D projects may make it impossible to generate a sufficiently high expected rate of return with a sufficiently low variance to encourage investment.) Consequently, there may well be an upper threshold of diversion beyond which the rate of technological development in the contributive sector is subject to dramatic collapse.

Given enough time, there may be so much weakening of the contributive technological sector that extraordinary measures will be required to rehabilitate it. Suppose, for example, that those attracted to electrical engineering are routinely shunted away from a contributive specialty like engineering of electric power plants into specialties with more prestigious and better-paid work opportunities in the distractive sector. Then not only the number of power engineers but also the capability for training them will decline over time. When the shortage of power engineers becomes severe and a social decision is made to increase their supply, it may be discovered that this cannot be quickly or easily done. There may no longer be enough power-engineering courses given at engineering schools, and perhaps not even enough capable teachers familiar with the state of the art in that field, to properly train those who are both interested and competent.

There is substantial variability in the rates of progress of different technologies—and hence in the rates of obsolescence of knowledge. This leads accordingly to differences in the critical size-duration combinations of any diversion thresholds that may exist. In any case, the possibility of such thresholds is an intriguing and basically empirical question. Whether thresholds exist or whether the decline of technological competence with resource diversion is smooth and continuous, it is clear that negative effects on productive competence will result.

Accelerating technological decline? There is yet another interesting and important question concerning the relationship between technological resource diversion and contributive technological development. Does the decline in the contributive technological sector's output (and so in productive competence) accelerate with continued diversion? Here there are two opposing forces. One might be called the problem of the "best and brightest"; the other is the question of whether technological inputs are subject to the law of diminishing marginal returns. Let us consider each in turn.

Technologists are, after all, a form of highly skilled labor. And like all highly skilled workers, technologists are not all equally good at what they do—even compared to other technologists with equivalent formal training and experience. Just as there are many highly talented professional ballet dancers but few Mikhail Baryshnikovs and many skillful professional tennis players but few Chris Evert Lloyds, so there are many physicists but few Albert Einsteins, and many inventors but few Thomas Edisons. However, unlike workers in many other endeavors, a brilliant scientist or engineer not only excels at what he or she does, but moves the entire technological base in that area forward. If the highest-paying, most prestigious job opportunities are in distractive work, a disproportionate share of the best and brightest technologists may be swept into the distractive sector. This is even more likely if heavy investment in R&D capital provides technologists in the distractive sector with extraordinary and thus highly attractive facilities. Because every employer has an incentive to choose the most qualified and capable applicant for a given position, there will be a tendency for the best trained, most promising technologists to be diverted first, and for others to follow in order of decreasing productivity. If this is so, it implies that the negative impact of technological diversion on technological development competence in the contributive sector worsens as diversion grows, but at a decreasing rate. Of course, employers can only use imperfect measures, especially in an area as uncertain as technological development, to determine which employees are likely to be the most productive. And some highly competent technologists may, for other reasons, not wish to participate in the distractive sector. So the selection process will not be as neat in reality as it is in concept; but on the whole, it will be reasonably similar.

The other side of the coin is the question of whether technological inputs are individually subject to diminishing marginal returns (as are other productive inputs) or collectively subject to decreasing returns to scale. If they are, then the loss of relatively few personnel from a fairly large contributive R&D sector will do little to impede the rate of contributive technological progress, since their marginal contributions will be small. But as the diversion grows, the negative impact it produces on the flow of contributive technology will grow at an increasing rate.

It is not at all clear which of these effects will dominate, and therefore whether the rate of deterioration of contributive-sector technology will accelerate or decelerate with increasing diversion. This is essentially an empirical question. One thing, however, is abundantly clear: the greater the diversion of technologists and associated R&D capital, the more the rate of contributive technological progress will slow down. And that is, after all, the critical matter.

For it is this negative effect on contributive technology that plays such an important role in the causal linkage between the growth of the noncontributive sectors and the decline of productive competence.

Capital Diversion

The question of diversion of technological resources, with which we have just been dealing, obviously includes a component of capital diversion as well as labor diversion, for a shift of R&D capital will naturally accompany the shift of technologists. But other aspects of capital diversion also have major impacts on an economy's productive competence.

Infrastructure capital. Underlying the system of production and consumption of goods and services is the web of transportation, communication, energy and water supply, waste treatment and disposal, and other systems—the infrastructure. This is a crucial part of the societal support system: it is difficult to conceive of how a modern society could function without a well-developed infrastructure. Even those who have as their ideal the replacement of large-scale power supply, for example, by individual or neighborhood energy self-sufficiency, do not generally argue for the desirability of chopping up the transportation network or disconnecting our intercommunications capability. To do so would be to bring about a kind of social isolation that would produce great cultural impoverishment, undoing one of the most positive accomplishments of modern technology—the increased capability for cross-cultural human awareness and interaction. In more narrow economic terms, the infrastructure is an important contributor to the efficiency of both production and consumption. And the quality and quantity of the capital component of the infrastructure are key determinants of its vitality.

Capital diversion affects the infrastructure in a different way than does the diversion of technologists. Engineers and scientists are diverted by being physically moved into distractive (or neutral) activity. Infrastructure capital is not so much moved into noncontributive activity as starved by the redirection of other capital and labor resources into such activity and away from the continued nourishment of the infrastructure. Infrastructure capital is, on the whole, very long-lived. However, without continuing maintenance it eventually falls into a state of disrepair and ineffectiveness. Furthermore, because of its crucial support function, failure to replace technologically obsolescing infrastructure capital with more efficient, newly developed versions will put a drag on the efficiency of the production system itself. If labor and production capital are directed away from the construction and maintenance of infrastructure capital, the effectiveness of this support system will be markedly degraded. And if the attention of technologists is also diverted from infrastructure improvement, the infrastructure will become even more debilitated.

Production capital. Production capital provides an interesting mixed case. On the one hand, it is directly divertible into distractive activity, as are technologists; on the other, it is subject to deterioration by starvation, as is infrastructure capital. To the extent that production equipment and facilities used in the distractive sector are sufficiently general in purpose to be usable in at least some part of the contributive sector, such production capital can reasonably be said to have been directly diverted. Part of the distractive sector's production capital is so specialized that it is useless elsewhere. In a sense it has been less directly, but more completely, diverted. The diversion is less direct because it is not so much pieces of capital per se that have been diverted as the labor, capital, materials, and other resources that they embody. The capital itself is symbolic of that underlying resource diversion. The diversion is more complete because the resources embodied by such production capital are not subject to redirection into contributive activity at some future point: from a societal viewpoint they constitute a sunk cost from which no future economic benefits can be derived.

In all likelihood, the vast majority of distractive-sector production capital will be transferable. While it may not be general-purpose in the ordinary use of that term, there will be at least some contributive-sector uses for which it is suited. It may be true, however, that the larger the size of the distractive sector and the longer it has been in place, the greater will be the fraction of its production capital that is not transferable into contributive activity. In fact, the degree of that transferability of resources in general may decline over time. The reasons for this are straightforward. The larger the distractive sector, the more resources it commands; the more resources it commands, the more influence it is likely to exert on the designers and producers of its production machinery. Its capital will therefore be more tailored to the particular needs of the distractive sector. In addition, production on a larger scale makes the use of more highly specialized inputs more attractive to producers. And the longer the period of heavy distractive activity, the greater the likelihood of divergence in design between the production capital used in the contributive and distractive sectors. The distractive sector ceases to be a mere offshoot of the contributive economy and increasingly establishes a distinct identity. This effect is strengthened by the diversion of technological labor and R&D capital to the solution of the increasingly specialized problems of the distractive sector. That is, as technologies of these sectors diverge, so will the particular characteristics of their production capital, which after all embodies a substantial part of those technologies.

Production capital, of course, also requires ongoing servicing and periodic replacement to maintain its competence. Consequently, as in the case of infrastructure capital, continuing diversion of resources needed for this purpose will result in a decline in the quality of the nation's stock of production capital. Furthermore, the economic impact of technological diversion's effects on production capital is greater than the economic impact of its effects on infrastructure. This is especially true in terms of relative productive competence. Deterioration of the infrastructure undermines the economy, producing definite negative effects on productive competence. The effects of a relative deterioration in the quality of production capital stock, however, more directly and completely degrades that competence. For example, while lagging behind other nations in transportation system quality will affect a nation's cost of supplying steel and thus the competitive position of its steel industry, competitiveness will be much more strongly affected if the steel industry's furnaces and collateral equipment are relatively old and technologically obsolescent.

Control capital.   Noncontributive activity also diverts a fraction of the stock of control capital. The nature of this diversion is conceptually similar to that of production capital. The impact on productive competence, however, tends to be far weaker. There are a number of reasons why this would be expected. For one thing, control capital is clearly not as central to the process of production. I have emphasized that the coordination and decision-making functions of management and administration are crucial to effective production—they are not to be underrated. Yet they only service production; managers and administrators do not directly produce the firm's output. Furthermore, control capital is not nearly as critical to management and administration as production capital is to production. Technologically obsolescent control capital (e.g., less than state-of-the-art word processors) will in general certainly not hamper effective management (let alone production) as much as technologically obsolescent production capital will hamper productive competence.

Moreover, the likelihood of technological divergence between the distractive and contributive sectors is much lower for control capital than for production capital. Although the management functions may be oriented differently, the performance requirements for the capital of management and administration (i.e., control capital) will tend to be fairly similar in the two sectors. For example, even if different types of labor are employed to do different things in a distractive firm than in a contributive firm, payrolls must be met, accounts kept, and personnel policy made; and the typewriters, calculators, and computers needed to do all this will be similar, if not identical. Finally, since much control capital is already engaged in neutral activity, its movement to distractive activity (one step further away from contributive activity, in a sense) would have little if any impact on the contributive sector. And management and administrative work are far more congenial homes for neutral activity than is production work.

Fuels and raw materials. Energy used up in distractive activity is clearly unavailable for use in the contributive sector. Certain forms of raw materials, for example most metals, can potentially be recovered from distractive-sector products through various forms of recycling, and thus are not entirely lost. This form of distractive capital use, however, does not so much affect productive competence as it does present output.

Resource Diversion and Productive Competence

In sum, then, nearly all forms of resource diversion have important effects on productive competence. The diversion of technologists drains the contributive sector by reducing the flow of contributive technology. Diversion of both R&D and production capital from activities servicing the infrastructure degrades the quality of the infrastructure services provided to production (and consumption). Hence, societal productive competence declines. Diversion of R&D capital (and technologists) eventually causes technological obsolescence of the stock of production capital relative to that of other nations not engaged in large-scale diversion. Direct diversion of production capital from reproducing itself—from constructing more contributive-sector production capital—greatly exacerbates this effect, as does physical depreciation. Control capital will tend to be less severely affected, and will have less effect on productive competence as it deteriorates. Fuels and raw materials diversion will not affect national productive competence as much as it will affect immediate production. And nearly all of these effects will be stronger in the long run.

In the next chapter, the relationships between productive competence, inflation, and unemployment are analyzed. The macroeconomic implications of the decline in productive competence caused by resource diversion can then be addressed.

7

Productive Competence, Unemployment, and Inflation

     In the preceding chapter, productive competence was defined as the capability for efficient production. The concept of efficiency is a relative one, in several senses. It is relative historically, since the quantity and quality of output achievable from a given input mix (or more generally at a given real cost) may change over time. We are accustomed to thinking of this change as rooted in the advance of technology—and this has in fact been the source of most if not all of this change in the past. But what is considered efficient production can also change because of the foreclosure of production options. For example, what constitutes efficient production in terms of the cost of producing a barrel of crude oil at the wellhead will change as the most easily recoverable oil deposits are used up.

    Even more important, the concept of efficient production may change as the social definition of what constitutes output changes. For example, as our society began to explicitly define environmental pollution as a form of negative output—a production "bad" instead of a production good—efficient production of automobiles required that they pollute less. Because a highly polluting automobile was no longer an acceptable output, its production became inherently inefficient. Furthermore, when efficiency is defined in terms of full output, as it should be, the negative output of a production process (in this case pollution) must be offset against its positive output (in this case the quantity of intended product). Considering full rather than conventional output can, and often does, alter the ranking of production processes in terms of efficiency.

Efficiency is also relative cross-sectionally. That is, even though a particular production system may be generating a high quantity and quality of output for a given cost relative to past history, it is not efficient if another contemporary production system is yielding that output at a lower unit cost. It is to emphasize this point that the idea of relative and absolute productive competence was introduced. Absolute competence captures the idea of efficiency in historical terms, relative competence in contemporaneous terms.

Competence and Economic Vitality

A fully competent contributive production system is capable of generating the maximum material standard of living that can be achieved at a given point in time by the society in which the system functions. This standard of living will be maximum within the constraints of the availability of resources to the society itself and the level of technological knowledge extant in the world as a whole. While it is by no means immune to economic, social, political, or technological shocks, it is maximally capable of dealing with them. It is dynamic, not only in the literal sense of the word, but also in the figurative sense of being vigorous and energetic. Like any healthy organism, it is widely adaptable in the face of changing environmental conditions.

In more concrete terms, one of the more important characteristics of the competence of a production system is the system's ability to cope with changes in the conditions of resource supply—particularly in the cost, availability, and quality of inputs. If, for example, the cost of labor rises for some reason (e.g., through the mechanisms of collective bargaining), a competent production system will be capable of at least partially offsetting the impact of that rise on unit production costs. This can be accomplished by developing and introducing improved manufacturing techniques to derive more output per unit of labor input—that is, by finding and using methods of augmenting labor productivity. Increases in other input costs will provoke similar reactions. The effectiveness of the production system in maintaining and improving this cost-offsetting capability will be critical to the success of the economy in maintaining and improving the general material standard of living. It is crucial to understand that such cost-offsetting capability is not a purely financial or monetary phenomenon. Far from it: it is a reflection of the deep-rooted ability of a society to take full advantage of its basic productive resources— to efficiently transform its factors of production into goods and services.

From a microeconomic point of view, a firm that is successful in offsetting any secular rise in the cost of its inputs will be able to short-circuit cost-push pressures that would otherwise force it to accept declining profits, raise its prices, or both. To the extent that it can implement productivity improvements that outrun the rise in input costs, it will be able to drop its prices over time. And whatever the structure of the market in which it operates, it will generally be profitable for the firm to do just that. Given some degree of active competition, a firm will be pressed to stay abreast of or even to develop and implement productivity-improving techniques—whether it is striving for competitive advantage or it merely wishes to avoid being squeezed by a more efficient rival. Similarly, unless there are extraordinary barriers to entry of rivals into the market, oligopolists and even monopolists will have to contend with the significant, though probably less severe, pressures of potential competition. Whether the competition is potential or current, continuing productivity improvements are an advantage to a firm in facing off against its competitors. And, independent of market power considerations, such improvements should increase the firm's ability to maximize its profits or achieve any other objective it may have.

The macroeconomic result of widespread, ongoing productivity improvement is a continuing rise in purchasing power (real income)— as long as total factor productivity outruns nominal input cost increases, this will be the case. Real prices will be falling; whether or not nominal prices will fall depends primarily on monetary policy. A sufficient expansion of the money supply may counterbalance the tendency for prices to fall, but it will not prevent real income from rising. Real income depends primarily on both the level of productive competence and the activation of such competence by proper coordination of economic activity. It does not depend on the nominal size of the money supply—especially not in the long run.

Furthermore, if the cost-offsetting process of productivity improvement is vigorous enough, it will generate secondary effects that further weaken any cost-push pressures on the production system. For one thing, to the degree to which firms at a lower position in the vertical process of production are successful in offsetting the input cost increases they face, they will not transmit these pressures to their customer firms. Thus, at every stage in the vertical stream of production a kind of safety valve will be operating, reducing the cost-push pressures with which subsequent processors have to cope. For another thing, as the cost-offsetting process proceeds, its very success in holding down the prices of final consumer products will tend to reduce pressure for wage increases. After all, the purchasing power represented by any nominal wage will be increasing, or at the very least will be falling less rapidly than it would in the absence of strong productivity growth. Therefore, smaller adjustments in the nominal wage will be needed to produce increasing real wages.

To those who would raise the specter of money illusion here and contend that workers would demand higher nominal wages even if prices were falling, I would respond that even if that is true, they would certainly demand less of a wage increase than they would if prices were rising. This mitigation of wage demands implies in turn that the production system in general would have less cost-push pressure to contend with from what is typically one of the most important and expensive inputs: labor.

It is the ability to *offset* high and rising wages—*not* the ability to hold wages down—that is the crucial skill. Most of the population receives the bulk of their income in the form of wages (and salaries). High and rising wages are desirable, provided that prices can be reduced, stabilized, or at least held to significantly lower rates of increase. For real income, and accordingly the standard of living, will then be rising for the vast majority of the population. Holding prices down by holding wages down is not particularly desirable. It tends to stagnate income gains for most of the society. But holding prices down by offsetting rising wages with productivity improvements is the key to generating widespread improvements in material well-being.

The Macroeconomic Consequences of Declining Productive Competence

Having considered the rather upbeat picture presented by a highly competent production system, it is now appropriate to look at the implications of declining productive competence. A secular decline in absolute productive competence must lead to reduced real income. A drop in the general material standard of living is the unavoidable result of the long-term deterioration of the efficiency with which a society transforms its available resources into contributive goods and services. In the face of declining competence, conventional monetary and fiscal policy cannot overturn this tendency. All that they can do is alter the mechanism through which the falling standard of living is transmitted.

The ineffectiveness of monetary and fiscal policy. Expansionist monetary or fiscal policy will ratify the cost-push pressures generated by the faltering of the economy's cost-offsetting capability. The result will be the transmission of the declining living standard through the erosion of real wages, as heightened rates of price inflation outrun the rise in the nominal wage. To this will be added the usual redistributive effects of inflation on real income—the pattern of which will be determined by the particular shape of the inflation. This is in turn influenced by the specific form of the monetary and fiscal policies implemented. However, these redistributive effects, though potentially serious and important, are secondary. The primary effect is a declining societal standard of living. Put simply, though the relative size of the pieces of pie may be changing, the main problem is that the pie itself is getting smaller.

If instead restrictionist monetary and fiscal policies are undertaken, their main effect will be to worsen recessionary tendencies, and the falling standard of living will be transmitted through rising unemployment, decreasing sales, and perhaps dropping nominal incomes (including falling wages). Tightening the money supply will tend to drive up interest rates, discouraging contributive investment. This will in turn produce both a decline in spending in the short run (worsened by the multiplier effect) and a further decline in productive competence in the long run. As for fiscal policy, cutbacks in government spending, increases in taxes, and other restrictionist measures will also aggravate short-run recessionary tendencies by reducing overall demand. To the extent that it is contributive government spending (e.g., on education or transportation) that is cut back, the long-run effects on productive competence will also be negative. Of course, these policies too will generate redistributive effects, though typically (but not necessarily) of a different sort than those that would result from taking the inflationary route. Nevertheless, the main effect—the reduction of societal real income—is the same.

But—it might be objected—the very point of expansionary policies is to encourage the sort of investment activities required to modernize and enlarge the stocks of production, infrastructure, and even R&D capital necessary to pull the economy out of its productivity doldrums. This would revitalize the cost-offsetting mechanism and thus rebuild productive competence. Why will this approach not work then, spurring productivity and so undoing the ultimate source of the real income decline? The answer is straightforward: monetary and fiscal policy, properly implemented, can *encourage* the investment in R&D, infrastructure, and production capital necessary to rebuild productive competence, but they cannot *create* the resources needed to achieve it. If there is a large distractive sector preempting critical labor and capital from the contributive sector (perhaps augmented by a considerable amount of neutral activity), no policy which fails to liberate these resources *and* rechannel them into contributive activity can hope to rebuild the nation's productive competence. After all, it is precisely the diversion of these crucial productive resources into noncontributive activity that generated the decay of productive competence in the first place.

Even so, one might ask, could not sufficiently stimulating monetary and fiscal policies draw these captive resources out of the distractive sector and out of neutral activity? The answer is no. The reasons lie in the nature of the mechanisms that bring neutral and distractive activities into existence in the first place and maintain or even enlarge them despite the fact that they do not raise the societal standard of living.

   Neutral activity. It has been argued that the most empirically important form of neutral activity is redundant or otherwise unnecessary management and administration. Part of the reason for the abundance of this type of activity may be ignorance of the fact that it is unnecessary (since, after all, it appears to be productive). But more of it is the result of the tendency toward bureaucratic empire-building by managers who, as their operational control of business decision-making increases, seek to augment their prestige as well as their salaries by expanding the number of their subordinates. For this reason, stimulating monetary and fiscal policy may—rather than drawing people out of neutral activity—increase the numbers of people so engaged: empire-building is easier in an expansionary atmosphere.

Restrictionist monetary and fiscal policy, on the other hand, may eventually force resources out of neutral activity through the recessionary pressure produced—but only after managers have cut back elsewhere in the attempt to avoid undermining their own power base. Furthermore, people engaged in neutral activity are already in the contributive sector. Therefore, these policies—if effective—will force at least some of these workers out of neutral activity and into unemployment lines. Rechanneling people from neutral to contributive activity may require some retraining and reorientation to allow them to shift careers; monetary and fiscal policy alone cannot provide for such transition. Furthermore, the very monetary and fiscal policies that tightened things up enough to force workers out of neutral activity will have created a recessionary climate. In the midst of recession, job opportunities will be hard to come by, even for people who have undergone whatever retraining and reorientation is appropriate.

Distractive activity. For a variety of reasons, the distractive sector may well be even less responsive than the neutral sector to monetary and fiscal policy. Unlike the neutral sector, the distractive sector typically exists not because many individuals are making private decisions to maximize their own economic and social status (consistent with their personal utility functions), but because there has been a social commitment of resources for extraeconomic reasons. To the degree that it is directed by a strong, centralized government, the distractive sector does not operate by market principles—even in a market economy. It is a command sector that draws on society's resources by decree rather than through the normal interaction of supply and demand forces. The inertia of the distractive sector will thus be greater than would be the case if it had come into existence, and was being maintained, purely as a result of misguided economic policy. There may be a great reluctance to recognize the distinctive economic nature of the sector. The proponents of any particular type of distractive activity need to prevent erosion of the political power base necessary to its continuance. The problem of maintaining political support would be that much more difficult if the activity were widely agreed to be economically damaging. Proponents may therefore feel compelled to argue that substantial economic benefits, not penalties, flow from its continued operation.

Proponents of distractive activity may thus wear a powerful set of ideological blinders, and may cling stubbornly to economic theories that ratify and rationalize this blindness. This is not to say that the economic theories they adopt were formulated in an attempt to foster blindness, or that they become widely accepted by economists for that reason. These theories may in fact have important virtues; it is just that there is a greater willingness to believe in theories that reinforce, rather than contradict, the things in which we already believe.

I have argued that the dominant distractive activity today is the production of military goods and services. How, then, does the pattern just described fit that case? To begin with, the military sector exists as a result of a political commitment made under the authority of a powerful central government. In the United States, that sector came into being in the period just prior to World War II, in response to dangerous political conditions in Europe and Asia that clearly constituted a threat to the future of the country. After World War II, a large military sector was maintained, for the first time in U.S. history, over a period of nearly four decades of what was officially peacetime.[1] This unprecedented maintenance of a large military sector apparently was and is the result of a perceived continuing threat to the nation's security posed by nations operating under different political and economic ideologies. At the time of its inception and ever since, the primary raison d'être of the military sector has been extra-economic: "national security."

In the euphoria following the end of the Great Depression, and in the postwar boom of previously pent-up demand, it was easy to ignore the long-term effects of this distractive activity. It was assumed that since the wartime boost in military expenditures had contributed to economic stimulation, continued large military expenditures would continue to produce positive economic effects.[2] The aggregate-expenditure, short-run approach of Keynesian theory permitted—in fact encouraged—the continuation of this illusion. It provided a theoretical framework which implied that any form of government expenditure (or for that matter private investment) had the same stimulatory effects regardless of what was being purchased. Keynesian theory was therefore certainly congenial to anyone who, for whatever reason, wanted to see the United States continually enlarge the capability of its military. It appeared that not only would we get guns *and* butter, but—because we were getting more and better guns—we would also get more and better butter.

As long as the ideology of a nation is locked into this set of beliefs, the resources in the military sector will be locked in place. Any incentives given to the contributive sector to encourage its firms to draw resources out of this distractive activity will surely fail; whether transmitted by monetary or fiscal policy or otherwise, the incentives will be met by countermeasures strong enough to insure that the resources will not respond. Ordinary monetary and fiscal policy thus become exercises in futility. While they may have some cosmetic effect, they will be unable to bring about the only actions that could effectively reverse the deterioration of productive competence caused by resource diversion.

Stagflation.   When productive competence is declining, it is perfectly possible to have high levels of inflation and unemployment at the same time. Rather than being a strange phenomenon, it is to be expected. The causal mechanism is not difficult to trace. Declining—and ultimately negative—rates of productivity growth frustrate attempts to offset increases in input costs, whatever the source of those increases. Since it is no longer possible to offset costs, modal cost behavior shifts from cost offsetting to cost transmitting. That is, even if managements actively try to minimize costs (according to the dictates of neoclassical microeconomic theory), they will increasingly discover that the best they can do is pass input cost increases along to their customers by a corresponding markup of their prices. When there is strong productivity growth, the tendency of firms to take the easy path and transmit rather than offset cost increases is held in check, in the absence of collusion, by the pressure of competition. In other words, when the capability of offsetting costs exists, a firm that fails to do so has no guarantee that its competitors will also transmit rather than offset cost increases; if competitors do not follow its lead, the cost-transmitting firm will find itself at a competitive disadvantage. But, given a broad failure of cost-offsetting options, cost-transmitting firms will discover that their rivals are also forced to transmit rather than offset costs. No competitive disadvantage will result—at least not among rival firms within the same economy.

There is a considerable danger that this behavior, as it continues, will weaken the cost minimization process itself. Removed from the world of abstract microtheory, the "real world" process of cost minimization is not simply a matter of mechanically applying some straightforward, constrained optimization algorithm. Rather, it is a time-consuming, difficult matter of continually monitoring and adjusting all facets of the firm's production system. Once managers learn that the much simpler process of transmitting costs is routinely ratified by their rivals, the incentive to spend the time and effort required to minimize costs will be considerably diminished.[3] The unintended collusion in which managers then find themselves seems agreeable and grows more and more routine. All of this, of course, worsens the problem of cost—and hence price—escalation. Even cost-offsetting options that are still available are increasingly overlooked.

The failure of productivity growth that results from extensive resource diversion does not affect cost-offsetting options in one industry alone. It will more likely be economywide, though some industries may not fit the overall pattern. Accordingly, increased cost-transmitting behavior will push prices upward throughout the economy, reinforcing itself as the higher-priced outputs of one industry become the basis for further cost transmission by its customer industries. And, of course, the wage-price spiral will further aggravate the problem.

But this supply-side, cost-push inflation also sows the seeds of unemployment, as it disadvantages producers in the domestic economy relative to those of other economies not subject to the drain of heavy noncontributive activity (and thus to declining productive competence). As the prices of domestically produced goods and services rise relative to the prices of comparable goods produced outside the country, firms producing domestically increasingly find themselves priced out of the market. Export markets decline. Imports increase, as long as there has been no compensating direct government interference with the international flow of trade (e.g., import quotas). The loss of both foreign and native markets to more efficient foreign production will in turn lead to domestic production cutbacks, with unemployment the result. Thus the same process that generates the inflationary pressures also generates pressure toward rising unemployment.

A review of various possible reactions to these inflation-recession pressures, on both the micro- and macro-levels, will demonstrate that there are no quick fixes available for what is basically a problem of structural economic decay. Some policies may appear to improve, to a limited extent, the condition of one part of the population, or may temporarily insulate one segment of the society from the negative effects. But they are inevitably ineffective in the broader societal sense even in the short term, and ineffective in both the broad and limited senses in the long term.

Migration of firms to low-wage areas.   Faced with declining productive competence, and hence severely compromised cost-offsetting capability, firms with rising resource costs may move production operations to places where productive competence is faring better and/or the costs of key resources are lower. If resource costs cannot readily be offset any longer, it is perfectly rational for the firm to go where there is not as much resource cost to offset. For many reasons—cultural, political, and otherwise—such moves may initially be concentrated within national boundaries and thus may have less effect on the rate of national unemployment than on its geographic distribution. But ultimately, the continued decline of productive competence will cause firms to move production operations beyond national boundaries.

This would occur even if general productive competence were lower (or declining) in the nations to which operations are being moved. As long as resource costs are significantly lower there, the move will seem attractive. Though low resource costs will tend to be the key motivator, other factors such as political stability, cooperativeness of the host government, and availability of the basic infrastructure the firm most directly needs will be significant as well. If relative productive competence at the new location were higher or were becoming higher, that would also be a major attraction—

especially if it involved the components of productive competence for which the firm would have to rely on the host economy, particularly a trained and well-motivated labor force and basic support infrastructure for transportation, communication, water supply, and so forth. Important though they may be, these last considerations serve mainly as enabling conditions. The prime motivator, at least initially, still is lower resource costs. Those resources whose costs loom largest are the most potent motivators. In the more developed countries, for nearly all manufacturing industries, labor cost is the largest part of unit manufacturing cost. Hence "cheap labor havens," as they have often been called, tend to be ceteris paribus the most attractive.

In the United States, the trend of industrial migration from the Northeast and Midwest to the Sunbelt greatly strengthened as the decline in general productive competence became stronger. For all the talk about amenities such as climate, the principal motivators in most of these moves were cheaper (mostly unorganized) labor and more laissez-faire state government attitudes, at least insofar as business (as opposed to organized labor) was concerned. The physical climate has, after all, not changed much in the past fifteen to twenty years. For that matter, labor was undoubtedly cheaper even in relative terms in the past and government might well have been as congenial toward business. But as long as productivity growth was good and productive competence strong, the geographic redistribution of industry was more or less evolutionary in character. It is the decline of national productive competence that turned the heat up under this process.

But, of course, the geographic redistribution of American-owned production did not stay within national boundaries for long. Acting rationally from their own point of view, firms began to move their production facilities out of the country, leaving behind a growing stock of idle factories and unemployed workers. This laying off of workers is profoundly different from that which has periodically accompanied recessionary downturns throughout the nation's economic history. It is not a temporary loss of work caused by a temporary decline in demand—that would be a problem of economic coordination. Rather, it represents a decision to service demand by production based outside the nation. That is a major problem of structural shift. Future increases in demand are now likely to be serviced by further expansion of foreign operations—by contributive investment abroad rather than at home. The idled factories and work forces are not merely waiting out the trough in the business cycle.

This reaction temporarily insulated the managers and stock-holders of these firms from the decline of productive competence within the United States. But it did so at the expense of accelerating the impact of that decline on their workers, and on the people and communities that depended on the workers' incomes for their own economic survival. Yet given the ongoing sapping of the nation's economic vitality by the large-scale diversion of productive resources, the failure of the firms to react in this way would have more rapidly rendered them economically nonviable. Thus, the impact on their work forces and the surrounding communities would have been softened and slowed, but not indefinitely forestalled.

Import controls.   Another reaction to the increasing competitive disadvantage of U.S.-based production has been growing pressure for import quotas, higher tariffs, negotiated export restrictions with major foreign suppliers to our economy (e.g., Japan), and other interferences with the free flow of trade. Of course, protectionist measures always look most appealing to the managements and workers of the least competitive and least efficient industries. This is perhaps more true of the workers than the managers because managers generally have more options available to them (as in the preceding discussion). If enforced with sufficient severity, such trade restrictions will stem the flow of imports. They cannot, however, stem the decline of exports and may, in fact, accelerate it by encouraging retaliatory measures. In any particular situation, it is therefore an open question whether these policies would either improve the balance of trade or curtail the overall loss of markets for domestically produced goods and services. Hence, it is questionable whether these policies will reduce the tendency toward rising unemployment. But there is no question that the result of these restrictive policies will be a net decline in *consumer* well-being.

If, on grounds of price and quality, consumers prefer domestically produced goods, there clearly will be no need for the restrictive policies. To the extent that consumers do not prefer domestic goods, these policies compel them to a second- or third-best choice. The utility of any consumer who would have preferred domestic goods will be unaffected by these policies, but that of any consumer who would have preferred foreign goods now unavailable or artificially overpriced will be reduced. (Consumers, looked at as a group, have undergone a kind of negative pareto change.) Their aggregate utility as *consumers* has been reduced. This does not, of course, mean that social utility or social welfare has been reduced. People are whole beings, not merely consumers. Those people who are producers within the industries that are being protected by the restrictionist policies gain utility insofar as their jobs have been preserved against the threat of foreign competition. For complex psychological and ideological reasons, these individuals, as well as others, may experience additional gain or loss of utility. And all the usual theoretical difficulties with the interpersonal comparison of utilities must also be considered. Taking into account all effects across the entire society, it is impossible to formally prove a priori that aggregate social utility has declined. But it is highly likely that more individuals will have experienced a net loss in welfare than a net gain or no effect. In any case, we can extract ourselves from the morass of theorizing on social utility by noting simply that because the consumer's opportunity set has been constricted, consumer welfare, in that sense, cannot have been increased.

Historically, the protectionist argument has been made with respect to "infant" industries, and has been an essentially long-term argument. Industries just beginning are unavoidably inefficient, so the argument goes, and thus need protection from already-established efficient industries abroad. This will enable the infants to mature, gain in efficiency, and thus be fully capable of competing without protection with foreign industries in the long term. Thus the consumer welfare loss associated with protection is a kind of social investment. A long-term gain is promised as a result of a short-term sacrifice.

But the argument is very different here. We are not dealing with newly born industries, inefficient because of their immaturity. We are instead faced with prematurely senile industries drained of their efficiency and competitive vigor as a result of having been parasitized by large-scale resource diversion to noncontributive activity. There is no promise of future viability to offset the consumer burden imposed by the protectionist measures; there is only the "promise" of societal subsidization without end, of a permanent place on the public dole. This is not the stuff of competitive capitalism, but rather its antithesis. It is the negation of one of the chief advantages of a competitive economy—the constant striving for greater efficiency under the pressure of competition. There is nothing in the policy of protection than can remedy the problems of such senile industries. That must await the correction of the resource diversion that is enfeebling them.

Government price controls.   Yet another policy advocated in reaction to the stagflation that has accompanied the decline of productive competence has been the direct governmental control of prices. If the control of prices is universal and strictly enforced throughout the economy it will, of necessity, prevent inflation. That is tautological. But it will do little to reduce the fundamental inflationary pressure. Hence, that pressure will make itself felt in different ways. Given the decline of productive competence, the failure to permit the transmission of any cost increases (some of which are either technical, as in the depletion of easily extractable mineral reserves, or external, as in the case of international prices) will lead to accelerated cutbacks in domestic production. This will occur as a consequence of nothing less basic than the upward slope of industry supply curves. Furthermore, fixing prices will intensify pressures to seek cheap resource havens abroad, resulting in still greater reductions in domestic production. Unemployment problems will thus be greatly increased, though perhaps only after a significant time lag.

Because rigid price controls interfere with the chief mechanism by which a market economy coordinates the allocation of resources among alternative types of production, they produce distortions that tend to grow with the passage of time. Firms operating in markets with declining demand will contract with or without controls, and will accordingly employ smaller amounts of productive resources over time; even if there are enough markets with rising demand to absorb these resources, they may fail to do so. The expansion of production within those industries may be inhibited because prices are not being allowed to rise there. If marginal costs curves are rising, higher prices will be required both to encourage existing producers to increase output and to attract new entrants to begin production. Thus, because of price controls, the resources cast off by the declining sectors of the economy will tend to remain unemployed.

Price controls may be made less than universal, or may be less than strictly enforced, in an attempt to mitigate some of these distorting effects. This will undoubtedly result in inequities paralleling the political strength of various vested interests. The distortions will change shape, but will not be eliminated. And if the controls are modified to allow the pass-through of various "legitimate" cost increases, the whole purpose of the controls will be defeated. After all, the inflationary mechanism they would be seeking to control is precisely the passing along of input cost increases, not inflationary pressure coming from excess aggregate demand.

One further note on the inequities of price controls. In the real world, control of prices requires the visibility of prices. It is clearly not list prices or other officially designated prices that need to be controlled, but actual transaction prices. There can be, and often is, a very substantial difference between list prices and transaction prices, at least for certain categories of goods (e.g., automobiles). When there is a substantial differential, it may be difficult to accurately determine transaction prices. But wages are nearly always more visible than other prices. Thus, price controls can easily be more effective in holding down labor prices than product prices. And this, of course, disadvantages those whose main income is in the form of direct wages.

About the only useful function widespread price controls have in fighting inflation within a market economy is in killing off inflationary expectations that themselves are contributing to inflation. To achieve this objective, however, the controls must be introduced with firm statements that they will remain in effect until other policies aimed at reducing the basic inflationary pressures become effective. Then they must be removed, preferably within a timespan that is reasonably short, yet long enough to be credible (perhaps six to twelve months). As the controls are removed, it must be announced that the other policies have become effective, removing the need for further price controls. If that is believed, inflationary expectations should be substantially reduced. If it is not, these machinations will have been ineffective. It helps, of course, if these statements about successfully turning off basic inflationary pressures are true. If they are not, inflationary expectations will be only too readily rekindled.

Policy ineffectiveness.   As long as productive competence continues to fall, the material standard of living of the population will decline. Under these circumstances, conventional macroeconomic policies amount to choices between various forms of decline. No policy which fails to directly address the source of the long-term secular deterioration of the economy—parasitism by overlarge noncontributive sectors—can come to grips with the fundamental economic disease.

The policies of conventional macroeconomics are essentially policies of coordination. They assume that the necessary resources are available, that the competence with which to combine them into desired goods and services with reasonable efficiency exists, and that effective demand is at least potentially adequate. But the existence of sufficiently large noncontributive sectors invalidates the first two of these assumptions. If a substantial fraction of key productive resources are held captive by a commitment to distractive activity, they are not available to the contributive economy. If sufficient capital and technological resources are held captive, then productive competence, certainly in relative and perhaps in absolute terms, will be continually evaporating. Under these conditions it is no surprise that the policies that derive from conventional monetarist and Keynesian economics are ineffective. It is not reasonable to expect the implications of a theory to continue to be valid if the assumptions on which the theory has been based no longer hold.

Resource Diversion in Differing Economic Systems

So basic are the effects of resource diversion that they not only render ordinary macroeconomic theory ineffective, but also are immune to changes in the form of the economic system itself. Economic systems as diametrically opposed as competitive free-market capitalism and centrally planned communism may show the symptoms of overlarge distractive (and neutral) activity differently; but neither will be able to override the economic deterioration they produce. In the context of capitalist economies, I have argued that the effects of resource diversion tend to be in the form of simultaneous inflationary and recessionary pressures whose surface manifestations may be shifted to some degree by various macroeconomic policies. In communist economies, the deterioration tends to be transmitted differently.

Since the government is the sole employer in communist economies, the government can provide paid work for everyone by decree. That, however, does not in any sense imply that the work will necessarily be fulfilling to the individual or socially contributive. The problems of job design and enrichment have more to do with workplace environment and production requirements than with whether the economy is operated under communist or capitalist principles. But the provision of paid work opportunities is in itself no real problem here.

There is somewhat less control over the inflationary problem. Though the government sets domestic prices, it must still deal with rising prices of imports. Nor is the system immune to cost increases due to technical factors such as depletion of natural resources. On the whole, however, the government clearly has more direct and ideologically legitimized means of holding down the growth of average prices than does the government of a capitalist country. The result is that the impoverishment of the contributive economy's resource base resulting from resource diversion tends to surface in other ways. Chronic and severe shortages of contributive goods and services may be commonplace—shortages in terms of insufficient quantities and of quality that falls short of the mark. These may be shortages of consumer goods, producer goods, or both, depending on the extent to which undiverted resources are directed toward investment activities or present consumption.

On the whole, it is probably more likely that the greatest part of the burden will fall on production of consumer goods and services. There are two reasons for this. To the extent that producer goods industries are seen as either presently or under some future contingency servicing distractive activity to which the nation is committed, they may be emphasized. Beyond this the grumblings of dissatisfied but disorganized consumers may not be as strongly heard as the complaints of enterprise managers trying to meet production quotas with insufficient or poor-quality materials and equipment. In any case, the effects of the long-term economic deterioration resulting from substantial resource diversion may surface in a very different form in a centrally planned economy—but surface they will. And they will surface strongly enough to produce drastically lower material standards of living than that economy is capable of providing.

Undevelopment

Resource diversion is not only a potential cause of inflation and unemployment, as discussed earlier in this chapter—it is capable of serving as such a powerful counterthrust to the engine of development as to halt and ultimately reverse it. Growth may keep rolling along for a while (and perhaps a great while), but development will not—and development, not growth, is the process that increases the material standard of living. Economic growth and economic development are very different things. Growth is a simplistic concept relating only to the expansion in the volume of economic activity. Development, on the other hand, is a concept more attuned to structural considerations, to the nature of outputs rather than merely their quantity. Whereas a single measure, such as increase in per capita gross national product, can reasonably be used as a measure of the narrow concept of economic growth, the many-faceted nature of economic development vastly complicates its measurement.[4] Even if noncontributive activity is set aside and its outputs ignored, effective measurement of economic development is difficult. It requires not only a measure of the raw volume of contributive goods and services produced, but also some concept of their interaction and balance, and their distribution.

Economic development is not a zero-sum game. The gains achieved by the "winners" do not come purely at the expense of the "losers." When a society engages in contributive activity, it can generate net societal gains, particularly as these activities are appropriately and effectively coordinated and interconnected (whether by the impersonal mechanisms of a free-market economy or by the more direct intervention of formal planning). If these gains were achievable only through the impoverishment of others outside this particular society, the problem of development would take on an entirely different cast and a wholly changed moral character. For in that kind of world helping a society to develop would directly imply the encouragement of exploitation elsewhere.

Fortunately, the world is not so inherently cruel. By developing and applying appropriate technology, by better coordinating the application of productive resources to contributive purposes, by improving the quality of the resources themselves (e.g., through the education of labor) the total world material standard of living may be raised. It is not especially easy to achieve such net gains, but it is clearly possible. However, once a given level of economic development has been attained, there is a certain amount of positive developmental activity that must continue to allow the society to maintain the status quo. Maintaining the standard of living and the level of productive competence of the developing society requires a portion of the available productive resources. If a society does not devote sufficient productive resources to various maintenance activities, it will not only fail to advance on the scale of development, it will go backward: it will "undevelop." For example, failure to invest in enough new production capital to offset the depreciation of the current stock will result in a shrinking base of production capital available to the industry. The consequence: less modern, less efficient industry over time. Economic development is not held in place until effort is expended to increase it. It is a reversible process.

Development raises the standard of living. To the extent that rising material well-being advances a society's quality of life, development leads toward the primary goal of economic activity. Therefore, insofar as resource diversion plays a prime role in generating "undevelopment," it is the very antithesis of what economic activity is all about. There is only one way to overturn the long-term secular decline of productive competence that is the source of such unavoidable economic decay—that is to undo the diversion of resources that underlies it. The economy is in some respects like a living organism, and like a living organism, a parasite-caused deterioration of its capability to function properly cannot be reversed by attacking the symptoms that the parasite causes. It is the parasite itself that must be attacked. Virtually all complex living organisms are parasitized to one extent or another at one time or another. Even continuous parasitization does not necessarily have noticeable effects if its magnitude is below some minimal threshold. Beyond that low threshold, however, weakening of the organism becomes increasingly severe. And, of course, there is also an upper threshold. If the parasite grows too strong for too long, the host will be permanently, irreversibly crippled or even destroyed—if not by the parasite itself then by some other assault, which the host has become too weak to defend itself against. So it is with an economy exposed to the parasitic action of noncontributive activity.

The shrinking of the noncontributive sectors by the redirection of diverted resources to contributive activity implies a complex and interesting problem in the political economy of transition; it is to that problem we now turn.

8

The Economics of Transition

Ignoring Transition

Though economists have devoted much thought to the desirability (or lack thereof) of various economic "states of the world," there has been little discussion about the nature of the problems of transition between these states. Given the lack of theoretical exploration of this area, it is difficult even to estimate how contentious these problems are. But contentious or not, they require much more attention than they have so far been given. Arguing that we have not been paying sufficient attention to the problems of transition is not the same as arguing that we have paid attention only to statics and not to dynamics (which is not true). Nor does it imply that the world consists of static equilibrium states between which we periodically move or contemplate moving (as comparative statics analysis seems to indicate). Even if there are static equilibrium states for something as dynamic as an economy, shifts in exogenous factors will probably guarantee that we are rarely (if ever) actually in those states. Owing to the considerable inertia of large and complex social systems such as our economy, we are more likely to spend most of our time slowly sliding between whatever static equilibria there might be.

Although the states of the world referred to here could be static equilibria, it is probably more accurate to conceive of them as different sets of opportunities. Perhaps the clearest analogy would be that of traveling on a rail system consisting of a number of different routes or lines. Riding on any one route (state of the world) does not confine the traveler to any one place: there are many possibilities. However, some travel plans require a transition to another route (state of the world). The destinations they involve cannot be reached without such a transition. What we lack are concrete, ameliorative analyses of how to smoothly move individual human beings and their social structures between different states of the world. People are neither as completely malleable nor as doggedly inflexible as our abstract theories seem to assume. We are not switches to be flipped or objects to be moved about to suit the purposes of the theoretical visionary. Neither are we frozen into place, taken as given. We are both the single most important means for altering the pattern of economic activity, and the masters whom that activity must serve. Any social alterations we choose to undertake should be accomplished by a process designed to be sensitive to the needs, desires, frailties, limitations, and capabilities of all individuals who find themselves at the fulcrum of the change.

Why worry about transitions?   The development of an economics of transition is not simply an interesting theoretical and empirical problem. The problems of transition can and do freeze societies into states of the world that are less desirable (in the societies' own judgment) than what could actually be achieved. Appropriate transitional strategies are needed to bridge this gap—and the greater the magnitude and the more fundamental the character of the required shifts, the more vital these strategies become. Real improvement in the social condition requires not only a vision of Oz, but also a workable plan for building the yellow brick road.

Societies are at times frozen into inferior positions even when the reality of suboptimality is acknowledged and the reasons for it understood, because the costs of transition are perceived as being too high. If these perceptions are correct, that is one thing. But they may also be a result of ignorance (in the sense of lack of information), and of the fear that ignorance engenders. Short of completely locking society into less desirable situations, misperception and lack of information can produce strong resistance to positive changes. Such resistance can add greatly to the direct cost of transition, as well as contribute to expensive and time-consuming delays. For example, virtually every time the U.S. military announces plans to close a base anywhere in the nation, "save the base" committees are formed,

congressional delegations pressured, and all manner of political resistance initiated by outraged local citizens. Dire predictions of job
losses and other severe local economic hardships are primary moti-
vations for this flurry of activity.

Yet long experience clearly indicates that the closing and conversion of military bases produces considerable job gains, not losses, in
addition to other substantial economic benefits. Over the period
1961–81, more than ninety U.S. military bases were closed in thirty-
nine states and Puerto Rico. The net result: a 25 percent *increase* in
civilian jobs after the bases were converted to alternative uses.[1] One
example of how this can come about is described in a 1979 *New York
Times* article on the reuse of Brookley Air Force Base in Mobile,
Alabama, closed in 1969:

> The base has been turned into a prospering industrial-aviation-
> educational complex; the city government has become an industrial
> landlord with a major new source of revenue, and the departure of
> so large a military presence has made the city more diverse and
> independent.[2]

To shift or not to shift.   If the costs of voluntary transition
do in fact outweigh the benefits, then the transition obviously should
not be undertaken. There is, after all, no conflict between the ends
and the means used to achieve them. The ends are what has happened, and what has happened is not only the final state achieved but
also the path taken to that state. Thus the costs borne in transition,
even though they may be transitory, must be included in any cost-
benefit calculation.

The relevant question however, is not whether the costs of any
given transition path are greater than the benefits, but whether the
costs of the *least costly* transition path are greater than the benefits
resulting from transition. A developed body of theory of transition
would be of great value in providing the necessary analytical framework; a developed set of empirical tools would be very useful in applying this framework to a particular situation. An economics of
transition would be of greatest value in finding the least costly path,
analyzing its characteristics, and developing a specific, pragmatic
plan for action. In the absence of such a plan, we may be kept from
improvements in our social condition that are, in fact, well within our
grasp.

Societies may also become stuck even if their members all perceive the desirability of an alternative state of the world and the vast majority find the transition costs acceptable. If the costs of transition fall disproportionately on a minority, the transition may be stalemated—either because the minority wields sufficient political or economic power to prevent the transition or because the majority does not believe it proper to force the minority to bear the pain. Here too an economics of transition would be most useful. With enough understanding of these problems, it might be possible to develop transition strategies that either average the costs or include compensation schemes that could overcome the inequity.

Evaluating Transition Strategies

The effectiveness of a transition strategy should be judged by two criteria: the extent to which the strategy minimizes the costs of transition and the rapidity and completeness with which it establishes the state of the world that is the object of the transition. The costs of transition should not be limited to purely financial or even purely economic ones. It may be irritating and frustrating to deal with factors that cannot be unambiguously quantified, yet in a way it is reassuring that not everything encompassed by the individual or collective reality of human beings—our needs, our hopes and aspirations, our pains—can be reduced to numbers.

Costs and benefits. The costs of transition include the economic costs of retraining, reeducation, relocation, capital modification or reconstruction, product (and thus real income) forgone, and what might broadly be called decommissioning costs. Decommissioning costs occur principally where transition is made from activities involving hazardous materials, expensive facilities with no alternative use, secrecy, or some combination of these. For example, a decision to shift from nuclear fission to an alternative non-nuclear means of generating electricity would involve significant decommissioning costs, primarily because of the radiation hazard. Radioactive materials themselves would have to be carefully disposed of, contaminated equipment would either have to be decontaminated or scrapped along with the nuclear materials, and portions of the plant itself might have to be sealed off and perhaps guarded as well. Because unrecoverable investment in an activity from which transition is contemplated is a sunk cost, such investment is irrelevant both to the choice of transition strategy and to the question of whether the transition should be undertaken in the first place. Remoteness and lack of alternative use, for example, are problems not because there is a greater sunk cost but because the cost of starting up an alternative activity may be higher, if wholly new facilities must be constructed to accommodate it.

In addition to the direct economic costs, transitions may also involve psychological and social costs related to the disruptions they can produce and the adaptations they require. These include, for example, the fear and worry associated with the termination of familiar work in familiar surroundings and the transfer to new and perhaps fundamentally different activities. There is also the possibility of social uprooting resulting from geographic relocation or a change in work schedule or character. Such shifts may isolate or alienate people from former colleagues, friends, and significant others. If relocation and other forms of transition are frequent and major, their psychological effects can be quite wrenching. Unable to establish or maintain the web of relationships to their social and physical environment (what we commonly call "roots"), people may come to feel disconnected, disoriented. These feelings of rootlessness can become so painful as to be impossible to bear. Some have argued that the rash of suicides in the past few years by teenagers from affluent, upwardly mobile families may be the result of stresses created by frequent corporate transfers of their parents. Reporting on teenage suicide in 1983, *Newsweek* focused on the seriousness of the problem in the affluent Dallas suburb of Plano, noting that

> Plano, despite its middle class comforts, has an abundance of both disruption and loss. It is afflicted by the rootlessness and isolation characteristic of places where nearly everything and everyone is new. . . . "I call Plano the nesting ground for the migratory American executive," says city manager David Griffin.[3]

As sex roles have become less rigid in recent decades, these feelings of disruption and loss have worsened. It is increasingly common to have two or more paid workers in the same family or social-emotional unit, who may be pulled in different directions by job-related transitions.[4] There may also be other social, economic, and political costs involved when transitions require significant reorganization of firms or other institutions. Ordinary "debugging" and learning costs are associated with any activity that is new to the people involved. These costs are that much greater when the institutions people work in are themselves rearranged.

Counterposed to these costs are the social and psychological benefits that can flow from the disruptions of transition. The breaking of boring old routines, the chance to learn new skills, a change of scenery, the excitement of a chance at a new life, are all potential benefits. Tibor Scitovsky has argued in another context that utility or pleasure derives not from the status quo, no matter how well off it may find us, but from positive changes in it.[5] Even if, after a time, the new activity to which transition is being made is no more exciting, no more utility-generating than the previous activity, it is still true that temporarily positive change has added some positive value to our lives.

Of course, the question of whether or not the transition itself has net cost or net benefit is separate from the question of whether the state of the world toward which the transition is moving is superior or inferior to the state from which transition is being made. Clearly the answers to both of these questions are critical to intelligent decision making about transition. Still, it is probably analytically useful to separate them.

Societal transitions are not always voluntary. There are times when external conditions force us to abandon a particular state of the world that we would prefer to maintain. The search for the best alternative situation still available and for the best transition path is, if anything, more important in this case. The problems posed by the depletion of natural resources, be they clean water and air, or oil and gas, have this involuntary character. Present levels and types of consumption serviced by present methods of production cannot be maintained indefinitely. Some shifting already has occurred and more will have to take place in order to come to a long-term viable alternative state.[6] For example, it matters not whether we would like to continue forever driving endless miles in petroleum-powered vehicles—we will not be able to do it. Transition is necessary. And the search for alternative futures must include the search for optimal transition paths to those futures.

Transition speed.   Nearly all the economic costs of transition are directly (i.e., positively) related to the speed at which that transition takes place. Modifications of facilities and equipment, retraining and reeducation programs, and relocation of facilities or labor are more expensive if they must be rushed. And, if done on a truly "crash" basis, they are likely not only to be far more expensive, but also less effective. Crash programs are often ill-conceived and poorly executed, requiring expensive patching up after the fact. Even when abbreviated schedules are more sensibly conceived, premiums must be paid for overtime labor and for rush orders, not to mention unforeseen bottlenecks and other disruptions.

Lost output is the only economic cost that does not follow this pattern: it is inversely related to the speed of transition. This forgone output may be seen in terms of either the origin activity or the destination activity; the choice is arbitrary, but it clearly does make a difference. If conceived in terms of the preferred output, these costs will be higher. Assuming rationality, this output will normally be that of the destination activity, except in the case of involuntary transitions. Choosing the more valued output as the one forgone affects both the relative and absolute costs of transition. The relative effect is to make slower transition strategies more costly, compared to faster strategies, than would be the case if forgone product were viewed in terms of the less highly valued output. In absolute terms, all transition options appear more expensive, since their "product forgone" cost component has been raised. The absolute effect of this choice is thus to bias the situation against choosing to make the transition in the first place, since this choice raises the apparent costs of transition. But this is paradoxical, since the source of this bias is the greater value placed on the output of the activity that will be the result of the transition! It therefore seems more sensible to value product forgone in terms of the origin activity while deciding whether or not the transition should be undertaken. Once a decision to go ahead has been reached, one may either continue to value product forgone in terms of the origin activity or shift to valuing it in terms of the destination activity. In fact, the shift of orientation seems more logical.

The social and psychological costs of transition also tend to be directly related to speed. In his book *Future Shock*, Alvin Toffler emphasized the personal and societal impact of the rapidity of change.[7]

In a mild form, novelty makes us more aware, more acute, more "alive." But as the degree of novelty increases—as the amount of change and the rate at which it occurs rises—so do mental and physical stress. We all periodically undergo major life transitions: leaving home for the first time, changing schools, moving, getting married, getting divorced, changing careers, losing a dear friend or family member. And whether the new situation is better, worse, or equivalent to the old, the change itself is always at least a little frightening. Since the sorts of social transitions we are dealing with include the personal life transitions of groups of individual human beings, the stresses they bear must be a part of our accounting of the costs of transition.

Furthermore, social transitions, particularly those large enough to alter the formal and informal institutions with which we interact or the structure of power within the society, have an impact greater than the sum of the effects on all individuals actually undergoing transition. By producing institutional change, power and influence are redistributed. This will affect the lives of individuals who were neither undergoing the transition at hand nor directly involved with the people who were. And again, the greater the speed of change, the more stressful the transition will be, for these indirectly affected individuals as well.

There are many examples of transitions that have had far-reaching effects because they produced institutional change. The 1949 revolution in China drastically altered the character of economic and political life, affecting the lives of millions of Chinese not even born at the time. Less dramatically, the development of labor unions, central banking, government regulatory commissions, and systems of social security substantially altered the economic climate. These changes did not merely rearrange individuals or modify the particular policy decisions of existing institutions. They have had widespread and long-term effects because they created or restructured institutions.

Completeness. As to the criterion of completeness, the complexity of significant economic transitions virtually guarantees that various elements of the destination activity will come on line at different times. Whether or not the destination activity is potentially viable is a property of that activity itself and not of the transition strategy used to establish it. However, a transition path could quite possibly cripple the ability of the destination activity to fulfill that potential, if the path chosen assembles the activity's parts in too piecemeal a fashion: if parts of the destination activity are subjected to heavy demands before other parts on which they depend are fully established, a perfectly viable activity may collapse, giving the appearance of unworkability.

For example, suppose a manufacturing company is changing its operations and entering a wholly new product area for which a well-operated distribution and maintenance system is crucial—say the production of automobiles. If the new production facilities come on line and start producing before the distribution and maintenance system is completely established, those who buy the cars may experience annoying delivery delays and even more annoying service problems. Customer difficulties in getting their newly purchased cars properly maintained, including long waits for parts, can give the firm a reputation of unreliability that will cut into sales and that may be very hard to overcome in the future. As a result, this product line may never realize its true, and perhaps considerable, profit potential; it may even be abandoned by the company as nonviable. Volkswagen's success in penetrating the U.S. automobile market in the early sixties, when many other foreign producers had failed, was no doubt at least partly due to its success in bringing a reliable distribution and maintenance system on line along with its production and sales operations.

Minimizing Transition Costs

Labor.   Whenever people are moved from one type of economic activity to another significantly different activity, some readjustments are required. Where major differences exist either in the nature or level of skill required, some sort of retraining and reeducation smooths the transition. The more that is known about the two endpoints of that transition, the easier it will be to design an effective retraining or reeducation program. It is patently insufficient to retrain displaced workers to some "useful" skill unless the workers can then be more easily reintegrated into the economy.

If job retraining and reeducation are planned within the context of a well-defined transition, it is possible to evaluate with some precision not only the skill type, skill level, and experience of each worker involved in the origin activity, but also the skill type, skill level, and orientation required by the jobs that will become available in the destination activity. It is therefore possible to make the best available match between the present labor force and the labor force required for the destination activity—and in so doing, to minimize the degree of retraining necessary for each worker and in the aggregate. This will minimize *all* of the labor-related costs of transition, economic and otherwise.

Labor force mobility, both in the geographic and in the skill-oriented sense, is a critical element of smooth economic transition. That which encourages the acquisition of new skills and locational flexibility thus enhances the economy's capability to accomplish both micro- and macrotransitions smoothly—with minimal economic, social, and personal disruption. Institutionalizing access to retraining, transitional income support, relocation assistance (in financial and other forms), and the like makes extremely good sense as ongoing economic policy. It maximizes the responsiveness of the economy to both socially desired and forced change and minimizes the likelihood of becoming stalled in socially suboptimal positions.

Planning.   Institutionalizing transition assistance does not require a centralized planning bureaucracy. In fact, such centralized operations are not well suited to tailoring the details of labor force transitional strategy to the specific workers involved and to the particular nature of the transition they must make. That is best done on a highly decentralized basis. To those who would argue that unaided market forces would take care of all such transitions, I would point out that market forces do not prevent people from getting severely crunched in the transition process, even if they do eventually redeploy the resources that have been released from the origin activity. The suffering that will almost certainly take place if transitional adjustments are left to market forces is both unnecessary and inhumane.

Furthermore, establishing an institutionalized transition capability is not aimed at overriding the market system but at smoothing the transition. Virtually all microentities within any healthy economic system do some sort of long-term planning, whether they be individual consumers or firms; this is a fact of economic life. In the risky and uncertain world in which we live, planning—often on a contingency basis—is all the more important. Planning the production of public goods (such as roadways and parks) is also common. It is rarely seen as a threat to the market system—it is normally just seen as common sense. If the planning of transitions is highly decentralized, there is no reason to see it as a source of serious ideological conflict.

At the same time, it is worth noting that centrally planned economies do not automatically do the sort of microtransitional planning being discussed, particularly not in advance or on a contingency basis. For that matter, there is no reason to believe that the leaders of the central planning bureaucracies of such economies are any more in tune with the factory floor realities of industrial production (or the operating details of other economic organizations) than are the government leaders or central corporate planners of large diversified enterprises in the market economies. Decentralization of microtransitional planning here would undoubtedly enhance efficiency as well.

Capital.   The nature and capabilities of major on-site capital and facilities, while not defining alternate use possibilities, clearly do set boundaries. For example, the prominence of metal-working equipment and large work areas in aerospace industrial plants makes conversion to the production of housing modules, mass transit vehicles, or large industrial machinery reasonable. On the other hand, the lack of vats and chemical processing equipment and the irrelevance of metal-working machines (among other things) make conversion to the production of cosmetics, processed foods, or detergents impractical.

Like labor, capital is neither as homogeneous nor as malleable as is typically assumed by microeconomists. On the other hand, there are very few types of capital or facilities so specialized that they cannot be transferred to any of a significant number of alternative activities. However, as with labor, capital typically will need to be modified somewhat to better fit the requirements of the destination activity. Production capital is most likely to require such modification, with R&D capital a close second. As a general rule, neither infrastructure nor control capital is so highly specialized that it cannot be easily transferred to a great variety of alternative uses with little or no alteration. And, of course, even if changes in the raw material and fuel requirements are substantial after transition, the new requirements will be met mainly by shifting to other materials and fuels and not by modification of existing stockpiles. Stockpiled materials not usable in the destination activity can be shifted to wholly different productive activity elsewhere.

Given the generally low mobility of major capital and facilities, it seems that these should be matched as closely as possible with the set of destination activities. This would minimize required capital modifications and hence associated costs. Labor, the more mobile resource, could then be brought to the appropriate facilities. However, this is not necessarily the best approach.

Relocation.   The relocation of labor involves costs as well. It may be that the total direct cost of relocating a work force may be greater than the cost of either relocating the capital directly or scrapping the old facility and rebuilding one more adapted to the destination activity. There are also costs associated with labor mobility that are not incurred with capital. Machines and buildings have no feelings, no friends to leave behind, no need for a sense of continuity, roots, or home. They also do not have families, with all the same needs, who will have to suffer the pains of transition. Factoring in all of these costs increases the total societal costs of relocating labor enough to warrant careful examination of the question of which resource to move.

If this seems like an unduly soft, "bleeding-heart" approach to a hard-nosed economic problem, that is only because we have grown used to paying attention mostly to costs we can easily quantify and monetarize. It is worth emphasizing again that such costs are no more real than the psychological and emotional costs we tend to ignore. The fact that they are easier to measure may make them more convenient, but it is hardly an index of their importance. Furthermore, since the only legitimate purpose of economic activity is to make people better off, *any* sense in which they are made worse off must be considered a cost. Therefore, any cost calculation that does not include these psychic costs is understated, perhaps seriously so. And decision making based on such flawed calculations is unlikely to result in wise choices.

Thus, transition costs will tend to be minimized by matching destination activities as closely as possible with origin activity, capital-labor force capabilities, and location, consistent with the full establishment of the destination state of the world. All of this boils down to the straightforward proposition that minimizing the *extent* of transition tends to minimize the *cost* of transition.

Maximizing Benefits

Apart from any advantage gained by reaching a better state of the world, the transition itself can convey benefits. The best transition strategy is thus not necessarily the one that minimizes cost, but rather the one that maximizes net benefits. The sense of challenge, excitement, even adventure in work-related transition—and more important, the sense of participating in a redirecting of one's life path—is heightened by some transition strategies, dampened by others. To the extent that the people involved (whether they be managers, technologists, administrators, or production workers) are simply being processed through a transitional path designed and directed by someone else, many of these potentially long-lasting benefits are lost. If instead employees are not only the subjects of the process but its conceivers, engineers, and operators, their motivation, their sense of pride, and their sense of proprietorship in the process will be much greater. There is something very empowering about having such a sense of participation in the control of one's present and future work.

Participatory decision making. To most of us, truly participatory decision making seems like a strange idea. Some of the strangeness comes from the tendency to equate management with hierarchy. Effective, "the buck stops here" decision making seems somehow inextricably linked with hierarchical decision structures. But there is not necessarily a one-to-one relation between the degree of hierarchy and the quality of decision making (let alone the broader societal flow of benefits). If not, why do so many people believe so? For one thing, we have precious little experience with a true participatory decision process whose object is not negotiation between adversarial parties (as for example in labor-management collective bargaining), but rather a mutually agreed-upon objective. The experience we do have is generally in committees functioning within either basically hierarchical decision structures or loosely formed organizations. That is, our limited experience of this sort of decision process is either within the context of one boss asking a small group to produce, for example, a policy analysis so that he or she can make recommendations to another boss, or as part of the refreshments committee of the local social club.

Because our experience of true participatory decision processes is so limited, when put into a participatory group situation we often tend to restructure it formally or informally on a hierarchical basis by choosing leaders. Nowhere was it decreed that human beings cannot make effective decisions under a nonhierarchical or minimally hierarchical decision regime. In a process so important and central as major economic transition, significant participant involvement could be socially beneficial. Given a fair trial, including time for the participants to learn how to function in that different environment, it's possible that it will not work well. But that is by no means a foregone conclusion—it may work very well indeed. In any case, it is not wise to let the bounds of our experience dictate the breadth of our vision.[8]

The value of participation. Though real participation in transition decisions generally yields benefits, this is even more true when the transition is involuntary. Assuming rationality and a reasonable degree of information, involuntary transitions must involve either destination states that are inferior to their corresponding origin states or transition paths whose net cost exceeds the net benefit of the destination over the origin state (otherwise, the transitions would not have to be forced). In other words, some degree of sacrifice is imbedded in a forced transition process, and perhaps in the final state as well. People's willingness to sacrifice depends at least in part on their belief in the necessity or virtue of that sacrifice, and in their sense that the burden of sacrifice is being equitably shared.

Perhaps most importantly, transition processes that involve real interactive participation by at least the most strongly affected parties can help lessen the feelings of anomie and alienation that have become such a common part of modern life. They can increase the sense of being taken seriously, of being important—something we all need. It is not necessary that our views always carry the day, or are met with great admiration. What counts is that they are heard, discussed, argued about—that they can be expressed, and that they will provoke a response. There is some evidence that apart from the positive personal benefits of open channels of communication and inter-action, there may be real societal benefits as well. The degree of violence and general social disruption surrounding situations of social and economic conflict may well be negatively correlated with the extent to which adversaries engage in a real process of communication, responsive interaction, or, in the lexicon of labor relations, "good faith bargaining." [9]

The potential benefits of establishing appropriate mechanisms of transition and transition planning are very great. Greatest among them is the increased fluidity of productive resources and the increased responsiveness and flexibility of the economy that such ongoing transition capability implies. For if economic activity, both small and large, is to be the servant and not the master of social decision making, it must be capable of smoothly and efficiently shifting gears in reaction to changing social goals.

9

The Theory of Resource Diversion

Having laid the foundation for a somewhat unconventional approach to aggregate economic behavior, we can now take on the challenge of fashioning a coherent theory from this primordial soup of ideas. Within the context of this theoretical framework, it should be possible to organize these ideas so as to achieve both the breadth of view and the specificity required to make effective policy.

The Basic Output Structure of the Economy

The economy is functionally divided into three *sectors* on the basis of the societal characteristics of each sector's output. It is not the durability, safety, reliability, or aesthetic value of the output that is critical here; the classification depends instead on the economic implications of the primary function the output is designed to perform and on the use to which it is actually put.

Assuming the enhancement of human well-being to be the only legitimate purpose of the economy, it is postulated that economic activity contributes to this goal in two main ways. In accord with the more traditional view, economic activity raises the standard of living by increasing the quantity and quality of goods and services available that directly contribute to *material* well-being. In addition, however, economic activity also affects human well-being by creating, or at least influencing, the conditions under which production and consumption take place. The positive and negative externalities of production—whether imposed on the work force, the community external to the producer, or both—are as much a part of output as the goods and services directly produced. They can have an impact on human well-being equal to or even greater than that of the direct good or service. Similarly, the conditions under which consumption takes place influence not only the enjoyment that the direct consumer derives from the product but also the enjoyment or penalty that others derive as a by-product of that consumption or from their own consumption of that or other products. Thus, the externalities of consumption can also have a major impact on the degree of general human well-being achieved through consumption of goods and services, and must be considered as real a part of the use value flowing from a product as the more directly derived part.

While recognizing the two-sided manner in which economic activity affects human welfare, I nevertheless choose to differentiate the sectors on the basis of the more traditional criterion: sectors are defined in terms of the degree of direct contribution their output makes, in quantity and quality, to the material standard of living. It is not compatibility with tradition that drives this choice. Rather, I believe that the question of how production is carried out is largely separable from the question of how the material standard of living is affected by the nature and use of the resulting product. Although these matters may well be of approximately equal importance, for the purpose of building a theoretical framework I think it is more analytically useful to focus attention on the nature of the product. However, it is important to recognize that concentrating on the product in no way diminishes the obligation to consider the effects of the process that brought it into being.

Those goods and services that directly contribute to the material standard of living define the *contributive* sector. Products may so contribute by increasing the present material standard of living, as do ordinary consumer goods, or by enhancing the economy's productive competence, as do producer (investment) goods. Enhancing productive competence increases the economy's capability for raising the future material standard of living in direct and obvious ways. Some goods, such as education and health care, are contributive in both senses, serving as long-term investments in the productivity of the economy as well as conveying advantages in terms of present consumption. The primary criterion of contributiveness is thus direct and positive impact on the material standard of living, not immediacy of effect.

Those goods and services that do not contribute to the material standard of living are termed *distractive*. These products, by their nature and design, are oriented to noneconomic purposes and do not typically have close counterparts in standard-of-living goods. For example, battle tanks or fighter planes do not have characteristics appropriate to consumer- or business-oriented land or air transportation. The value of such goods to human society in general is *not* at issue here. What is clear is that they were not intended to—and do not—fulfill either consumer- or producer-oriented functions. Therefore, they are not economically contributive.

It is worth noting that although many of the goods and services produced to support the distractive sector are distractive, not all such production is so classified. Food produced for consumption by military personnel is a contributive good; so is most housing. This reinforces the earlier point that it is the nature of the good or service itself that determines whether it is classified as distractive or contributive. Yet it also points out that essentially contributive goods can be used for distractive purposes. Thus, there is asymmetry here. Distractive goods and services are oriented only to distractive use, but contributive goods and services can often be used in either contributive or distractive activities.

Since the sectors are being defined in terms of the nature of output, and since all goods and services are either contributive or distractive, it seems there is nothing left to define as the output of the third sector. And that is correct, for the third sector is defined precisely by its lack of output. This peculiar *neutral* sector is essentially a resource sink. It is a theoretical construct to represent what was ealier termed neutral activity, activity that occurs in the context of essentially contributive processes but is irrelevant to the effective operation of that process. In other words, resources engaged in neutral activity have zero marginal product; they could be eliminated without effect on output quantity or quality. Redundant or unnecessary administration is perhaps the main empirical example.

All three sectors absorb, or are capable of absorbing, labor and capital of all the various types defined in chapter 5. However, the transferability of resources between sectors is restricted. Resources used in the contributive or neutral sectors are assumed to be transferable (within the same resource category) to use in the distractive sector, but resources used in the distractive sector are assumed to become specialized to use there. They are not permanently captured, yet they can only be reclaimed for contributive (or neutral) use after being subjected to a defined and nontrivial transition process. It would be most realistic to assume that this transition process required both time and contributive resource inputs. However, it should be possible to make the simplifying assumption that only time is required.

It is assumed that resources can move freely, i.e., without the requirement of a formal transition process, between the contributive and neutral sectors—providing only that they remain within the same resource subcategory. As long as managers, administrators, and engineers remain managers, administrators, and engineers respectively, it is postulated that there is no need for retraining. If a manager wants to become an engineer, however, some sort of retraining process is obviously required.[1]

For simplicity, it is assumed that labor or capital of a particular subcategory (e.g., production workers, infrastructure capital, R&D capital) remains in its particular subcategory when it transfers among sectors, whether or not a formal transition process takes place. In practice, both intersectoral movement and movement among subcategories can of course occur, with widely varying degrees of difficulty and hence of cost. However, only intersectoral movement is considered here.

The Social Material Product

At any given time, a society has a certain stock of productive resources and a certain level of organization- and production-related knowledge to work with. The magnitude and nature of that knowledge and resource pool is the ultimate constraint on the economy's ability to generate the material standard-of-living component of its ultimate goal—the maximization of human well-being. The part of the full output of the society's production system that involves the material standard of living is defined as the *social material product* (SMP). There will be some combination of contributive activities, not necessarily unique, that constitutes the maximum SMP that the society is capable of generating at any given time. This potential

SMP is called the *social material optimum* (SMO). Assuming a reasonable human planning horizon, the combination (or combinations) of activities that constitutes the SMO will contain an appropriate trade-off between contributive consumption and investment activities (in accordance with time preferences, rates of discount, and so on).

Because of differences in personal preferences and worldview, the SMO will tend to differ when seen through the eyes of different individuals in the society. The achievement of social consensus on the precise nature of this optimum (or set of equivalent optima) may be extraordinarily difficult, intolerably costly, or just plain impossible. Nevertheless, insofar as attention is focused solely on the material standard of living, the optima will share at least one characteristic: they will allocate all resources to the contributive sector. What about resources that may, as a result of previous use, have become specialized to the distractive sector? Such optima would call for them to be converted to contributive use (by an appropriate transition process) as long as the net costs of transition are less than costs of abandonment (in the case of most capital) or maintenance (in the case of labor and some capital). The net cost of transition is the difference between the net transition cost itself and the value of contributive output (treated as a negative cost) derivable from those converted resources over the course of their remaining productive lifespans.

Whereas trading off resources among various forms of contributive activity might result in a product mix closer to or further from any given individual or group's conception of the SMO, diverting resources to either distractive or neutral activity cannot result in moving closer to *anyone's* conception of the optimum. Such resource diversion shrinks the resource base of the sector that generates the material standard of living, thereby tightening the resource-knowledge constraint. It is a basic principle of constrained optimization theory that tightening a constraint can never improve the optimum. If we are willing to make the following two additional assumptions, it can be demonstrated that such resource diversion must always unambiguously reduce the optimum: (1) all individuals can agree on which goods are contributive (without any necessary agreement on how contributive they are); and (2) although the marginal utility of contributive goods may diminish as their output expands, it never drops to zero or becomes negative. The assumptions imply that resources used in the contributive sector always yield some increase in the material standard of living. Accordingly, taking them out of such use and directing them to sectors whose output (if any) has zero contribution to the material standard of living must result in a lowered living standard. In other words, every good produced in the contributive sector, at any output level, is seen as having positive impact on the society's material standard of living. Therefore, in everyone's conception of the social material optimum the resource-knowledge constraint will be binding. Since tightening a binding constraint must always diminish the optimum, resource diversion will lead the society away from everyone's concept of the optimum.

The concept of SMP is related to but significantly different from the more conventional gross national product (GNP), and the relation of SMO to "potential GNP" is analogous. The similarity lies in the fact that both SMP (SMO) and GNP (potential GNP) represent conceptual measures of the aggregate material product that an economy generates. One major difference is that GNP treats products assigned equal monetary value as fully equivalent, whereas SMP does not. SMP includes only the output of the contributive sector. Theoretically, the SMP concept encompasses both product quality and the positive and negative externalities generated by economic activity—neither of which form part of GNP. Hence SMP is intended to represent a kind of full-output, quality-adjusted gross national product of the contributive sector.[2]

While it is relatively easy to conceive of a measure such as SMP (or SMO) theoretically, translating this theoretical concept into an empirical measure is not such an easy task. As a first approximation one could probably use the gross national product of the contributive sector alone, preferably adjusted by at least some rough measure of externality effects.

Economic Coordination and the Short-Run SMO-SMP Gap

In terms of the concepts just outlined, the key macroeconomic problem is keeping SMP as close as possible to SMO. The difference between SMP and SMO measures the gap between the actual material standard of living of the population and the standard of living attainable given available resources and knowledge. It is a measure of societal opportunity cost. There are essentially two main sources of this gap: (1) failures of economic coordination; and (2) resource diversion (i.e., the channeling of resources to the neutral and distractive sectors).

If the distractive and neutral sectors did not exist—or, more realistically, were negligibly small in their use of *all* subcategories of labor and capital—coordination would be *the* primary macroeconomic problem, and Keynesian or monetarist theory might well serve. Of course, this is precisely the context in which Keynesian theory was developed. It is difficult to know the extent of neutral activity in the United States in those times, but it is clear that the distractive sector, at least, was small and historically had been so (with periodic, short-lived exceptions). Shortly after Keynes's *General Theory* was published, the distractive sector (and less spectacularly, the neutral sector) underwent a substantial and protracted enlargement which has continued to this day.

If restricted to the problem of short-term coordination within the contributive sector alone, most, if not all, of the apparatus of Keynesian theory could be applied. Consumption functions based on disposable personal income or wealth, government expenditures treated as exogenous, liquidity preference schedules interacting with money supply to determine interest rates, and private investment determined by interest rates through the marginal efficiency of investment: all of these have relevance here.

Intersectoral leakages. The main problem in applying Keynes's theory as the theory of economic coordination restricted to the contributive sector is the "openness" of this sector to the neutral and distractive sectors. Rather than being self-contained, the system is quite leaky. For example, given the demand for money (liquidity preference schedule), a change in the money supply alters the interest rate. Ceteris paribus, the same interest rate is available to producers of distractive goods as to producers of contributive goods, since financial capital markets concern themselves only with monetary rates of return, not with questions of the generation of inherent economic value per se. Hence monetary policy intended, for example, to stimulate contributive sector investment may also stimulate distractive sector investment, producing intersectoral competition for limited physical capital. If the capital goods industries are near enough to capacity at that time, the pressure of this two-sided competition might be sufficient to drive the price of capital goods upward, to deprive the contributive producers of the full measure of capital goods they wish to acquire, or both—phenomena that would be far less likely to occur if there were no distractive sector. This is especially true if both sectors require capital inputs of essentially similar character, at least to the point of being complements in production. Furthermore, the distractive sector will typically have the upper hand in such input competition. Since it exists for extraeconomic purposes, it is unlikely to be subject to an ordinary market test of its efficiency. Therefore, insofar as there is a sufficiently strong commitment to distractive production (on whatever noneconomic grounds), the distractive sector may well be in a stronger position than the contributive sector (which *is* subject to a market test) to bid for the inputs. Consequently, monetary policy employed to raise investment in the contributive sector to supplement insufficient aggregate demand there may have unintended and undesirable "back-door" effects. Policy used to combat contributive sector unemployment may instead produce cost-push inflationary pressures there, and perhaps in the distractive sector as well. It may not even alleviate the unemployment problem it was originally intended to solve.[3]

Intersectoral coordination?   What about applying Keynesian theory to the problem of economic coordination across all three sectors? It seems as though that might improve its effectiveness by eliminating the intersectoral leakage problem. But this cannot work, since the causal systems underlying the behavior of the three sectors are different. In an essentially capitalist economy, the contributive sector operates primarily according to market principles toward what are clearly economic goals. The neutral sector is to a much greater extent driven by sociological and psychological factors (mainly related to the operation of bureaucracy) in the pursuit of personal power and status by the key decision makers involved. Activities in the distractive sector, on the other hand, are likely to be motivated by political considerations, though psychological, religious, and general cultural factors may well play a significant role. Because the underlying mechanisms are so different, any theory that treats activities as homogeneous across sectoral boundaries is very unlikely to be useful as a descriptive analytical framework, let alone as a source of effective policy.

For example, suppose the problem is rapidly escalating inflation that has its statistical source in the distractive-sector goods and services component of some generalized economywide price index. One Keynesian prescription is to raise taxes to depress consumer spending (essentially on contributive goods) in order to reduce aggregate demand and relieve the inflationary pressure. But if there is no excess demand in the contributive sector, the tax increase will depress consumer spending, resulting in deficient contributive demand, and will thus lead to unemployment in that sector. At the same time, the influx of new revenues to the government might well be taken as a golden opportunity to press for the expansion of government spending on distractive activity, which its proponents view as important to the nation on noneconomic grounds.[4] If they are even partially successful, the result will be somewhat increased distractive demand—which will aggravate the inflation in the distractive sector without necessarily alleviating the newly generated unemployment in the contributive sector. Consequently, because of sectoral differences, a counterinflationary policy that would have been completely sensible within the context of a totally contributive economy might not only generate unemployment but might also aggravate the very inflation it was designed to counteract.

Inflation and unemployment.   There is yet another issue to raise with respect to conventional macrotheory: the definition of the macroeconomic problem itself. Viewed from the somewhat different perspective that has been developed here, inflation and unemployment are not the root macroeconomic problems—they are surface manifestations of a more basic economic problem, the existence of a gap between SMP and SMO. Inflation under circumstances of equality between SMP and SMO is purely a monetary and not a real phenomenon, and as such is easily handled. On the other hand, full employment is a necessary (though not sufficient) condition for the equality of SMP and SMO.

The existence of inflation, unemployment, or both can have very considerable effects on the *distribution* of the SMP among a population, the other central macroeconomic issue. Yet there are many other phenomena (including quite a few that are not generally thought of as economic, such as ethnic discrimination) that also have a substantial effect on the distribution of SMP. And it is important to distinguish the problem of optimal aggregate economic performance from that of appropriate distribution: they are essentially different, though often mutually interacting, issues.

Resource Diversion and the Short-Term SMO-SMP Gap

Apart from failures of economic coordination, a gap between SMP and SMO may be generated by the diversion of productive resources to the noncontributive sectors. All resources available to the society that are potentially capable of generating contributive product must be considered in the calculation of SMO. Consequently, if some of those resources are presently engaged in noncontributive activity, that alone will guarantee that SMP is below the level the society is capable of producing, regardless of how successfully economic coordination is carried out.

Noncontributive activity vs. unemployment. From an *economic* perspective, there is little difference between capital and labor being unemployed and being employed in noncontributive activity. In either case, those resources are not contributing to the improvement of material well-being. If those resources employed in neutral and distractive activity were to become unemployed, the SMP of the society would not be reduced one iota, just as it would not be increased one iota if all unemployed resources were to be put to work in neutral or distractive activity.

Surely, this cannot be true. Putting capital resources aside, how can it be possible that workers are not better off with jobs than without? In the first place, it is not argued that the individual workers themselves wouldn't be better off employed than unemployed, but simply that the SMP would not be affected. And SMP is, after all, an aggregate concept. But are not the workers involved a part of society, and is their well-being not higher employed than unemployed, regardless of the nature of the work they are doing?

The answer lies in the earlier discussion concerning the nature of work. Work was divided into two categories, paid and unpaid. The only essential difference between them is that paid work provides income. Unpaid work has all of the physical, sociological, and psychological characteristics normally associated with work—there is simply no remuneration in money or kind. In this taxonomy then, paid work is what has traditionally been referred to in both the lay and social science literature simply as "work." The primary reason for creating this dichotomous view of work was to separate what are in fact two separate aspects of work, seen from the viewpoint of the worker: the pay received and the nature of the work itself. There is no reason why a society must always provide both of these needs within a single package. Income may be distributed in any of a great variety of ways that may or may not be coupled with the performance of any particular tasks. And unpaid work opportunities can be furnished relatively easily by either the public or private sector.

The distribution of income by a society to individuals, not coupled to the performance of work by those individuals (or to the sale or rental of an asset they own) is, of course, a transfer payment. Ordinarily the mechanism by which such transfer payments are distributed by society is referred to as a welfare system. The defining characteristic of a welfare system is that it provides to individuals not participating (or minimally participating, in the case of supplemental benefits) in the production of the society's economic product (SMP) the wherewithal to share in the consumption of that product. From this perspective, the neutral and distractive sectors constitute one form of societal welfare system. Individuals employed in those sectors are thus, in lay terminology, on welfare. Therefore, those workers employed in the neutral and distractive sectors are personally better off than if they were unemployed only because they are in effect both on welfare and provided with unpaid work. If they were unemployed and provided with more traditional welfare payments (of equivalent amount) and with unpaid work opportunities, they would be just as well off. The belief that people engaged in neutral and distractive activity are economically employed because they are working hard and generating visible individual or collective product is simply a societal delusion. From the standpoint of contribution to the generation of economic product, they *are* unemployed.

There is no question that people engaged in neutral activity, since they are not producing anything, are contributing no more to society than those who are unemployed. But, it might be objected, this cannot be true of those engaged in distractive production. After all, they are producing something, and even if that something has no economic value, it must have some sort of value (political, social, or otherwise) or it would not be produced. It is certainly true that economic value is not the only kind of value and it is true that the distractive sector does produce some product. But it is also true that those who function in the distractive sector must live off the product of the contributive sector, a product that they have not participated in generating. In this respect they are in precisely the same situation as the unemployed. And the value of the product they do produce is not necessarily reflected in the money value attached to that product— nor, for that matter, is it even necessarily positive.

   Evaluating noncontributive product. It is difficult to assess the true value of the distractive sector's product. Since there is no market exchange involved, it is not clear that the money price of the product reflects anyone's assessment of the value of that product to him or to her. Typically, the decision makers in charge of purchasing such products (ordinarily government officials and politicians) are spending someone else's money. The wisdom of the valuations reflected in their purchasing decisions is not subject to any direct test, market or otherwise—and only to a generally uninformed and infrequent evaluation by the people whose money is being spent (ordinarily the taxpayers). Furthermore, the product itself is often hard to measure—national defense, for example. Consequently, the "price times quantity" (or "factor cost") figure typically used to assess the value of distractive product is at best highly misleading and at worst completely fallacious. The value of distractive product, as a total or at the margin, seems extremely difficult if not impossible to determine.

   In fact, it is often not quite as difficult to assess the value of distractive product as it seems—particularly at the margin. But the perception of difficulty, interacting with the other characteristics of the purchase process, allows for distractive production to be carried out on a scale unrelated to its value. In fact, the "fog" may be sufficient to permit distractive activity to be pushed beyond the point of negative marginal returns, even in terms of the stated purpose for which it is being carried out.[5] Therefore, while some of the people employed in the distractive sector may be contributing something with positive noneconomic value to the society, it is by no means certain that all people distractively employed are doing so. Some, possibly many, may be generating negative value even in the noneconomic sense. Those producing positive noneconomic value are therefore contributing more to society than those who are unemployed. But those producing negative noneconomic value are contributing less. Society would be better off both economically and noneconomically if they were unemployed (although clearly best off if they were instead contributively employed).

Let it be understood that there is absolutely no implication in the foregoing discussion that individuals employed in distractive or neutral activity are, in some personal sense, of lesser worth; that is a completely separate issue. To be sure, individuals have a right—indeed an obligation—to ask to what end their efforts are being put and to decide for themselves whether participation to that end is personally acceptable. Yet the variation in human moral systems and in more general human judgments on such matters is such that a wide variety of viewpoints may be honestly held. Furthermore, given the aforementioned "fog" that surrounds the social valuation of distractive activity and clouds the determination of whether a given activity is in fact neutral in character, individuals may find it very difficult to perceive the true social character of their work. In fact, such character may be difficult to assign on an individual basis, even though it is perfectly clear in the aggregate.

For example, suppose four managers are doing managerial work that could, from the perspective of forwarding the goals of the organization, be readily accomplished by three. That is, unnecessary memoranda, analyses, and reports equivalent to one manager's full workload are being produced. It is clear that one manager is engaged in neutral activity. But which one? The question may be unanswerable. It is possible that each manager spends one-quarter time generating such useless paperwork. That does not alter the fact that one managerial job's worth of neutral activity is going on from the societal viewpoint. No one need be loafing or covering up or even individually aware of being engaged in neutral activity. Similarly, a determination that the nation's military system is operating in an area of negative marginal national security returns does not in itself assign negative noneconomic contribution to any particular soldier or military industrial worker.

The noncontributive model.   With some modification, a

conventional macroeconomic model (Keynesian or otherwise) is serviceable as a theory of economic coordination within the contributive sector. What of the neutral and distractive sectors?

The output of the noncontributive sectors is fundamentally noneconomic in character. Neutral activity is driven largely by such noneconomic forces as bureaucratic imperatives, while distractive activity is driven chiefly by political, psychological, and other noneconomic factors. But there are economic factors involved in the causal system of noncontributive activity. Managers motivated by the desire to increase their salaries or perquisites may press for hiring additional subordinates as a step toward justifying higher compensation for themselves in the future on grounds of increased managerial responsibility. By this route, much neutral activity may be generated. Similarly, firms engaged in distractive production may be internally motivated by ordinary considerations of profit or sales maximization, their workers by a desire to maintain or increase their incomes, and the communities in which they operate by a desire to maintain the tax base. All of them, therefore, may press for continuation or expansion of distractive activity in general and their piece of the action in particular. Furthermore, in addition to arguing on noneconomic grounds the necessity of at least their species of distractive activity, they may point to either the short-term economic costs of its cancellation (e.g., lost jobs) or the short-term economic benefits of its expansion (e.g., jobs created). To the extent that the resources involved are, in the short term, specialized to the distractive sector, there is some surface validity to the economic argument—particularly in the case of job maintenance. The transition process required to move these resources back into the contributive sector is not instantaneous. So in the short term, cutbacks in distractive activity would cause some of these resources to become unemployed.

However, as I have argued above, these resources are already unemployed from the point of view of the economy. Accordingly, what this short-term "jobs" argument boils down to is an argument to maintain these workers "on welfare" in the part of the welfare system associated with distractive employment, rather than in the part of the welfare system normally associated with the lack of paid work. As such, it is an extremely weak argument. From a societal viewpoint, it is positively foolish to base levels of distractive expenditure on anything other than its noneconomic benefits, balanced against the opportunity costs of such activity (the economic component of which is measured by the magnitude of SMP forgone). To do otherwise is to remain trapped in the short term, condemning the society to a permanent and ongoing diminution of its material standard of living simply because of its inability to instantaneously redirect resources to contributive activity. Such myopic reasoning is an economic disease which if allowed to spread would undermine both capital investment (human and physical) and expenditure on technological advance, neither of which makes the slightest bit of sense in the short run. Yet, without all these forms of investment, human economic activity would first stagnate, then decline.

It is clear that both failures of economic coordination and diversion of resources to noncontributive activity play a role in generating a gap between SMP and SMO in the short term. But what of the long term?

The SMO-SMP Gap in the Long Run

Failures of economic coordination and resource diversion have key long-term effects on the SMO-SMP gap by way of two intervening variables: investment and productive competence. Failures of coordination depress investment chiefly through their impact on expectations, though they may also depress investment by drastically shortening decision makers' time horizons. If, for example, poor economic coordination results in sustained inflation, expectations of further inflation may be generated, producing a shift toward present consumption and away from saving. On the other hand, poor coordination resulting in sustained unemployment may well give rise to expectations of continued recession, leading business people to view the time as hardly propitious for undertaking substantial investment projects. Business people operating in such an environment may rationally try to maximize flexibility and minimize the extent to which their capital is tied up in longer-term projects. The result: a bias toward quick-return, short-term profits. The economic pressure put on individuals in such periods of downturn may lead them to focus their attention on immediate concerns and to neglect the longer-term view appropriate to investing heavily in the future. Under such conditions, investment does not flourish.

Resource diversion may depress investment by an entirely different route. For all its special properties, the market for investment is two-sided, just like other markets. Neither the demand for investment per se nor even the accessibility of financial capital to support that demand alone determines the actual level of investment. Rather, it is the interaction of the perceived need for investment, the enabling financing, *and* the supply of investment goods and services that sets the actual *physical* rate. And it is through the supply side of the investment market that resource diversion has its greatest impact.

For the time being, we will focus our attention on two major forms of investment activity: augmentation of the stock of physical production and infrastructure capital, and technological development. Both of these have had enormous impact on the secular growth of SMP over the long term, and of course they are interrelated. But whereas it is the condition of the former that provides a picture of a society's level of economic development at any given time, it is the status and progress of the latter that has increasingly become the hallmark of the modernity, vitality, and prospects of an economy. So let us begin by considering the impact of resource diversion on the progress of technology.

Resource Diversion and Technological Development

The most fundamental prerequisites to the development of new technology are the availability of appropriately skilled engineering and scientific personnel and, nearly as important, proper R&D capital with which they can work. If these critical resources are not available in sufficient quantity and quality technological progress will be frustrated, no matter how great the demand for it. There are two interrelated reasons why this might happen: insufficient generation of technological resources, and resource diversion.

It is simply not true (nor should it be true) that people's occupational choices are determined solely by considerations of rates of pay, fringe benefits, and other related conditions of work; there is far greater diversity in human society than that. Differences in inherent capability, individual psychology, and social conditioning are also reflected in these choices. In fact, the degree to which they are reflected is an important measure of the level of freedom in a society. Human diversity also implies that people will exhibit different performance capabilities in the occupations they do ultimately choose. Consequently, there will only be a subset of the population that would want to be scientists and engineers, even under very favorable conditions, and only a subset of that subset will be capable of performing at least adequately in those roles.

Of course, that is just as well, since there are a great many other important roles that need filling in any society, and there is great richness available in permitting the fullest possible flowering of human diversity consistent with a coherent society. In fact, the ability of a society to foster the development of the capabilities and traits that make each human being unique is a measure of its success in advancing human well-being. For it is primarily the society that must accommodate to the capabilities, personalities, and dreams of its individual members, and not the other way around.[6]

None of this is to say that people do not also respond to the incentives or disincentives of salary and work conditions—they most assuredly do. Rather, it is to say that the supply of labor to various broad categories of occupations is not perfectly flexible even within the constraints of population size. This is particularly true of highly skilled categories, such as scientists and engineers. There is some empirical evidence that for scientists and engineers, changes in social emphasis—backed up by corresponding changes in salary, job availability, and work conditions—are more likely to shift individuals among the various specific fields of science and engineering than to increase the flow of individuals into science and engineering as a whole.[7] One would expect this to be generally true. It seems logical that the elasticity of supply of labor to a specific field within a broader occupational category would be greater than the elasticity of supply of labor to that broad occupational category as a whole. There are simply closer substitutes available within the broad categories of occupation than between them.

In any case, if the supply of labor (adjusted for quality) to engineering and scientific disciplines as a whole is fairly inelastic to begin with and becomes even less elastic as the quantity supplied expands, the society will face a limited R&D capability. This will be especially true if the supply becomes unresponsive to positive incentives (as the previous argument indicates it will do) at a low enough level. The effect of resource diversion here is to substantially tighten this constraint for the contributive sector.

Contributive and distractive technology. Technologists (and for that matter, R&D capital) employed in the distractive sector are more completely diverted than those engaged in neutral activity. They are not presently producing contributive technology; they are also less capable of doing so in the future without a formal transition process. Their experience and training orient them to the special characteristics of the distractive sector. The greater the divergence between the conditions of distractive and contributive sector technological development, the more severe this trained incapacity becomes. It is not merely differences in the nature of contributive and distractive technology per se that causes this problem, though these are very important: it is also differences in the contexts within which the technologies are developed.

Since the distractive sector operates for primarily noneconomic purposes, its functioning will not typically be subject to evaluation by the same sort of efficiency criteria (e.g., a market test) as in the contributive sector.[8] Consequently, technology-developing activities will be affected. In the development and application of technological knowledge, choices made will affect costs incurred. For example, the particular engineering specifications chosen from the wide range of choices consistent with the product's primary design objective can and usually do have major impact on cost of manufacture. For instance, the tighter the dimensional tolerances specified (i.e., the less margin for error permitted in the dimensions of parts), the greater the machining costs tend to be. Higher-precision work will be required, and more rework and scrap generated. Engineers and scientists operating in a highly cost-sensitive environment must therefore pay close attention to the implications of design for manufacture and product operation costs; technologists operating in a relatively cost-insensitive environment, such as is likely to prevail in the distractive sector, do not. This renders them inappropriate for contributive-sector employment unless they are retrained and reoriented. A similar argument applies to the design of research projects and to the judgment of which research problems are interesting and promising.

Inevitably, the nature and characteristics of distractive technology diverge substantially from those of contributive technology. For one thing, one of the major emphases of the latter is the development of efficiency-increasing production techniques aimed at reducing the total cost per unit of contributive goods and services. Scant attention will likely be devoted to that sort of technology in the distractive sector, precisely because of its relative cost insensitivity. The nature of the goods and services produced and the uses to which they are put differ so greatly between the contributive and distractive sectors that technological development aimed at improving their quality will also be sharply different. The design emphases, degree of field specialization, and even fields of training necessary to the development of the two types of technology are likely to differ as well. These are further reasons why engineers and scientists in the distractive sector are unlikely to be suited to contributive employment without undergoing transition.

This sectoral differentiation may explain what would appear to be anomalies, seen through the eyes of more conventional theory. It is, for example, entirely possible to observe shortages of engineering and scientific labor in one sector existing side by side with substantial unemployment of engineers and scientists in the other. Furthermore, it is likely that unemployed distractive sector technologists will have difficulty finding jobs in the contributive sector. Contributive sector producers may not be willing or able to absorb the costs of the retraining and reorientation necessary to turn them into efficient generators of technology suited to contributive sector needs. Contributive sector engineers and scientists, on the other hand, may have much less difficulty finding employment in the distractive sector; this is primarily because distractive producers are less concerned with absorbing the transition costs (e.g., retraining) of relocating contributive technologists to the distractive sector—for the same reasons that they are less concerned with other costs.

Therefore, to the extent that a society's pool of engineering and scientific talent is directed to distractive activity, it is unavailable for contributive R&D. But is the actual technical knowledge developed in one sector really so different from that useful to the other sector? Is there not likely to be a substantial degree of intersectoral transfer of technology, if not of technologists?

Spinoff. Of course, there will be some intersectoral technology transfer—or spinoff, as it is commonly called—and it will typically be two-way. The real question is, is this spinoff effect substantial or marginal? The answer to this question depends on several factors. In general, the results of basic research will be more transferable than those of applied research or development. Greater knowledge of the laws of nature cannot help but widen the horizons of all scientific research. Hence, the more fundamental the research activity is, the more likely that its results will be transferable. The inverse is, of course, also true. Since distractive activity is so different from contributive activity, the more the R&D is oriented to a particular application, the less transferable it will tend to be.

Intersectoral differences in cost sensitivity again enter the picture. Even technologies developed in the distractive sector that are technically applicable to contributive activity may be so expensive as to render them unusable in a cost-sensitive contributive sector. It is possible that further developmental activity might reshape them into a form appropriate to contributive application; but this commercialization or development is anything but trivial. It may well be a long, difficult, expensive process, requiring much engineering and scientific talent and creativity. The development stage is often looked down upon as being of lesser scientific value or achievement. Yet from an economic standpoint, it is crucial: it is what transforms an interesting possibility or a laboratory curiosity into an invention with real impact on society.[9] Thus, if a great deal of commercialization remains to be done after an innovation has been spun off, the original innovation was not really all that transferable.

Summary propositions. The following propositions summarize the effects of resource diversion on technological development:

1. There is an upper limit to the pool of scientists and engineers potentially available to a society over time as well as at a given time.

2. This pool is not likely to be large, compared to the needs of a vigorous, modern, technology-based economy.

3. Without time-consuming retraining and orientation, technologists working in the distractive sector are unsuited to contributive technological development.

4. For the most part, technologies developed in the distractive sector will be only marginally transferable to the contributive sector.

As a result, a significant diversion of engineers and scientists seriously hampers investment in contributive R&D from the supply side. Furthermore, such diversion raises substantial barriers to the future availability of these engineers and scientists to the contributive sector—barriers that cannot be overcome quickly. Thus, resource diversion yields serious present and future constraints on contributive R&D investment.

Since R&D activity is critical to maintaining and improving a society's productive competence, it follows that resource diversion can seriously undermine productive competence over the long term. This in turn implies at the very least a reduction in the secular growth of potential SMP (i.e., SMO)—and perhaps its stagnation or decline, should the diversion be sufficiently large. If technological resource diversion is great enough, it will bias scientific and engineering education toward that most appropriate to functioning effectively within the distractive sector. The institutional capability for properly operating and maintaining certain types of contributive technologies may thus atrophy. This institutional effect is unlikely, however, unless the diversion of engineers and scientists is both large and protracted.

Resource Diversion and Capital Investment

Resource diversion also has important effects on investment in production and infrastructure capital. On the supply side, the argument is similar to that made for R&D investment. The capacity of capital goods industries is essentially fixed over the short term. The portion of that capacity being directed to the servicing of distractive sector demand is unavailable for supplying capital goods to the contributive sector. In the competition for this scarce capital production capacity, the contributive sector is at a decided disadvantage, for it is operating in a relatively cost-sensitive environment while the distractive sector is not. If the societal commitment to the distractive sector is sufficiently strong, the financial constraints on that sector will tend to be weak. It *will* be successful in preempting a portion of the economy's capital capacity by simply outbidding the contributive sector.

Expanding capital goods production.   The capacity for

producing capital goods may be fixed in the short term, but what of the long term? Cannot the capital goods industries expand sufficiently over the long term to satisfy the demands of both sectors? Will they not in fact do so, in response to the financial incentive of rising capital goods prices caused by excess demand?

The answer to the first question is yes, they can expand. But such expansion is not free—it comes at the expense of the production of consumer goods. The inputs needed for such expansion—capital *and* labor in all their various forms—must come from somewhere. They will not come at the expense of the distractive sector, as long as the societal commitment to that sector continues; they must therefore come from the ranks of the unemployed (or underutilized, in the case of capital), or from consumer goods producers. If there is an unemployed pool of appropriate resources from which to draw, the society is already forfeiting consumer goods, so drawing off these resources will not add to the forfeiture (but neither will it reduce it). If employment is full, then there will be a direct diminution of consumer goods production matching the capital industries' expansion. In either case, the society will be experiencing an opportunity cost—a cost that could be expressed in terms of consumer goods forgone, and thus reduced standard of living.

As to the second question, it is true that competition between the two sectors will drive the price of capital goods up. But because of the relative cost insensitivity of the distractive sector, its demand for capital goods will tend to be far less elastic than the capital goods demand of the contributive sector. Consequently, though the rising price of capital will cause a reduction in the quantity of capital demanded by both sectors, that drop in demand will tend to be larger in the more cost-conscious contributive sector. At the higher price, effective demand for capital may well be satisfied (i.e., the market will clear), but the contributive sector will wind up with a smaller quantity of capital than it originally wanted. Thus, contributive investment will be lower than it would have been in the absence of a distractive sector. On the other hand, distractive sector investment will come pretty close to meeting its original targets. The incentives for expansion of the capital goods industries are thus unlikely to be sufficient to secure an expansion large enough to accommodate the full measure of contributive and distractive investment originally planned.

But what of contributive infrastructure capital investment? Is not most of this done by government and thus also not subject to a market test of the sort faced by the contributive private sector? Shouldn't that type of government investment therefore be less cost-sensitive?

Infrastructure capital. It is true that the government is much more likely to be a heavy investor in infrastructure capital than in production facilities and equipment under normal conditions (owing to the greater externality effects of the former as well as the higher likelihood of natural monopoly). However, there is no inherent reason why the private sector should not or could not supply infrastructure services as well. Empirically, of course, it often does. Much of the communications and transportation infrastructure of the United States, as well as portions of its education, health care, and other types of infrastructure, is at least partly supplied by the private sector.

Public investment in infrastructure capital is substantial, though, and is presumably subject to a different set of constraints than private investment. But to the extent that such investment is being made for basically economic purposes, it is more likely to be evaluated by the criteria of economic efficiency than is distractive investment servicing noneconomic objectives. For example, the decision of whether to improve mass transit by building a surface passenger rail system, building a subway, or buying and operating more public buses will probably be subject to a more thorough analysis of cost effectiveness than will alternative designs for a new governor's mansion or public monument. Public contributive sector infrastructure investments will generally be much more cost-sensitive than infrastructure investments of the distractive sector and may, in some cases, approximate the cost sensitivity of private contributive infrastructure investment.

Additional considerations. Over the long term, the effects of resource diversion on the supply side of the market for capital goods will be greater than these quantitative arguments imply. For just as technologists are not directly interchangeable between the sectors, capital may not be either. The difference in function between the products of contributive industry and those of distractive industry may give rise to a difference in the characteristics of the required capital goods themselves. If so, it is possible, even likely, that the production facilities and capital equipment necessary to produce distractive-sector capital will be different from those required for production of contributive-sector capital. Under those circumstances, capital goods industries may divide into contributive and distractive components. This kind of second order diversion will probably not occur unless the noncontributive sector's claims on capital resources are significant and long-term.[10] In any case, it is clear that the supply-side effects of resource diversion on capital investment are serious and negative. Through its effects on technological progress, discussed earlier, resource diversion may also exert a serious negative effect on capital investment via the demand side.

By definition, embodied technological progress can only be applied by obtaining the equipment that embodies those advances. Even some forms of disembodied technological progress may require more capital of existing design. Since resource diversion retards contributive technological progress, it will weaken this stimulus to investment demand.

Summary propositions.   The following set of propositions emerges with respect to the impact of resource diversion on investment in production and infrastructure capital:

1. The capacity of the capital goods industries is roughly fixed in the short term. The distractive sector demand for capital goods preempts a portion of this capacity. This hinders contributive sector capital investment from the supply side, producing long-term effects on the economy's contributive capital capacity.

2. Long-term expansion of the capacity of the capital goods industries in order to accommodate the intersectoral competition for capital goods will occur at the expense of contributive consumption, reducing the material standard of living.

3. Intersectoral competition for capital goods will drive up the price of these goods, both in the long and the short term.

4. The rise in the price of capital goods will depress contributive investment more than it will depress distractive investment because of the greater cost sensitivity of the contributive sector.

5. If the resource diversion is large and long-lived, it may give rise to distinct contributive and distractive capital goods in-

dustries, thus aggravating the supply-side shortage of contributive sector capital goods.

6. Because resource diversion retards contributive technological progress, it reduces the capital investment demand stimulus associated with technological advance.

Resource diversion thus has a potent negative effect on SMO in the long run, through its depressive effect on both contributive R&D and capital investment. Since SMO is the upper limit of SMP, this will eventually (and perhaps fairly quickly) depress SMP *whether or not* economic coordination has been effective. Therefore, if resource diversion is large and continuing, it will produce serious negative effects on the contributive economy's ability to function in the long run, resulting in an unavoidable decline in the society's material well-being.

The Investment-Consumption Trade-off

Apart from resource diversion and poor coordination, the path taken by SMP and SMO depends on the set of choices made between contributive investment and consumption activities. Clearly, a high-investment, low-consumption strategy will depress the present material standard of living but sharply raise SMO in the future. The inverse is also true. While it is likely to be judged suboptimal for a society with any reasonable planning horizon to focus completely or nearly completely on consumption, it also makes very little sense for a society to indefinitely pursue a strategy of very high investment and low consumption. It only makes sense to invest if you intend to reap a return on that investment at some reasonable future point. Investment merely represents deferred consumption, and it makes no sense to defer consumption indefinitely. It is easy to become enamored of high-growth strategies because they seem so dynamic, constructive, and powerful. But the central purpose of an economy is not to grow—it is rather to provide the material component necessary, in the minds of the population, to maximize the quality of life.

Different people and societies have different ideas about the optimal consumption-investment trade-off. Other than cautioning against following either path to an extreme, there is very little to be said about that here. Consequently, any gap between the actual path of SMP (or SMO) that a society follows and some other path that might have been attainable with a different secular consumption-investment mix is a matter of differing time preferences for consumption, and thus of patterns of SMO through time. However, gaps between the SMP and SMO paths that arise from poor coordination, resource diversion, or both are not of the same character: they represent not simply differing concepts of SMO, but an absolute opportunity cost—in forgone consumption, investment, or both—that is being borne by the society.

The Distortion of Fiscal and Monetary Policies

Fiscal and monetary policies, as ordinarily understood, are useful tools for short-term economic coordination in the absence of resource diversion. They cannot, however, overturn the fundamental deterioration of productive competence caused by a large and continuing societal commitment to locking up productive resources in noncontributive activity. Hence, they are unable to assure effective and efficient functioning of the economy over the long run. Furthermore, fiscal and monetary policies forced to operate in a context of decayed productive competence will ultimately fail to operate properly even as techniques for short-term economic coordination.

Why? Because fiscal and monetary policies operate by attempting to manipulate demand—final demand for goods and services or intermediate demand for capital and labor by producers. They do this either by impacting purchasing power directly or by affecting purchase incentives (such as interest rates, in the case of consumer durables and capital goods purchases)—which often amount to practically the same thing. But they cannot guarantee the ability to carry out purchase plans. This depends on the availability of appropriate capital goods, engineering and scientific personnel, and other inputs. It is these supply-side considerations that are directly affected by the existence of a substantial distractive—and to a lesser extent, neutral—sector.

Thus, policies aimed at encouraging capital investment by, for example, lowering interest rates, may run up against problems of insufficient contributive capital goods availability (and perhaps insufficient capital goods production capacity as well), owing to pre-emption of these goods by the distractive sector. Such incentives are not necessary to secure increased distractive investment, and may be incapable of generating increased contributive investment. To the ex-tent that lowered interest rates do encourage distractive investment as well, the policy may be counterproductive, lessening the contributive capital goods availability in the long run through increased intersec-toral competition, as earlier discussed.

If, as was argued for technological personnel, it is easier for the distractive sector to use contributive capital goods than for the con-tributive sector to use distractive capital, we are in the worst of all possible worlds. This unequal relationship means that expansions of distractive investment can result in preemption of additional con-tributive capacity, but surpluses of distractive capital goods produc-tion capacity will not be available to service contributive investment in periods of high demand. The same effect will occur if the distrac-tive sector, for one reason or another, hoards capital or capital pro-duction capacity. Parallel arguments exist for sectorally specialized labor, such as engineering and scientific personnel. Since the distrac-tive sector is inherently noneconomic, it can potentially get away with such hoarding behavior even in the face of contributive sector shortages. And, in that situation, distractive producers may wish to hoard in order to be ready for possible future demand increases.

The central fact, then, is that resource diversion results in a na-tional standard of living that is lower than what it could be in the absence of this diversion and that is either growing more slowly than it could be, stagnating, or actually declining over time. That is a "real" phenomenon. Whether it surfaces as nominal price inflation, nominal income decline, unemployment, or some combination of these affects the distribution of SMP but not its magnitude. Fiscal and monetary policies can determine, or at least strongly influence, in which of these forms the negative effects on real standard of living surface—but they cannot forestall the decline.

Until now, we have been tacitly assuming an essentially "closed economy" context. It is time to consider what the effects of opening the economy to international trade and other international economic interaction will be.

The Open Economy Context

In an "open economy," the issue of *relative* productive competence—the productive competence of the economy at hand relative to that of all other economies with which it interacts—is critical. If the level of competence of the domestic production system is sufficiently high relative to that of other economies, it is possible for domestic industry to be highly competitive with foreign industry in price and quality of goods and services produced. This is true even if domestic industry faces higher costs of all productive resources. In other words, a more efficient production system is capable of off-setting higher input costs effectively enough to keep its price low and its product quality high relative to the production systems with which it competes. Of course, if its resource costs are lower as well, the domestic economy will have a double advantage.

On the other hand, productive competence is not a simple, static phenomenon. It is very much affected by the kinds of dynamic processes that have been discussed, particularly capital investment and technological development. If, because of lagging investment and retarded technological progress, the competence of the domestic production system does not grow as fast as that of other societies, the product of domestic industries will be less and less attractive relative to the product of foreign industries. If this decline in *relative* productive competence is permitted to continue over a sufficiently long time span, even a substantial initial competitive advantage will be eroded and finally reversed. Note that it is not necessary for *absolute* productive competence to decline—that may, in fact, continue to increase. It is only *relative* competence that is important to competitive advantage.

If it does not come only at the expense of lower present consumption, large and persistent resource diversion *will* cause relative productive competence to erode. This is especially true if the economies of the competing countries are not so heavily drained by noncontributive activity. Consequently, foreign industry *will* make progressively larger inroads into both the foreign and domestic markets of domestic industry. This eventual loss of markets will lead to cutbacks in production and hence to progressively higher domestic unemployment.

The inflation-unemployment trade-off. In the closed-economy context, it was argued that the legacy of sustained resource diversion is "real" inflation—the decline of the material standard of living. To this inflationary effect is added rising unemployment, once competition from foreign producers is allowed. Nor is this unemployment of the cyclical variety, though cyclical unemployment may from time to time be added to it. It is structural unemployment, and as such will resist the traditional cyclical unemployment remedies. Hence, it is perfectly possible to experience both high and rising inflation and high and rising unemployment at the same time.

This does not, however, mean that no trade-off exists between inflation and unemployment. In the first place, the particular economic coordination policies pursued will tend to add either to the inflation or to the unemployment over any given short run, but not usually to both. There is in effect a (cyclical) trade-off between unemployment and inflation sitting on a base of growing inflation *and* unemployment. In other words, the persistence of a substantial noncontributive sector shifts the economy's Phillips curve outward over time.[11]

More importantly, manipulation of the degree of openness of the economy can itself trade the structural unemployment effects of resource diversion for the inflationary effects, and vice versa. A more open economy, free of trade restrictions and trade-discouraging exchange rate interventions, will give the domestic population access to less expensive and higher quality contributive goods supplied from foreign sources. Thus, though domestically produced SMP will be reduced, the slide in the society's material standard of well-being will be slowed, at least for a time. However, this will be achieved at the expense of a higher rate of contributive sector unemployment. Closing the economy off through one means or another of protecting domestic industry from foreign competition will reduce the unemployment problem, but only at the expense of cutting off access to these cheaper foreign goods. Therefore, the rate of "real inflation" will increase. Either way, it is a devil's bargain. Furthermore, unless the society is exceptionally well endowed, it is likely that significant amounts of at least a few particularly important resources will have to be imported. Thus, closing off the economy completely is not really feasible. There is always the possibility that partial measures will antagonize trading partners, leading to retaliation of one sort or another. In any case, the limitation of competition generally tends to reduce the pressure to produce efficiently. Protecting domestic industry is therefore almost certain to accelerate the decline in productive competence.

An open economy poses a more difficult coordination problem than a closed one. This is mainly because economic policies undertaken by foreign trading partners can have a significant impact on the domestic society, and conversely. Second-order effects are then generated as each society reacts to the effects its partners' policies have had on its economy. And so the action-reaction process continues.

Expanding foreign noncontributive activity.   Since *relative* productive competence is what is crucial to economic competitiveness, it might seem that one way of regaining position would be to convince competitive societies to engage in expanded noncontributive activity. It is hard to imagine how an expansion of neutral activity in another society might be encouraged. Distractive activity, however, is an entirely different matter. After all, the distractive sector *does* exist to service societal objectives, and the neutral sector does not. And if it is possible to increase the importance of those objectives to the competing societies, those societies may be encouraged to respond by expanding the level of their distractive activity.

For example, if it is possible to make them believe that some other society poses a serious military threat to them, they may respond by expanding the level of their own military forces and military support industries. If the threat, real or imagined, can be maintained at a high enough level for a long enough time, sustained resource diversion will cause their economy to deteriorate as well. This will come to inhibit the growth of, stagnate, or even diminish the productive competence of these competitor societies. Accordingly, the retardation of *absolute* productive competence caused by your own society's extended resource diversion will not produce as large a loss of *relative* productive competence. Hence your own industries will not be at as great a competitive disadvantage.

But this is a fool's game. This policy of trying to even the contest by infecting your opponent with the same disease that is debilitating you results in everyone's being sick. There may be some short-term economic advantage to be achieved—or more accurately, some economic disadvantage to be temporarily offset—but in the long term everyone is worse off. And the seeds of distractive activity planted elsewhere, as in the military case, may ultimately result in pressures to expand your own distractive sector, reinforcing even your original *relative* disadvantage. Finally, it has already been argued that the decay of material well-being that results from long-term resource diversion occurs even in a closed economy, and that some degree of openness may slow the decline in the domestic standard of living. It should therefore be obvious that the policy of encouraging foreign distractive activity can only change the mix of surface effects of resource diversion—it is impotent to deal with the basic SMP deterioration that diversion generates.

Exporting distractive products.   It might be argued that the deleterious effects of diversion-induced incompetence in the contributive sector could be offset, in an open economy setting, by simply trading the products of the domestic distractive sector for those of foreign contributive industry. After all, distractive products presumably have some sort of value. Hence, if there is a spontaneous foreign-based demand for these goods and services, or if such demand can be created, it should be possible to trade these products for goods whose value *is* inherently economic. A large and well-nourished domestic distractive sector presumably has developed some capability for more effectively producing distractive goods than the smaller (or even virtually nonexistent) distractive sectors of other societies.

If it is possible to trade distractive for contributive goods, then such trade would of course increase the domestic availability of contributive goods, ceteris paribus. The domestic society would therefore experience a slower slide in material well-being. This trade would, in effect, help to finance the importation of contributive goods that the domestic contributive sector was no longer able to produce efficiently. But to the extent that this trade centered on importing consumer goods, it would not halt or even slow the decline in the competence of the domestic contributive sector's production system. As a result, the distractive sector would continually need to enlarge in order to offset by trade the declining ability of domestic contributive producers to maintain the society's material well-being. This, in turn, would accelerate the deterioration of the contributive base, increasing the need for expanding distractive production to maintain the availability of contributive goods by trade. The end point of this process would be an economy turned upside down, with the major portion (or, in extremis, all) of the society's productive resources devoted to fundamentally nonproductive, noneconomic activity. This is not an economy at all, but a caricature of one.

Such a society would be not only economically grotesque but also extraordinarily insecure. It would be heavily dependent on other societies for most of its material existence. Disruptions of supply, for whatever reason, would be potentially catastrophic. And what if the societies that have become its economic lifeline decided they could do without such heavy spending on distractive goods? Or if their levels of expenditure on imported distractive products grew large enough that they moved to establish or enlarge their own distractive sectors? Since distractive products lack inherent economic value, these last possibilities could not be forestalled by appealing to the economic self-interest of the competing societies. And if we felt compelled to forestall them through political, military, or other forms of coercion, we must ask ourselves what sort of society we had created.

Furthermore, the supply of distractive goods to other nations might be counterproductive, in light of the reasons for which we created the goods in the first place. This is particularly true in the case of military goods. The arms trade might backfire, resulting at some point in the exported weapons being used in a conflict against the arms-exporting nation or one of its allies.[12] The availability of larger quantities of more destructive weapons might not create conflict, but it would surely escalate the damage caused when existing tensions erupt, as they do from time to time. Consequently, the contributive capacities of trading partners could be severely damaged. Further, the arms exporter's military position could be weakened by the release of technical information about the capabilities and operation of its own weapons systems—which would inevitably accompany the sale of these systems to other nations. No, it does not make sense to pursue economic policies whose logical conclusion is to cause the tail of the distractive sector to wag the dog of the contributive economy.

If the exportation of distractive products were used to finance the importation of state-of-the-art capital goods (especially production—and to a lesser extent infrastructure and R&D—capital), some of these problems could be mitigated. The importation of appropriate capital goods could slow the decline in domestic productive competence. But there are a number of reasons why this would not solve the problem entirely. Most importantly, investment in physical capital is only one component of what is needed to maintain or improve productive competence. As long as a sufficiently large fraction of critical categories of labor, particularly technologists, remained locked in the distractive sector, productive competence would continue to decline. And direct trade restrictions, or simply normal competitive practice, might make it impossible to import the most up-to-date capital and all the necessary disembodied technology that goes with it. Furthermore, if this trade resulted in importation of capital rather than consumer goods, the open economy would not be as effective in slowing the decline in present standard of living. Public opinion might thus be antagonistic to this approach. And finally, it would seem that if the domestic population were so concerned with the decline of the society's productive competence as to focus its trade policy on capital importation, it would be willing to shift its domestic priorities enough to move resources out of the domestic distractive sector and undo the decline in productive competence more directly.

This last point can be broadened. The production of distractive goods and services reduces the resource base available to the contributive economy. Thus the very existence of the distractive sector creates an internal trade of contributive goods for distractive goods. If distractive goods are then going to be traded externally (i.e., to other societies) for contributive goods, would it not be more efficient to produce only enough distractive goods to satisfy domestic demand, and return the excess resources directly to the contributive sector? This would allow strengthening and expansion of domestic contributive production and so lessen the need to import foreign contributive goods and services.

In the short run, the price of exports relative to imports determines whether it is better to trade distractive exports for contributive imports or to produce more contributive goods domestically. This seems to be a question of comparative advantage. But the lack of inherent economic value of distractive goods inserts a considerable degree of arbitrariness into the establishment of the terms of trade. Or, put differently, since distractive goods have no inherent economic value, the money value they do have compared with contributive goods is determined by political and other noneconomic considerations—many of which are subject to arbitrary change. In the long run, however, for all of the reasons we have been discussing, the deck is stacked heavily in the direction of minimizing the size of the distractive sector.

There may be noneconomic reasons for exporting distractive goods. The validity of these (or lack thereof) can be quite a complex issue, and in any case is simply not addressed here. But there are only the most fleeting and marginal economic reasons for exporting distractive goods. In the long run, and perhaps in the short run as well, it is simply poor economic policy.

Work and the Workplace

I have so far discussed two reasons why there may be a gap between SMP and SMO—resource diversion and failures of economic coordination. There is a third: the failure to carry out production in a way that maximizes the quality of life of the work force in particular and the society in general. For if we take seriously the mandate of the economy to maximize the contribution of economic activity to the quality of life, we must consider not only what is produced but also how it is made. It is the full output of the production system that needs to be the focus of our attention. "Full output" has been defined to include everything that the production organization does to the society. Thus, to the value of goods or services produced must be added positive and negative impacts of the work environment on the workforce (physical, psychological, and otherwise), and the positive and negative externalities (e.g., technology transfer, air pollution) the operation imposes on the part of society that lives beyond its doors.

Looking only at direct output of goods and services, because of the analytical and empirical difficulty of considering full output, in no way alters the reality of these indirect impacts or their societal significance; it merely leads to a fixation with numbers and things, turning means into ends. That is, production of goods and services is simply one means by which people attempt to make themselves better off. Whether we recognize it analytically or not, that is the reality. The production of goods and services is not, and should not be, an end in itself.

The social material optimum will not necessarily be, and in fact will generally not be, the point of maximum output of contributive goods and services: the achievement of the maximum possible production of things from a given resource-knowledge base will typically require levels of specialization, work simplification, and fragmentation that are inconsistent with producing a psychologically and sociologically healthy work environment. It is also likely that maximum physical output will require some laxity in the safeness and healthfulness of the workplace and a significant degree of general environmental pollution. In short, maximum production of goods will also tend to produce a substantial collateral output of "bads." When the latter are offset against the former, full output will be less than maximum and the society will not be operating at the SMO. Workplace utility and general societal utility are legitimate and serious considerations in trying to close the gap between SMP and SMO.

If there are additional direct costs imposed on domestic producers as an immediate and traceable effect of pollution abatement or work enhancement, it may be necessary to place equalizing tariffs—equal to and no higher than those costs—on foreign producers, to avoid unfairly disadvantaging domestic industry. But this should only be done to the extent that it can be demonstrated that foreign producers are achieving lower costs specifically because of their lack of attention to these concerns. This is probably one of the few forms of tariff that could legitimately be considered in the interest of true efficiency.

Applicability to Planned Economies

The arguments that have been made with respect to the impact of the noncontributive economy, particularly in the long run, apply essentially intact to planned economies as well. The main theoretical alteration necessary is to replace the modified Keynesian (or monetarist) theory of economic coordination with that of state-based socialism. The solutions to the problems of short-term economic coordination are entirely different under the Keynesian and socialist paradigms, but the sorts of long-term deterioration of productive competence generated by resource diversion are remarkably similar.

Actually, that is not at all surprising, since it is not the mechanism of resource allocation that is crucial to the generation of effects on productive competence but the resulting allocation itself. It matters little whether the contributive economy operates under market or planned economy principles: what makes the difference is the extent to which its resource base has been shrunk by preemption of resources by the noncontributive sectors. Similarly, it is not important whether the distractive (or neutral) sector is wholly government-operated or is government-financed and contracted out to private firms. In neither case (socialist nor capitalist) will the distractive sector operate according to free-market principles. In fact, the distractive sector may be the closest thing to state socialism that exists in an essentially market economy like that of the United States. In such a sector, the government may not only direct production, but may also actually own some or all of the means of production. In any case, given sufficient priority the distractive sector of either market or socialist economies will be able to effectively preempt critical resources, and hence will produce the same general negative effects on productive competence.

What is likely to differ between essentially socialist and essentially market economies are the ways in which the effects of decayed productive competence surface. In general, market economies have advantages in terms of incentives and motivation, socialist economies in terms of coordination and stability. Consequently, the effects of deteriorating productive competence tend to surface in the form of inflation and unemployment in market economies, and in the form of chronic shortages of contributive products in socialist economies. It is possible to prefer one or another symptom, I suppose, but it is rather like being asked to choose between a backache and a headache—neither is a very pleasant prospect.

I shall not develop further here the validity of applying the same macrotheory (with different coordination theory embedded) to market and socialist economies. But a question naturally arises from this attempt. How is it possible that two economic systems as different as market capitalism and socialism could conceivably be analyzed by the same macrotheory? The answer is that the theory focuses on fundamental economic issues that cut across all systems of economic organization. The division of the economy into three sectors—contributive, distractive, and neutral—is based not on ideology, ownership, or control, but rather on the basic economic properties of the output of those sectors. The argument that a long-term deterioration of productive competence will be produced by sustained, large-scale noncontributive activity also has nothing to do with the system of internal exchange and control over production, but rather concerns the fundamentals of resource allocation—and not so much the mechanisms of that allocation as its result. Furthermore, one of the most central concepts of the theory, productive competence, is much more concerned with the realities of the factory floor and other microeconomic issues than with the structure of the overall economic system.

10

The Theory of Resource Diversion: A More Technical Look

Basic Propositions

The core of the theory of resource diversion is contained in the following set of propositions:

1. The purpose of economic activity is the improvement of the well-being of the population. The annual aggregate contribution to the material component of that well-being is referred to as the social material product (SMP).

2. Over any time horizon, reasonable in comparison to the human lifespan, there exists a stream of SMPs that represent the highest achievable state of material well-being aggregated over that time horizon. These SMPs are referred to as the social material optima (SMOs).

3. The central macroeconomic problem is assuring that the SMP for any given year is kept equal to the SMO.[1]

4. The SMP in any given year depends on the *functional* nature of the goods and services produced, their quantity, their quality, and their full output characteristics.

5. The SMO in any given year depends on the nature and availability of productive resources and the nature and level of applied technical knowledge.

6. The economy is differentiated into three sectors, defined by the functional nature of their output:

   a. *Contributive:* The goods or services produced augment the present material standard of living or the capacity to produce material standard-of-living goods and services in the future.

   b. *Neutral:* No goods or services are produced; this sector exists for noneconomic reasons and is essentially a resource sink.

   c. *Distractive:* Goods or services are produced but are not of the type that either add directly to the present material standard of living or add to the economy's capacity to produce goods or services that will contribute to the future material standard of living.

7. The demand for neutral and distractive activity is exogenous to the economy.

8. In the short run, divergence between SMP and SMO occurs for two reasons:

   a. failure to equilibrate aggregate demand with full-employment aggregate supply;

   b. allocation of productive resources to the noncontributive sectors.

9. In the long run, 8a produces divergence between SMP and SMO *only* to the extent that contributive sector *investment* has been depressed below optimum levels as a result of poor coordination.

10. In the long run, the maintenance and improvement of contributive-sector productive competence (i.e., the ability to produce efficiently with respect to both price and quality) requires a continuing and substantial flow of resources to that sector—particularly production, infrastructure, and R&D capital, and technological labor. Thus 8b produces divergence between SMP and SMO to the extent that it has involved diversion of resources from contributive activity in the past. This divergence is cumulative.

11. Resources may be efficiently redirected from the distractive to the contributive sector only after a nontrivial formal transition process.

Implications for the Short Run

The full-employment aggregate supply of contributive sector goods (Y_F) depends on the quantity and quality of the resource pool available to that sector and on the level of contributive production technology extant. It differs quantitatively from the SMO in that SMO is the full-employment contributive supply that would be producible if there were no productive resources engaged in noncontributive activity. It differs qualitatively in that the SMO includes consideration of full output, which is strongly influenced by the way work is performed and by the nature of production externalities.

Since contributive-sector output is the only output that adds to the material well-being of society, only the increase in the level of prices of this output constitutes inflation directly relevant to the real income (purchasing power) of the general population. It is thus a sufficient condition for the generation of inflation that aggregate demand for contributive-sector output, denoted X_C, is greater than Y_F.

If no noncontributive sectors existed, we would be in an essentially conventional macroeconomic world. In such a world, since the source of all income is the production and supply of contributive goods and services, it is only necessary to pump up the level of aggregate demand through injections of investment and government spending to make up for the leakage of demand represented by savings. But the existence of distractive and neutral sectors vastly alters this picture. The output of these noncontributive sectors is valued in money terms and hence gives rise to money incomes, a fraction of which (measured by the average propensity to consume, *apc*) gives rise to demand for contributive goods. Thus, the leakage from contributive demand represented by the saving of a portion of the income earned in contributive production is offset by the injection of contributive demand arising from the consumption activities of those who earn their incomes in the noncontributive sectors. Added to this are the demand for contributive investment goods and the contributive component of government spending.

Avoidance of inflation therefore requires that the total of consumer demand plus contributive investment plus contributive government spending be less than or equal to the savings of those consumers whose income derives from the contributive sector. It is plausible to assume that there is no systematic difference between the consumption habits of those who derive income from contributive activity and those deriving income from noncontributive activity. If the ratio of money income generated in noncontributive activity to that generated in contributive activity is equal to $(1 - apc)/apc$, consumer spending by those earning income in noncontributive activity will *by itself* completely offset the leakage from contributive demand represented by the savings of those whose income derives from contributive activity. In such a situation, *any* investment activity by contributive industries or *any* contributive government spending will push total contributive demand beyond total contributive supply. This tends to increase contributive supply and expand employment of productive resources available to the contributive sector, as long as it occurs when there is unemployment or idle capacity among such resources. But if it continues to occur once Y_F has been reached, sustained inflation will be generated.

In other words, at Y_F the volume of savings by those deriving income from the contributive sector defines the amount of slack available to accommodate other injections of contributive spending without necessarily generating demand-pull inflation. But contributive demand by those whose money income derives from noncontributive activity uses up some of this slack and therefore reduces the volume of contributive investment and contributive government spending that can be carried out without forcing inflation. In this sense, there is a kind of "crowding out" effect. If the noncontributive sectors are very small, the ratio of noncontributive to contributive money incomes will be very small and little crowding out will occur. But as the ratio approaches $(1 - apc)/apc$, there will be a greater tendency toward inflation. When the ratio exceeds this boundary, there will be inflation even under conditions of no contributive government spending and zero contributive gross investment.

The differentiation between sectors also allows the simultaneous occurrence of high inflation and high unemployment, even in the short run. It is perfectly possible for an excess of contributive demand over Y_F to exist at the same time that insufficient demand exists to call forth employment of all of the labor (and capital) that has become specialized to the distractive sector. Under these conditions, there will be inflationary pressure in the contributive sector side-by-side with unemployment in the distractive sector. In the absence of a formal transition process, which will *not* automatically occur (particularly not in the short run), the unemployed distractive-sector resources will be frozen into that sector. Bearing in mind that distractive-sector resources are really unemployed from the standpoint of the economy even when they are working, the loss of distractive paid work may create personal difficulties for the workers involved, and that is a matter of concern. But it is of no consequence to the wider economy or to the material well-being of the general population: it is merely a shift from hidden unemployment to open unemployment.

If the same capital goods industries produce contributive capital and distractive capital (assuming that these different forms of capital are substitutes in production but not in use), simultaneously high *contributive* inflation and *contributive* unemployment are also possible. If high distractive demand leads to an attempt to rapidly expand distractive sector capacity, there will be a heavy component of investment demand coming from that sector. The distractive sector may thus preempt a sufficient portion of the capital goods industries' output to drive up prices of contributive capital goods. This cost-push pressure may generate inflation in the contributive sector even in the face of overall slack demand there. There will thus be both inflation and contributive unemployment. For this to happen, though, one must assume that some contributive industries continue to buy capital in sufficient quantity to generate this effect even though overall contributive demand is slack and part of present capacity is thus unused. Expectational factors may make this possible, as may ordinary capital replacement.

If there is excess distractive demand, resources will tend to be drawn out of the contributive sector. If there is unemployment in the contributive sector or readily convertible idle capacity, this labor or capital will be put to work producing distractive output. This is less advantageous than it may seem, since resources engaged in distractive activity are still unemployed in the sense that they are not contributing to economic well-being. However, although putting these unemployed resources to distractive use may not involve any economic benefit, there is also no short-term economic cost to doing so. Paid work in the distractive sector is likely to be a more lucrative form of welfare assistance to the workers involved than the alternative of unemployment compensation or more conventional welfare assistance. If so, there will be an increase in money income that will drive up consumer demand. Consequently, in the second round the deficiency of contributive demand will be somewhat abated and paid-work employment in the contributive sector will increase.

This does convey real economic benefits. However, precisely the same result could have been achieved by diverting the funds financing excess distractive demand to increase unemployment compensation to the contributive sector labor force—and by providing unpaid work opportunities as required. An economically superior result is achievable by redirecting these same funds to financing additional contributive activity (say by a shift in government spending priorities or by a tax cut). This strategy is superior in the pareto sense in that it provides all the same benefits as the preceding situations *plus* a greater net contributive output.

If excess distractive demand exists when there is full employment in the contributive sector, the picture is quite different. To the extent that the distractive sector is still willing and able to outbid the contributive sector for the latter's resources, there *is* a net economic penalty involved. Success in drawing contributive resources out of contributive activity will produce an immediate drop in contributive output. If the drop occurs in consumer goods production alone, the reduction in present material well-being will be maximized. If the drop occurs in capital goods production, there will be no immediate drop in the standard of material well-being, but the future standard will be adversely affected to the maximum degree. How the drop in contributive output is shared between diminished consumption and diminished investment depends on a great many things. Perhaps the most important determinant, however, is the nature of the resources the distractive sector seeks to hire away.

Regardless of which particular industry employs them, technological resources (i.e., R&D capital, engineers, and scientists) are by nature oriented primarily to investment. The generation of technology is not typically a short-term process with immediate returns:

it requires present expenditure in the hope of future gains, i.e., investment. Consequently, to the extent that the marginal expansion of distractive activity draws more heavily on technological resources, the primary impact will fall more heavily on investment than on present consumption. As long as attention remains focused strictly on the short term, this will seem an advantage. But because of the impact on productive competence, the long-term picture will be very different.

If there is an excess of contributive demand at a time when there is unemployment in the distractive sector, only two categories of workers will flow to the contributive sector: production workers—primarily the less skilled—and administrative personnel. This will reduce the unemployment problem somewhat, provided other factors do not get in the way. For example, geographic separation of concentrations of contributive and distractive activity may impose high costs on the transfer of labor or capital goods. Or barriers to information flow may prevent workers from learning about available job opportunities and employers from locating available workers. On the whole, the intersectoral flow of resources will be much more restricted in this direction. For whole categories of unemployed distractive-sector workers, excess contributive demand will mean nothing more than a source of inflation that will diminish the purchasing power of their incomes, which are likely to be quite restricted. Such workers are too specialized to distractive activity to transfer to contributive work without a formal transition process. It is therefore not surprising that workers in the distractive sector constitute a powerful and highly motivated vested interest in opposition to any curtailments of distractive activity, no matter how socially beneficial such curtailments may be. Given a society (and a theoretical world view) captured by the short term and blind to the importance of developing and activating effective transitional mechanisms, what else could be expected?

Implications for the Long Run

A society's level of productive competence is the principal determinant of its potential real income in the short run and in the long run. It is necessary to take the longer-term view, however, in order to understand the processes that alter productive competence and the macroeconomic policies needed to maintain or improve it.

Investment is the process through which productive competence is altered. The physical wearing out of capital, and its analog, attrition from the labor force and secular deterioration of labor force skills, represent ongoing, natural disinvestment processes. The rates of depreciation of production capital, infrastructure capital, and (to a much lesser extent) control capital are the primary capital resource determinants of this natural rate of decline in absolute productive competence; the attrition and skill deterioration of production workers (especially the highly skilled), managers, administrators, and those engineers involved directly in production and management activities (rather than research and design projects) are the primary labor resource determinants of this natural rate. Hence maintenance of productive competence requires sufficient contributive capital production, worker education, and appropriate job experience to offset this natural rate of decline. If, for whatever reason, the investment in each of these categories is not enough to offset the rate of decline, the real income of the society must diminish over the long term.

In the long run, resources specialized to the distractive sector are not inherently unavailable to contributive activity. It is possible, through defined transition processes, to reclaim all of the labor and most if not all of the capital resources for the contributive sector. Hence the quantitative difference between Y_F and the SMO is largely eliminated, though the conceptual qualitative difference remains. As a result, the existence of any noncontributive sector creates a quantitative gap between actual contributive supply (Y) and Y_F. The society's material standard of living is thus forcibly held below its maximum. If the noncontributive sectors expand their share of resource usage over time, even effective coordination of aggregate contributive demand and supply will not prevent a widening of the gap between Y and Y_F and hence a decline in real income.

A certain minimum mix of capital and labor resources must be devoted to the maintenance of absolute productive competence. Let us refer to this minimum mix (or vector) of resource types and quantities simply as the *maintenance resource investment* (*mri*). Note that the *mri* need not be unique (in general, it will not be), and that it must be defined in terms of a share of resources rather than an absolute amount so that it is scaled to the size of the society's infrastructure and productive capacity.[2] Taking the present standard of living as given, productive resources of certain types and in certain quantities will be necessary to sustain that standard in the short term. This mix (or vector) of productive resources will be called the *consumption resource requirement* (*crr*).

Long-term *and* short-term stability of the material standard of living therefore requires a mix of adequate quantities of appropriate types of productive resources equal to the sum of *mri* (for long-term stability) and *crr* (for short-term stability). If the noncontributive sectors absorb an amount of *any* resource greater than the difference between the total amount of that resource available and the sum of its quantity included in *mri* and *crr*, the material standard of well-being must decline. (That is, if any component of the difference between the vector of resources available to the society and the vector of resources claimed by the noncontributive sectors is less than the corresponding component of the sum of the *mri* and *crr* vectors, the SMP will be reduced—presently or in the future.) If that excess of noncontributive resource absorption comes at the expense of *crr* alone, only a short-term decline will occur—after which, if the society is content with its lowered present consumption standard and if the noncontributive sectors do not expand further, the slide in living standard will cease. If, however, the excess noncontributive resource absorption comes at least partially at the expense of *mri*, a continuing reduction in the material standard of living will occur—even if the noncontributive sectors do not expand their share of resource use. However, as the capital and skilled labor pools contract because insufficient resources are being devoted to their maintenance, the *mri* (which is scaled to the size of that pool) will shrink as well. Thus the decline in the living standard will continue only until the *mri* eventually shrinks to the point where it can be satisfied with the smaller amount of resources still available for investment. At that point the decline will cease, unless the diversion of resources expands further.

Because the results of slower, more chronic processes are not as clearly visible or as obviously painful as those of more spectacular acute events, considerations of political expediency will almost guarantee that at least some of the trade-off of resources—and perhaps much of it—will come at the expense of *mri*. This is perhaps especially true in a democratic society. The exception would be a society that had achieved prior general consensus in support of the present sacrifice because of some (rightly or wrongly) perceived crisis. Even under these conditions, however, the tendency will be to divert some portion of the distractive resource requirement from *mri*, as well as from *crr*.

It is thus quite possible to generate a sustained fall in real income—a growing gap between Y and Y_F—without any growth in the relative size of the noncontributive sectors. Even a mild shrinkage of the relative share of noncontributive activity might still be consistent with falling real income over an extended (though not indefinite) period. There are, however, good reasons to expect that the share of noncontributive activity will be highly resistant to decline—and will perhaps expand persistently, over the long term—once the noncontributive sectors become well-established and large. For example, the chief present-day form of neutral activity appears to be excessive management and administration, whose driving force is bureaucratic expansionism. This expansionism is the result of status seeking and of institutionalized personal economic incentives to which managers and administrators respond, incentives that are not necessarily congruent with social benefits: it is the end product of personally rational acts that aggregate to socially irrational actions. Since the expansion of neutral activity is socially irrational to begin with, and is driven by personal incentives that may even intensify in the face of a generally declining standard of living, there will be a tendency for neutral activity to expand—unless, of course, major institutional revisions occur.

The chief present-day example of distractive activity is the maintenance, expansion, and use of military systems. Militaries are typically constructed, maintained, or expanded because of internal or external forces perceived as posing a threat to a society, or at least to its present system of governance. Yet as a society's military systems are enlarged, opposing forces to whom those systems appear as a threat (or obstacle) tend to expand their militaries in reaction. The strengthening of these opposition forces is a powerful motivation for the further enlargement of the society's own forces. This kind of action-reaction phenomenon so common to arms races constitutes what engineers refer to as a positive feedback loop—a self-reinforcing and self-justifying process—and fuels the continuing expansion of this type of distractive activity.

A long-term tendency toward continuing decline in material well-being ("real" inflation) thus results from the existence and operation of the noncontributive sectors. But what about unemployment? Does the inflationary bias just analyzed imply a counter-recessionary bias? In a closed economy, unemployment of contributive-sector resources will occur only as the result of poor economic coordination. The fundamental process by which the operation of the noncontributive sectors erodes productive competence will not of itself create contributive unemployment in this setting. The inflationary bias produced by the existence and operation of the noncontributive sectors does produce a bias against contributive unemployment. But it is not a countercyclical bias. What it does, in a sense, is to shift the business cycle upward, exaggerating its peaks and moderating its troughs.

It is important not to fall into the trap of applying conventional economic reasoning to this wholly different setting. It may seem worthwhile to trade off worse inflations during peaks against shallower recessions during troughs. But the operation of noncontributive sectors always produces this shift in the business cycle within the context of a longer-term, more persistent and more fundamental shift: the progressive—in fact cumulative—deterioration of productive competence and hence of material standard of well-being. In other words, there may well be sharper nominal inflations and shallower recessions than in the absence of noncontributive activity, but these altered cycles will be occurring simultaneously with a continuing impoverishment of the society. It is difficult to see that as an advantage from any perspective.

Implications of an Open Economy

The single most important implication of considering the economy as an open system is the partial disconnection of domestic demand and domestic supply. Increases in domestic demand for a given category of goods or services no longer necessarily imply the calling forth of domestic production as a means of meeting that demand. Similarly, domestic supply may be expanded as a result of demand emanating from foreign sources. The apportionment of demand and supply between foreign and domestic sources then becomes a crucial issue. The openness of the economy places the domestic production system in direct competition with the production systems of every other society that exports. This radically alters the macroeconomic situation for essentially microeconomic reasons. Competition is no longer confined to rivalry among firms operating under the same societal deployment of productive resources. Firms operating within a society whose sectoral resource allocation hampers productive competence are likely to find themselves at a serious disadvantage in this competition. This has especially important implications for employment.

In the short term, the relative competences of the foreign and domestic production systems are given. Suppose that foreign contributive producers are more efficient across a broad range of industries. Assuming no compulsion or restriction is involved, demand will be apportioned among foreign and domestic producers in accordance with relative prices and qualities. Demanders will tend to purchase less expensive goods for a given level of quality. If it is assumed that all products are homogeneous (except for place of origin), all demand will shift toward the purchase of the least expensive source. Even under such an extreme assumption, as the cheaper supplier expands output in the short run, its price will rise because of increasing marginal costs. Since the goods are homogeneous, and assuming there is no inherent consumer preference for either foreign or domestic suppliers, this process will continue until the price charged is the same for foreign and domestic suppliers of the good. The market will then be apportioned according to the relative output levels at which marginal cost equals marginal revenue for each producer, giving rise to the identical price. The more efficient producer will then have the largest *share* of the market, but will not necessarily take the entire market.

Allowing for international nonhomogeneity of product will alter this result by biasing the market shift in favor of whichever country's version of the product is preferred by the majority of demanders, ceteris paribus. This preference may stem from differences in quality or even biases owing to country of origin. The result will be the persistence of a price differential at equilibrium, the product generally preferred bearing a higher price. If the higher-cost producer is also the higher-quality producer, the shift of market in favor of the lower-cost producer will be mitigated. However, if the more efficient producer (in terms of cost) is also considered to have the higher-quality product, it will take an even larger share of the market.

If the cost differences between foreign and domestic producers are not the result of microeconomic factors per se but rather are manifestations of widespread differences in societal productive competence, cost and quality advantages will be positively correlated to a high degree. Thus foreign contributive producers operating in an economy less heavily burdened by noncontributive activity than that of domestic producers will have the advantage in both cost and quality. Accordingly, in an open economy the short-term inflationary bias resulting from the existence of large noncontributive sectors will not imply a bias toward higher employment among resources operating in the contributive sector: the economy is simply too leaky. High contributive demand is perfectly consistent with high levels of unemployment in the domestic contributive sector in short-term equilibrium. There will, in fact, be a tendency to just such a short-run equilibrium in open economies with large noncontributive sectors.

Conventional macroeconomic policies that look to demand stimulation as a means of countering high unemployment will be severely debilitated, if not rendered completely impotent, in such a setting. Stimulation of consumer demand through tax cuts, for example, may well result in increased imports, with little effect on domestic employment. Of course, if domestic demand stimulation is large enough, it will relieve domestic unemployment—unless all demand leaks away to foreign markets at the margin. However, this relief will come at the expense of a hemorrhage of currency flowing out of the country to support a vast increase in imports. This might be tenable in the short term, but it is clearly insupportable over the longer term.

Neither fixed nor floating exchange rates will insulate the country from the basic, real-income–deteriorating effects of the economic drag produced by a large burden of noncontributive activity. If exchange rates float, and hence reduce the value of domestic relative to foreign currency, this import surge may be somewhat restricted. Consequently, domestic contributive employment will benefit more from the demand stimulation policies than it would if exchange rates were fixed. But because consumer options have become more restricted and less favorable, this will merely be a matter of trading off unemployment against inflation; real income will decline in either case.

Maintenance of absolute productive competence requires continuing investment in both human and physical capital. The least investment that will achieve this objective at any given time has been called the maintenance resource investment (*mri*). Investment beyond this level is thus required to raise absolute productive competence over time. Maintenance of *relative* productive competence between societies, on the other hand, requires that sufficient appropriate investment is carried out by each society to match the growth in productive competence of the others.

In fact, there is another strategy open to a firm caught in a situation of deteriorating productive competence: close down domestic production facilities and move to areas where input costs are lower. This action may temporarily maintain the firm's financial position, but only at the price of higher domestic unemployment. Again, this action—rational for the firm—generates no real benefits for the domestic society. It merely transfers the pain resulting from declining competence from the managers and stockholders to the work force. More precisely, it merely speeds the unemployment of workers who would ultimately become unemployed anyhow as the firm became less and less competitive and lost more and more of its market share.

A deteriorating trade balance produces pressure to devalue the domestic currency. If other factors do not overcome this pressure, the falling value of domestic currency will contribute to inflation by raising the price of imports. This will, of course, counter the loss of markets to some extent, and thus mitigate unemployment somewhat. If, for other reasons, the international exchange value of domestic currency is stable or even increasing, inflation will be reduced because of the dropping price of imports to domestic consumers; but this will aggravate domestic unemployment. In no sense does exchange rate adjustment either mollify or intensify the basic problem: it merely affects the rate of trade-off between inflation and unemployment while the secular trend toward increases in both inflation and unemployment continues.

Conventional macroeconomic policies are relegated to the role of changing the symptoms of the degenerative economic disease caused by persistent, substantial levels of noncontributive activity over the long term. For example, attempts to lower unemployment by demand stimulation via consumer tax cuts will mainly lead to higher import levels, and thus to larger trade deficits and further weakening of the international value of the domestic currency. This approach may therefore add to inflation without significantly reducing unemployment. Attempts to stimulate investment are just as likely to stimulate distractive investment as contributive investment. Hence temporary mitigation of unemployment may be achieved at the expense of even greater enlargement of the distractive capital drain. For that matter, it is very possible that if contributive investment is stimulated at all, capital goods will be obtained from foreign producers. If so, the short-run domestic multiplier effect of such investment will be minimal.

Direct job creation schemes by the government will tend to reduce unemployment by straightforwardly creating paid work. However, only if these jobs are of the type that augment productive competence (e.g., infrastructure maintenance and development) will this have any longer-term effect on the secular undermining of domestic jobs by foreign competition. If they are distractive sector jobs—if, for example, the government increases the military budget as a jobs policy—the long-term deterioration of the economy will be accelerated, and will be more difficult to overturn as these resources become less capable of producing contributive output in the future. Furthermore, present inflation will be aggravated by increasing the demand for contributive goods without increasing the supply, and the trade deficit will likely widen.

Of course, the method of financing the government job creation will also influence its economic impact. And the efficiency of this policy depends on the extent to which the skill mix of the unemployed contributive workers is utilized. Government job creation, if it is not aimed at work that augments the productive competence of the society, will need to expand over time to absorb the increasing numbers of contributive-sector workers displaced by foreign competition. This growth of the government sector is not supportable in the long run unless the government itself moves into contributive production on a large scale. After all, someone in the society must be creating the real wealth to support the subsidies which in effect are being given to distractive producers. Yet this would mean the progressive abandonment of the free market system, a system which is a significant part of the ideological and operational social structure that much present-day distractive activity is allegedly protecting in nations with market economies.

On the other hand, conventional policies aimed at abating inflation may be ineffective, or may worsen unemployment while having only mild success against inflation. Driving interest rates up will tend to depress investment spending, lessening aggregate demand in the short term; but contributive investment will be reduced more than distractive investment. In the long term, this will further reduce productive competence, worsening the basic problem. Raising taxes will also tend to diminish aggregate demand; but since the inflation is essentially cost-push in nature, this policy too will exacerbate unemployment more than it will abate inflation. In fact, higher interest rates (and perhaps business taxes as well)—to the extent they can be passed along to customers—may actually worsen inflation by adding to the cost-push process. The higher domestic prices that result will put domestic industries at an even greater competitive disadvantage: even though they will lose markets by raising prices, they will not be able to avoid doing so as their costs of doing business increase under conditions of deteriorating relative productive competence. Consequently, such policies will worsen unemployment, and may aggravate inflation as well.

In short, applying conventional discretionary policies to what is a highly unconventional economic disease will either make things uniformly worse or merely generate short-term oscillation about a steady trend of economic decline.

Implications of Method of Financing Distractive Expenditure

The way in which distractive expenditures are financed cannot alter the extent of the economic damage they produce when sustained at a high level for an extended period of time. Financing can, however, very much affect the surface manifestation of that damage. Ordinarily, the distractive sector will be largely, if not totally, government-financed. Accordingly, there are three basic modes of financing available: taxation, borrowing, and money creation. Let us consider each of these in turn.

If distractive spending is financed wholly by taxation of consumers, the result is an unambiguously lower contributive demand, since both those deriving their income from the contributive sector and those deriving their income from the distractive sector will have lowered disposable income compared with a pretax situation. Thus, any tendency toward slackness of demand for contributive-sector goods and services will be strengthened, causing deeper contributive unemployment. Since a portion of consumption goods is purchased from foreign suppliers, financing distractive expenditures in this way may reduce the flow of imports relative to a pretax situation. In any case, the economic sacrifice of supporting distractive activity by taxation is extracted primarily in the form of a lowered present standard of living.

If consumer goods demand is depressed by this mode of financing, contributive investment demand will also tend to be reduced as the result of accelerator factors. That is, slack contributive demand reduces the incentives to contributive producers to improve or expand their productive capacity. In the absence of strong countervailing incentives, contributive investment will be lower, adding to the long-term decline of productive competence. Thus, the future standard of living will tend to be somewhat affected as well.

If we look at the situation from a purely marginal point of view, financing increased distractive expenditures wholly by taxation may have no effect on the demand for contributive goods if the *marginal* propensity to spend on contributive goods is the same regardless of whether the income being spent is derived from contributive or noncontributive activity. This, in fact, seems the most plausible case. Only if the spending propensities differ will an increase in non-deficit spending on distractive goods affect contributive demand in the short run.[3]

Suppose distractive spending is instead financed wholly by borrowing. Here the primary effect will be on credit markets. Large-scale government borrowing will drive up interest rates, thereby depressing both contributive investment and the interest-sensitive component of consumer demand (mainly durables, presumably). Consumer demand in general will be higher than under the taxation financing option. Depending on the interest elasticity of investment demand (and the interest-sensitive component of consumer demand), there may be higher or lower aggregate contributive demand in the short term than under the taxation approach. There is little doubt, however, that contributive investment will be more depressed, which, as mentioned earlier, accelerates the decline of productive competence. For that matter, high interest rates will depress investment not only in contributive physical capital, but also in research and development—perhaps even more crucial for productive competence. High interest rates imply a lowered present value to any given expected stream of returns, making *all* investments evaluated by such criteria less attractive, ceteris paribus. In an open economy over the long term, depressing domestic investment in contributive capital and R&D virtually guarantees a continuing relative loss of domestic cost-offsetting capability and further shifting of markets to foreign producers. Hence this mode of financing will significantly aggravate both cost-push inflation and unemployment over the long term.

The third financing option is running the printing presses, i.e., creating more money and using it to finance the distractive expenditure. Since no money income is directly extracted from consumers, their demand should not be reduced. Furthermore, the increase in the money supply should drive interest rates down and stimulate both investment demand and the interest-sensitive component of consumer demand. Unless serious bottlenecks occur in the capital goods industries as contributive and distractive investment demands compete with each other (which, as previously discussed, is a real possibility), total contributive spending will be higher than under either of the previous conditions. Hence unemployment in the (assumed) slack contributive sector will be lower. In the short term, then, this option for financing the distractive sector seems best, if there is considerable slack in the contributive sector: it is the only financing technique that stimulates both sectors. Hence, if distractive spending is being carried out under conditions of full employment or excess demand in the contributive sector, this financing option is, for the same reason, the worst. However, this result is strongly dependent on assuming a closed economy and on myopically viewing only the very short term.

Over the long term, financing distractive expenditure by money creation will foster sustained inflation rather than real growth. The expanding money supply will not be balanced by an expanding supply of contributive goods and services, since the contributive sector will be progressively debilitated by the distractive sector, not stimulated by it. In the long run, this running of the printing presses is dangerous, possibly touching off high rates of inflation that could even, if pushed hard enough, explode into hyperinflation—a clear predecessor of dramatic and sharp economic collapse.[4] And economic collapse has more than once led to social and political disaster.[5]

We have seen that it is possible to have substantial contributive unemployment in the face of high, even excess, contributive demand, if foreign-produced contributive goods take a large share of the market. Furthermore, this importation must be financed somehow. It can be financed by the export of distractive goods, if there is sufficient foreign distractive demand and if we are willing to ignore the problems of such a strategy as earlier discussed. It can also be deficit-financed—by a large net flow of domestic currency out of the country. Even in the short term, this would create pressure toward devaluation of the domestic currency. To the extent that fixed exchange rates are appropriately adjusted, or the exchange rate is simply permitted to float, this outgoing flow of currency will lower the international value of domestic money and hence will raise prices for imports. This, in turn, will of course make imports less attractive. However, if the competence of the foreign production system is substantially greater than domestic productive competence, it is likely, at least in the short term, that rising import prices will not fully offset the competitive advantage of foreign industry. In the long run, it is simply not possible to indefinitely finance a trade deficit with exports of money.

Conclusions

It has been argued that (1) the inflation-unemployment problems generated by lack of productive competence are not amenable to cure by conventional short-term macroeconomic policies; (2) a long-term perspective is crucial to understanding the process by which noncontributive activity leads to simultaneous inflationary-recessionary pressures via the deterioration of productive competence; (3) the way in which distractive activity is financed does make a difference—but no method of financing can seriously ameliorate the basic negative effect on the contributive economy; and (4) in the presence of declining relative productive competence, closing off the economy through trade restrictions will tend to reduce contributive unemployment—but only at the cost of a very substantial exacerbation of inflation.

Conventional macroeconomic policies and financing choices thus manipulate the surface manifestations of the economic decay. No matter how the symptoms are manipulated, however, the long-run consequence of sustained high levels of noncontributive activity is the same. The legacy of persistent resource diversion is an ongoing structural deterioration in the economy leading to a progressive inability of the economy to achieve its primary objective—the maintenance or improvement of the material well-being of the society.

11

Applying the Theory of Resource Diversion

Relevance to the Present Economic Situation in the United States

The second half of the twentieth century has seen a vast expansion of both neutral and distractive activity in the United States. The noncontributive burden on the economy has been heavy and prolonged. If the theory of resource diversion has any validity at all, then, it should apply with some force to this nation during this period. Does the theory in fact correspond to the realities of American economic experience over the past few decades?

In chapter 1 it was argued that for all the talk of recovery and economic strength, the American economy is neither recovering nor strong. It is a peculiar blindness that insists on measuring economic well-being in terms of surface phenomena like GNP growth and international exchange rates, while overlooking something as fundamental as the declining ability of industry to compete—not to mention such things as rising poverty, stagnating real income, increasing bank failures, high rates of mortgage foreclosures, and astounding accumulations of debt. It is a blindness that arises from misdirected attention rather than from ignorance or malice. Yet it is dangerous, causing us to see strength where there is weakness and moving us to follow policies that increase the burden on an economy less and less able to bear it.

The fact that the United States is experiencing serious economic problems after a long period of noncontributive activity does not in itself establish the relevance or power of the analysis developed in the previous chapters. It is necessary to examine in greater detail the correspondence between the mechanisms of the theory and the evidence that these mechanisms have been operating. While it is true that the ultimate test of a theory's usefulness lies in its ability to predict, it is also true that a theory whose internal structure has no connection with reality is less likely to continue generating reliable predictions than one that is more "realistic."

Again, I stress that this work is not fundamentally empirical but rather is intended to be mainly theoretical and conceptual. In that spirit, the evidence for the applicability of the theory of resource diversion presented in this chapter should be taken as indicative. A great deal more investigation will be required to pin down the details and rigorously test the various hypotheses of the core theory and its periphery. Nevertheless, this brief look should provide a useful measure of concreteness.

The burden of neutral activity.   The growth of management and administration relative to production work has its roots early in the century. It is not quite clear when this process reached the point where its further growth no longer contributed to the productivity gains that were its raison d'être; it is clear, however, that it has long since reached that point, in the aggregate. There is by now a considerable body of empirical analysis supporting the proposition that the rise in the size of management and administration relative to production has been substantial and that this rise is unrelated to the pattern of output per worker. To the extent that managerial and administrative activity is economically contributive, it adds to the output of the firm (quantitatively or qualitatively) without adding to the number of production workers—or, equivalently, maintains output with fewer production workers. In either case, there will be a *positive* relationship between rising output per production worker and the expansion of management and administration. A lack of relationship between increases in management and administration and changes in output per production worker is therefore an indication that management and administration have expanded into the zone of neutral activity.

Initial studies by Melman in the 1950s, and subsequent refinements and expansions by Dogramaci, Boucher, and Fraiman, have built a strong case for the lack of correlation between managerial and administrative expansion and the productivity of production labor.[1] There are, of course, methodological difficulties and limitations, such as the measurement of output in quantitative terms alone and the measurement of managerial and administrative activity in terms of numbers of workers. Nevertheless, the evidence is so strong and consistent that it seems highly likely that what we are seeing is the vague outline of a large and growing neutral sector.

In addition to these formal, systematic analyses of the overall contribution of increased management and administration to output per production worker, an increasing number of examples of clearly neutral activity are emerging within particular managerial and administrative arenas. For instance, on 27 July 1985, the NBC television network aired "The Biggest Lump of Money in the World," a documentary on the roughly $1.3 trillion of pension fund money in the United States, which grows by some $100 billion each year. Most of that money is invested in corporate stocks by "money managers" hired for that specific purpose. The documentary describes the constant, fruitless shuffling of stock certificates back and forth among these pension funds, an activity which on occasion reaches absurd levels:

> They pass stock certificates from one of their hands to the other. . . . A big corporate pension fund may have $2 billion to invest. It would farm that out among a dozen or more money managers, each a specialist in one sector of the market . . . that is called diversity, investing prudently. . . . The inevitable result is that on a given day, one money manager, using Company A's money, buys IBM, while another money manager, also using Company A's money, sells IBM. Company A's pension fund then owns exactly as much IBM as it did before, but it has paid brokerage fees on both ends of the deal.

Thus—though there do not appear to be any quantitative estimates available to date—it is reasonable to suppose that some significant fraction of the present structure of managerial and administrative capital and labor is, in fact, engaged in neutral activity. Further, on that same basis, it seems reasonable to suppose that the neutral sector has been with us for some time now, perhaps for decades.

The distractive burden. On the matter of distractive activity, there is considerably more clarity. World War II inaugurated an unprecedented expansion in the size and scope of military spending in the United States. More importantly, in the postwar period high levels of military expenditure have for the first time in U.S. history been maintained for decades (decades in which, it is interesting to note, there was not a single officially declared war). The American economy has never before been burdened by so large a distractive sector for so long a period of time.

It has been argued that the military burden during the postwar period has never been a large percentage of GNP (peaking at about 14 percent in 1953 and averaging only about 7.6 percent, according to Department of Commerce figures)—and that it has in fact substantially declined over the past three decades (from the 1953 high of 14 percent to a 1978 low of 4.9 percent, then back up to 6.7 percent in 1984).[2] Since at least 86 percent of the GNP—and on the average more than 92 percent—has been nonmilitary over this period, how could such a small fraction of economic activity be that important? How could the tail wag the dog? In the first place, because GNP is an aggregate of the money value rather than the inherent economic value of what has been produced, it is a poor measure of the volume of real economic activity. Second, and more important, it makes no sense to judge the significance or impact of any one part of a system of interconnected components by comparing the size of that part to the size of the total system. Rather, to understand the impact of a particular component, one must consider what role it plays in the system—how its operation interacts with the operation of other components and with the system as a whole.

For example, consider the human body. It is a complex biological system of interacting components, just as the economy is a complex social system of interacting components. Following the argument that the fraction of GNP (total system size) is a reasonable indicator of the importance of a part of the economy, the importance of body parts should be indicated by their fraction of gross body weight (total system size). This approach implies that the leg is much more important than the brain, since it makes up a much larger fraction of body weight. It could further be argued that the brain could not really be that important to the body—after all, it accounts for less than 4 percent of body weight. How could something that small have any major effect on the remaining 96 percent of the body? Clearly, it is the role the brain plays and not its size that measures the importance of its impact on the system. The distractive sector is an economic parasite. It may be small relative to the total economy, while at the same time diverting substantial amounts of critical economic resources. Its impact on the functioning of the economy, therefore, can also be dramatically out of proportion to its relative size.

Throughout this analysis I have stressed the importance of looking beyond aggregates, not merely in the usual sense of disaggregation, but also in considering the internal structure of the system and the functions and interactions of its components. The drag effects of noncontributive activity are visible even at the aggregate level. The process by which these effects are produced is not. The distractive sector has not been a minor economic phenomenon in the United States. Capital and labor of all subcategories have been diverted to distractive activity. Yet the drain has not been evenly distributed throughout. The single most important labor resource diversion has been that of technologists, while the primary capital impacts have been on infrastructure and production capital.

Diversion of technologists. Since the beginning of World War II, and especially since the mid-1950s, the United States has channeled a large part of its engineering and scientific resources into military-related research. Some of this has been direct, through priority allocation of federal grants; some has been indirect, through the use of a considerable portion of the annual discretionary federal budget to purchase increasingly sophisticated weapons and related systems. The research, development, and production of these technology-intensive goods has required military-industrial firms to hire large quantities of technologists.

According to National Science Foundation (NSF) preliminary data for 1984, nearly two-thirds of all federally funded R&D was directed to "national defense," up sharply from the seventies, during which the figure was roughly one-half.[3] The NSF figures are clearly understated, since they do not include any of the R&D performed as part of the space program—a program which has always been partly oriented toward military purposes and which is rapidly becoming more so (witness the fraction of the space shuttle missions devoted to these purposes). If the so-called Strategic Defense Initiative (more popularly known as the Star Wars program) proceeds, the military dominance of America's space research will become even greater.

Table 3 details federal R&D funding for the eleven-year period 1974–84. Along with NSF data for national defense R&D, data are given for the excluded space program. If it is conservatively assumed that the only federal R&D funds used for distractive purposes are the "national defense" funds plus half of the space program. research funds, then over the past decade an average of roughly 60 percent of federal R&D money has been spent for essentially distractive research. Looked at from another angle, as of 1974, 77 percent of the nation's research and development engineers and scientists (excluding social scientists) receiving federal support received it from the Department of Defense (DOD), the National Aeronautics and Space Administration, or the Atomic Energy Commission—more than 50 percent from the DOD alone.[4] Nearly three-quarters of the engineers and scientists employed by business and industry who received federal support in that year received it from the same three agencies.[5]

Trying to estimate the fraction of the nation's total engineering and scientific talent engaged in military-related research is a more tortuous task than it should be. I shall not attempt here to disentangle the available data and make a serious attempt at an accurate, up-to-date estimate of the preemption of engineering and scientific talent by the military sector. However, it is possible to produce reasonable and fairly conservative rough estimates by manipulating some of the published data.

According to data provided for 1981 in the Defense Economic Impact Modeling System (DEIMS) of the Department of Defense, only about 12 percent of the nation's engineers and scientists are included in "defense-induced" employment.[6] However, the methodology used in DEIMS excludes from the "defense-induced" category employment related to arms exports, programs for nuclear weapons research, design, testing, and production (none of which are part of the DOD budget), and the military-oriented part of the space program. Perhaps even more significantly, the methodology assumes that the percentage of engineers and scientists in any given industry is the same in the military-serving part of the industry as in the civilian-

Table 3 Federal Funding of Research and Development in the United States, 1974–84

Year	Total Federal R&D Funds	Federal Funds for Military R&D[a]		Federal Funds for Space R&D		Estimated Federal Funds for Distractive R&D[b]	
	(billions of $)	(billions of $)	(as % of total)	(billions of $)	(as % of total)	(billions of $)	(as % of total)
1974	$17.4	$ 9.0	51.8%	$2.7	15.5%	$10.4	59.8%
1975	19.0	9.7	50.8	2.8	14.5	11.1	58.4
1976	20.8	10.4	50.2	3.1	15.1	12.0	57.7
1977	23.5	11.9	50.1	2.8	11.9	13.3	56.6
1978	26.0	12.9	49.6	2.9	11.2	14.4	55.2
1979	28.2	13.8	48.9	3.1	11.0	15.4	54.4
1980	29.8	14.9	50.0	2.7	9.1	16.3	54.5
1981	33.7	18.4	54.6	3.1	9.2	20.0	59.2
1982	36.1	22.1	61.2	2.6	7.2	23.4	64.8
1983	38.8	24.9	64.2	2.1	5.4	26.0	66.9
1984 (est.)	44.4	29.3	66.0	2.3	5.2	30.5	68.6

Source: National Science Foundation, Federal R&D Funding by Budget Function, cited in Department of Commerce, Bureau of the Census, Statistical Abstract of the United States, 1985 (Washington, D.C.: Government Printing Office, 1984), table 991, p. 576.

[a] The category defined by the National Science Foundation as "national defense," including "all the programs of the Department of Defense (except civil programs of the Army Corps of Engineers) and the Defense-related programs of the Department of Energy."

[b] Calculated conservatively by assuming that only one-half of the space program is military-related and adding that half to national defense R&D as defined by the National Science Foundation.

oriented part.[7] Yet it is clear that the technological intensity of the labor force in military-oriented segments of industry is much greater. It is not unknown for military-industrial operations to employ one engineer or scientist per production worker, as for example in the Rockwell Industries B–1 bomber plant in the late 1970s. Such ratios of technologists to production workers are insupportable in civilian-oriented industry. Conservatively assuming a 50 percent greater intensity of technologists in the work force of military-oriented segments of industry, and making a rough correction for all of the military-oriented activity excluded by the DEIMS methodology, it is hard to see how the fraction of the nation's engineers and scientists engaged in this form of distractive activity could be less than 25 percent. More than likely it is 30 percent or even higher.

The estimate can be approached from another direction by extracting from NSF data for 1970–80 the number of full-time equivalent R&D scientists and engineers for three major military-oriented industry categories—electrical equipment and communication, aircraft and missiles, and machinery.[8] Assuming that roughly two-thirds of the R&D engineers and scientists in the first two industries and only one-quarter of those in the third industry are engaged in military-related work, and ignoring all other industries completely (industries ignored would include tank manufacture, ordinance, and nuclear submarine production), an average of just over 32 percent of engineering and scientific industrial R&D employment is military-oriented. Interestingly, this estimate of the fraction of the nation's technologists engaged in military-oriented R&D is roughly consistent with the estimate of the National Science Foundation that the United States devoted some 30 percent of its national R&D expenditures to military and space programs as of 1981.[9] Thus, though it is inappropriate to rely heavily on the accuracy of estimates so crudely developed, it would appear likely that an important fraction of the engineering and scientific personnel in the United States has been devoting its talents to the development of military-oriented technology. This fraction probably is not less than 30 percent; in all likelihood, it is much higher. And whatever the precise figure may be, it is important to understand that this magnitude of preemption of technological resources has been maintained for three decades or more.

As I have earlier argued, the kind of new technical knowledge developed is strongly conditioned by the nature of the problems being studied and the types of solutions being sought. Since 30 percent or more of U.S. engineering and scientific personnel have been seeking military-oriented solutions to military-oriented problems over most of the post–World War II period, it should not be surprising that the development of this type of distractive technology has proceeded at a rapid pace. But what of the effects of this resource diversion on the progress of *contributive* technology?

There are, conceptually, two ways that diversion of technological resources can fail to retard contributive technological progress. One possibility is for the aggregate pool of technologists to grow enough to offset this distractive-sector drain. However, there is some evidence to indicate that the elasticity of the size of the technological labor force with respect to enlarged job opportunities and higher salaries is rather low. What tends to happen instead, in response to changed economic conditions, is a shifting among fields of science and engineering of those who have already demonstrated competence and interest in those broad areas. As Hollomon and Harger have written,

> The fraction of college graduates opting for science, mathematics, and engineering has changed very little since World War II. . . . Hugh Folk has pointed out that the choice of a broad field by students does not appear to be affected by demand, which influences only the choice of lucrative activities *within* broad fields. Changes in salaries and stipends affect the choices between specialties.[10]

Even if the pool of technologists were more responsive in the aggregate, those people must come from somewhere. Thus society must bear the opportunity cost of doing without them in whatever other areas of skill they would have otherwise entered.

It is interesting to note that the United States, with a 1982 population of about 230 million, produced almost 10 percent fewer engineering graduates in that year than Japan, a nation of about 120 million people. At the same time, the Japanese economy bore an insignificant burden of distractive R&D compared with the conservatively estimated diversion of 30 percent of American engineering graduates. Combining these two considerations implies that the Japanese contributive R&D effort received *nearly 56 percent more* newly graduated engineers in 1982 than did the contributive-sector R&D

effort in the United States.[11] Under these conditions, it is not surprising that American contributive producers are having difficulty generating a sufficient flow of commercial technology to remain competitive with their counterparts in Japan.

Furthermore, high salaries and other benefits in the distractive sector (such as a free spending environment that allows access to the latest equipment) attract those who might otherwise be training future generations of technologists. As of 1984, "fully one-tenth of the Nation's engineering faculty positions are currently vacant. In critical fields, like electrical engineering and computer science, some universities report half of their positions as unfilled. . . . We are 'eating our own seed corn.'"[12] The current distractive-sector diversion of technologists is therefore affecting not merely the current capacity for contributive technology but the future capacity as well.

The second way that the diversion of technologists can fail to retard contributive technology is if there is a great deal of intersectoral transfer of technology—commonly called spinoff or spillover. There is, of course, some such technology transfer (in both directions). Only at the height of theoretical abstraction would the distractive and contributive sectors be considered completely sealed off from each other. Yet given the nature of technology and the technological development process, and the clear distinctions between distractive and contributive output, this transferability should be quite low—especially going from the distractive to the contributive sector. It is difficult to see how it could be otherwise—how directing attention to one area of technical research could routinely and *efficiently* generate knowledge related to an entirely different area. The real issue, then, is not whether there is spinoff, but whether there is enough spinoff to offset the negative effects of the "brain drain" from contributive to distractive research activity. There are two effects working in opposite directions—a "diversion effect" that reduces the flow of contributive technology by removing technologists from the contributive sector, and a "spinoff effect" that stimulates contributive technology by transferring technology developed in distractive R&D back to contributive-sector applications. The question is, which of these contrary effects is stronger—and by how much?

In 1980, Simon Ramo, formerly chief scientist of the U.S. Intercontinental Ballistic Missile Program and chair of the President's

Committee on Science and Technology, and cofounder of TRW, Inc. (a company with heavy military involvement), expressed the following judgment on this issue:

> The military technology programs of the United States over the past several decades have advanced technology enormously on several fronts. . . . However, the fallout has not been so great as to suggest that for every dollar of military technology expenditure we realized almost as much advance of the nonmilitary fields as if we had spent it directly on civilian technology. Probably our relative productivity increases and our net rating in technology vis-a-vis other nations have on the whole been hurt rather than helped.[13]

An earlier report, issued in 1974 by a committee of the National Academy of Engineering, stated:

> With a few exceptions, the vast technology developed by federally funded programs since World War II has not resulted in widespread "spinoffs" of secondary or additional applications of practical products, processes and services that have made an impact on the nation's economic growth, industrial productivity, employment gains, and foreign trade.[14]

Given the huge amounts of funds and technological personnel that have indisputably been lavished on distractive research and development in the United States over the past decades, high transferability would have meant rapid contributive technological progress. The stimulus of military technology would have spurred improvements in contributive product and production technology. But if the intersectoral transferability of invention and innovation was and is actually low, the diversion of such a large fraction of the nation's technological talent could not have helped but produce a serious slowdown in contributive technological progress. So which is it? What has been happening to the rate of progress of contributive technology in the United States?

By the mid-1970s, the signs that the development of contributive technology in the United States was in a severe state of deterioration were so widespread and obvious that they began to be recognized by both the scientific and business establishments. The seventh annual report of the National Science Board, governing body of the National Science Foundation, expressed concern over the serious erosion of U.S. predominance in science and technology. In several international comparisons, the empirical indicators behind this concern were detailed:

> The "patent balance" of the United States fell by about 30 percent between 1966 and 1973. . . . The decline was due both to an increasing number of U.S. patents awarded to foreign countries and a decline (in 1973) in the number of foreign patents awarded to U.S. citizens. Overall, foreign patenting increased in the United States during the period by over 65 percent, and by 1973 represented more than 30 percent of all U.S. patents granted. This suggests that the number of patentable ideas of international merit has been growing at a greater rate in other countries than in the United States.[15]

The report goes on to describe the shares of the United States, the United Kingdom, Japan, West Germany, and France in 492 major innovations spanning the two decades from 1953 to 1973:

> The U.S. lead . . . declined steadily from the late 1950's to the mid-1960's, falling from 82% to 55% of the innovations. The slight upturn in later years represents a relative rather than an absolute gain, and results primarily from a decline in the proportion of innovations produced in the United Kingdom, rather than an increase in the number of U.S. innovations.[16]

More recently, the National Science Foundation has pointed to a continuation of these downtrends:

> U.S. patenting has decreased abroad as well as at home. . . . From 1966 to 1976, U.S. patenting activity abroad declined almost 30 percent in ten industrialized countries. . . . The decline in U.S. patenting abroad could be attributable to a number of factors, including . . . a relative decline in U.S. inventive activity.[17]

The relatively poor showing of the United States is even more remarkable considering that these data do not specifically exclude military-related technology and hence are biased in favor of the United States, the heaviest military R&D spender of the group.

Japan and West Germany did quite well in these comparisons:

> Since 1963, inventors from West Germany have received the largest number of foreign-origin U.S. patents (83,220). In fact, among U.S. foreign-origin patents, West Germany was first in 11 of the 15 major

product fields and second in the remaining four. . . . Japan ranks second in the total number of U.S. patents granted to foreign investors
between 1963 and 1977 (61,510). Japan has the largest number of foreign patents in three product groups . . . and is second in an additional five categories. . . . Since 1970, Japan has dramatically increased its patent activity by over 100 percent in every product field
except the two areas in which it already had a large concentration
of patents.[18]

Not so coincidentally, these two countries spend on defense and
space only about 4 percent (Japan, 1961–75) and 20 percent (West
Germany, 1961–76) of overall government R&D expenditures,
as opposed to a U.S. average of about 70 percent over a comparable period.[19]

The nation's business community also began in the mid-seventies
to recognize the retarded progress of American contributive technology. According to a 1976 *Business Week* article, "The Breakdown
of U.S. Innovation," "from boardroom to research lab there is a
growing sense that something has happened to U.S. innovation." Apparently that "sense" continued to grow, because by 1978 the story
had made the cover of that journal. That article, titled "Vanishing
Innovation," began: "A grim mood prevails today among industrial
research managers. America's vaunted technological superiority of
the 1950's and 1960's is vanishing."[20]

Governmental recognition of the severity of the problem was
demonstrated by the Carter administration's massive (eighteen-month,
twenty-eight–agency) domestic policy review of the influence of the
government on industrial innovation. More recently, the 1985 report
of the President's Commission on Industrial Competitiveness, established by the Reagan administration, placed heavy emphasis on technology. One of its four main recommendations was stated succinctly
as "Create, apply, and protect technology"—not the sort of advice
that would be offered were technological progress healthy and strong.
Although the report still refers to the American lead in technology,
the commission's concern about the economic implications of the direction of American technology is clear:

Roughly half of the total R&D done in the United States is funded by
the federal government, which spends most of its money (about two-
thirds) on defense and space programs. And in those two areas, any

commercial spillover is not a prime objective. Thus when we look at what the United States spends on civilian R&D—areas of innovation from which we reap the greatest commercial reward—we find ourselves behind both Germany and Japan.[21]

It is worth noting that this commission was headed by John Young, chief executive officer of Hewlett-Packard Company, and included other top-level executives from such military-oriented corporations as Rockwell International and Texas Instruments.

In 1980, Simon Ramo wrote a book with the revealing title *America's Technology Slip*. On the basis of his long experience in science, government, and business, he assessed the overall situation in the United States:

> In the past thirty years, had the total dollars we spent on military R&D been expended instead in those areas of science and technology promising the most economic progress, we probably would be today where we are going to find ourselves arriving technologically in the year 2000.[22]

This assessment is particularly striking coming from an individual who spent most of his life in high positions in the distractive sector. In the terminology of the present analysis, Ramo is saying that the United States is now experiencing a roughly two-decade contributive technology lag as the result of three decades of high levels of technological resource diversion. This obviously would not have happened if the spinoff effect had been anywhere near as strong as the direct "brain drain" effect.

It therefore seems clear that the transfer of technology between the distractive and contributive sectors is relatively low and that the theoretically predicted deterioration of contributive technological progress has in fact followed as a result of the diversion of a substantial fraction of the technological labor force to distractive activity.

Diversion of capital. Empirical analysis of the distractive capital drain, even in this rough indicative sense, is a bit more complicated. As the predominant present-day noncontributive sector, the military clearly preempts a substantial amount of capital resources. However, producing a comprehensive estimate of the extent of this diversion is a large and complex problem. Part of the difficulty lies in finding and aggregating all the pieces of the vast network that is the military sector. A comprehensive estimate would have to add to the capital directly used by the military agencies of the federal government all of the capital taken by the 20,000 or so prime military contracting firms and the more than 100,000 subcontractors. If all the data were readily available in the proper form, one could theoretically use techniques such as input-output analysis to derive reasonable estimates. Even so, this would be a major project.

However, the data are not readily available in the proper form. For example, though it is relatively easy to obtain data that identify prime military contractors and give the values of their contracts, data on such matters as capital equipment investments and number of engineers and scientists employed by the military-serving divisions of these firms are much harder to come by. Furthermore, it is no easy task to fully identify all of the subcontracting firms, let alone get these data for them. Beyond this, the effects of distractive activity on infrastructure capital do not really come from direct resource diversion. The distractive sector does not so much preempt infrastructure as divert investment activities away from infrastructure maintenance and development. This occurs primarily through its effect on the priorities with which the government operates.

There is also some effect on infrastructure operated by the private sector, through the same process as that which affects production capital. From the microeconomic point of view, this part of infrastructure capital is the production capital of firms that supply infrastructure services—telephone companies, private garbage collection firms, airlines, and so forth. Hence it is appropriate to focus separately on government-supplied infrastructure and leave private-sector infrastructure for the discussion of the diversion of production capital.

Before discussing the production and infrastructure capital subcategories, it is worth looking at the extent to which physical capital in general has been preempted by the distractive military sector in the United States. Much of the physical capital used in military industry is in fact privately owned, though its use is in practice largely controlled by government contracting decisions. However, the various military agencies of the federal government do actually own a substantial amount of physical capital. And there are some data available on the size of this stock of government-owned, distractive-sector capital, which comprises landholdings, structures, and highly specialized maintenance or test facilities, as well as a substantial amount of direct production equipment such as metalworking machine tools. Table 4 provides data on the stock of physical capital owned by the Department of Defense and its various subagencies as of the end of September 1983. At that time, the total reported value of all physical capital owned by the military was $474.9 billion. That there may be some understatement here is indicated by the fact that the nearly $300 million value of the roughly 12.2 million acres owned by the U.S. Army implies an average land value of under $25 per acre. Nevertheless, it will be assumed that the reported values are essentially accurate; if they are indeed understated, the analysis will then be conservative.

Not surprisingly, the largest single category of capital in this summary is "weapons and other military equipment in use," valued at $267.1 billion, more than 56 percent of the total. The vast majority—perhaps nearly all—of this type of capital is frozen into a form specialized to noncontributive use. The second largest category, inventories of equipment, material, and supplies—valued at $114.0 billion—makes up another 24 percent of total capital. It is likely that much of this category is also specialized to noncontributive use. Thus, the largest part of more than $380 billion, roughly 80 percent of the physical capital owned by the military, may have been cast into forms essentially without contributive use. The economically valuable services of vast quantities of productive resources embedded in this capital have consequently been permanently lost to the contributive sector. Real property, in the form of land, buildings, utilities, and other structures, accounts for $57.4 billion, some 12 percent of the total. Though it is less than 5 percent of the total, the $20.2 billion of plant equipment directly owned by the military represents a large stock of equipment with considerable productive capacity; it is important enough to warrant further attention later.

The huge amounts of capital diverted to this noncontributive sector are impressive enough in absolute terms. But it is also worth comparing this claim on capital to that of sectors that do generate economic value, in order to get a feeling for the relative capital drain. At the end of 1983, the value of the combined net stock of all capital equipment, structures, and inventories owned by all manufacturing

Table 4   Department of Defense Holdings of Physical Capital as of 30 September 1983 (Billions of $)

	Dept. of Defense[a] (Total)	Army	Navy[b]	Air Force	Defense Logistics Agency
All Physical Capital	474.9	114.6	213.4	131.6	14.3
Real Property	57.4	18.8	17.6	21.0	—
Land Cost	—	0.3	—	0.2	—
	—	12.2[c]	—	—	—
Buildings	—	13.1	—	13.3	—
Other Structures	—	5.5	—	7.5	—
Construction in Progress	9.3	4.3	3.0	2.0	—
Other Physical Capital	408.2	91.5	192.8	108.6	14.3
Weapons and Other Military Equipment in Use	267.1	45.7	153.2	68.3	—
Equipment, Material, and Supplies in Stock	114.0	37.4	30.3	35.7	10.6
Plant Equipment	20.2	7.9	8.2	2.4	0.6
Excess and Surplus Property	5.6	0.4	0.6	1.6	3.0

Sources:
Department of Defense, Directorate for Information, Operations, and Reports, Washington Headquarters Services, *Department of Defense Real and Personal Property* (Washington, D.C.: DOD, 1983).

Department of the Army, "Cost and Rentals of Military Real Property Controlled (30 September 1983)" and "Acreage of Military Real Property Controlled and Located at Installations (30 September 1983)," both unpublished.

Unpublished data from Department of the Air Force, Office of the Assistant Secretary, provided to author in correspondence from Chief, Policy Control Branch, Real Property Division, Directorate of Engineering and Services.

Notes:
[a] Includes Army, Navy, Marines, Air Force, Defense Logistics Agency, and other defense agencies.
[b] Includes Marine Corps.
[c] In millions of acres.

establishments in the U.S. was $1,011.9 billion.[23] This stands against the $474.9 billion value of the stock of all physical capital owned by the Department of Defense as of 30 September of that year. The two numbers are not precisely comparable, since they are not for the same point in time, and since the Department of Defense figures include landholdings. However, unless the physical capital inventories of the Department of Defense were decreasing during the last quarter of 1983 (which is highly unlikely, given the rapid military buildup the Reagan administration was pursuing at the time), using the 30 September Department of Defense figure as an estimate for the end of 1983 would be conservative. Furthermore, land costs are very small in comparison with other forms of physical capital for the Army and Air Force (for which separate data on landholdings are given in the table)—less than 0.3 percent of the capital stocks held by those services. To remain conservative, it will be arbitrarily assumed that land costs for the Department of Defense as a whole are more than three times as high—1 percent of the total.

The adjusted Department of Defense capital stock figure for 1983 is thus $470.0 billion, compared with the $1,011.9 billion value of the net stock of capital equipment, structures, and inventories in manufacturing industry. Thus, the book value of the stock of physical capital preempted by the noncontributive military sector was *more than 46 percent* the value of the combined stock of physical capital owned by *all manufacturing establishments in the United States*! This comparison is even more striking when one considers that all the physical capital owned by private military-industrial firms is included in the manufacturing industry figure. If a reasonable estimate of this privately owned distractive capital were available, it would be added to the numerator and subtracted from the denominator, making the estimate still higher.

It might be argued that it is inappropriate to include weapons in the military capital stock since they are not capital goods in the same sense as factory buildings, metalworking machines, and the like. On the other hand, weapons are without question created by the military system as an important class of "tools" with which that system attempts to produce its "product," national security. In that sense, weapons are capital goods of the military in the same way that furnaces are capital goods of the steel industry. However, it is possible to look more closely at the issue of physical capital drain in ways that avoid this objection. In particular, we can focus on the diversion of industrial plants and plant equipment.

Production capital. To some extent, the diversion of production capital occurs by a process similar to the diversion of technologists. That is, the distractive sector outbids the contributive sector for the products of the capital goods industries. Part of the capital bid away from the contributive sector is essentially the same as that with which it normally operates; part has characteristics more oriented to the needs of distractive activity. But virtually all of it preempts the productive capacity of the capital goods industries and hence lessens (through price escalation or product characteristic distortion) the availability and attractiveness of production capital to contributive producers. Furthermore, the slowing of contributive technological progress that has resulted from the diversion of engineers and scientists also puts a sharp brake on investment in contributive production capital. Since new machines do not embody much technological progress, the efficiency advantage of purchasing them is sharply reduced.

For reasons cited earlier, a comprehensive estimate of the fraction of the nation's stock of production capital operated in the service of distractive activity is difficult to make. But again, it is possible to look at the part of government-owned capital held by the Department of Defense. As shown in table 4, that inventory of plant equipment was valued at $20.2 billion as of 30 September 1983. According to the Defense Department, the book value of this stock of plant equipment had increased by $3.3 billion over fiscal year 1982.[24] In 1982, net capital investment in equipment *and* structures by all manufacturing establishments in the United States was only $1.4 billion.[25] Of course, 1982 was a deep recession year, with unemployment rates almost half as high as those prevailing during the Great Depression. Yet the following year, during the "recovery," the situation was far worse: net investment in plant and equipment in manufacturing industries dropped well below zero, to −$6.6 billion.

Rather than comparing the 1982 figures directly, it would be more reasonable to compare the military sector's rate of net investment in plant equipment with an average rate of net investment in plant equipment alone by manufacturers. The average net investment in plant equipment by all U.S. manufacturing over the three-year period 1980–82 was $8.8 billion. The 1982 net investment in plant equipment by the Defense Department was, as previously stated, $3.3 billion. Thus, in 1982 the Defense Department's investment in plant equipment was *nearly 38 percent* of the (three-year average) combined annual net investment in plant equipment *by all U.S. manufacturing establishments*. And again, the data on investment by manufacturing establishments is overstated because it includes military-industrial manufacturers; this comparison is thus conservative.

The expandability of the supply of production capital is not likely to be as low as the elasticity of supply of engineers and scientists. The gestation time for most production capital is generally shorter than that for engineers and scientists, and the latter are subject to all sorts of noneconomic considerations not applicable to the former. Therefore, distractive-sector preemption of production capital is less a case of withdrawal from a relatively fixed supply than is preemption of technologists. The effect will be most visible as a discouraging of contributive-sector investment.

As the erosion of productive competence proceeds, business expectations of future sales are likely to become more pessimistic. If the economic malaise is seen as widespread, chronic, and resistant to conventional remedies, this pessimism will tend to deepen. Regardless of interest rates, capital goods prices, or capital goods availability, contributive producers will *not* invest in production capital if they do not expect to be able to profitably sell what that capital will allow them to produce. Hence a sustained distractive drain of production capital is likely to result in an aging and increasingly obsolescent contributive capital stock. In its 19 October 1973 issue, *American Machinist* commented on the state of the U.S. machine tool inventory (which it surveys every five years).

The number of young (less than ten-year-old) machine tools in U.S. industry declined slightly, as shown by the fact that only 33 percent of the present total is less than ten years old. This is the lowest level that has been recorded for the young machines since 1940, just before World War II when—after ten years of depression—the level was 30 percent.[26]

Ten years later, the "13th American Machinist Inventory of Metal Working Equipment" (published in 1983) indicated some improvement: the percentage of metalcutting machines less than ten years old had risen slightly to 34 percent. However, this rise was offset by a dramatic aging of the stock of metalforming machines. The fraction of such machines under the age of ten years dropped to an all-time low of 27 percent. Overall, then, the percentage of U.S. metalworking equipment less than ten years old still did not exceed 33 percent.[27] Thus, after nearly four decades of heavy distractive activity, the American stock of machine tools had been left in an aging condition comparable to that which existed after ten years of the most severe depression in U.S. history. Furthermore, these data do not specifically exclude distractive producers, whose capital stock is likely to be much younger than average. This capital has been particularly significant since 1980, when the Reagan administration's weapons-oriented military buildup began. The overall post–World War II estimate of the percentage of machine tools less than ten years old is therefore likely to be biased upward, especially in recent years. Consequently, the *contributive* production capital stock is almost certainly older than indicated.

In certain major contributive industries such as automobile and steel manufacturing, the picture is even more bleak. Something under 25 percent of the machine tool stock in the automobile industry was under ten years old in the late 1970s; the Office of Technology Assessment estimated 33 percent of steel production facilities (not machine tools) to be more than twenty years old by that time.[28]

Infrastructure capital. In a market economy, the government achieves command over the resources, goods, and services it needs to perform its various functions by taxation, money creation, or borrowing. Taxation amounts to direct confiscation of private wealth, money creation to indirect involuntary shifting of purchasing power away from private organizations and individuals, and borrowing to voluntary acquisition of present private wealth in exchange for the future promise to return more than is borrowed. All of these are subject to political-economic constraints: the government can take only so much of a society's private wealth at any given time. If this ill-defined yet very real limit is exceeded, political backlash will either enforce the constraint, disenfranchise those in control of the government, or both.

Given these constraints, a substantial distractive sector supported by the government (as is typically the case) will claim a portion of societal resources and output to which the government has access. As a result of overnourishment of the distractive sector, the other, contributive, activities for which the government bears responsibility will tend to be undernourished. This is particularly true if the government is operating at or very near the point at which the political economic limits on the size of its total activity are binding. Government operating under this kind of budgetary pressure can generally be expected to neglect longer-term projects in favor of meeting current operating needs. Infrastructure capital, because it is so long-lived, tends to become the poor stepchild. In the short term, this seems to make sense. Road maintenance and preventive replacement of water mains are easier to ignore than garbage collection or snow removal. But in the long term, this is a prescription for disaster.

It might be argued that since the main form of distractive activity in the United States today is military expenditure—a responsibility of the federal government—and since much infrastructure maintenance and improvement is the responsibility of state and local government, the trade-off between distractive activity and infrastructure should not be as strong as I have indicated. But this is not so. The political-economic limits on the size of government activity relate to government as a whole. The intergovernmental allocation of funds is a zero-sum game. If federal taxes and borrowing were lower, it would be possible for state and local taxes to be higher, and it would be easier for state and local governments to borrow. As a result, the persistent expenditure over the past several decades of roughly half of federal income tax dollars on the military, combined with the gigantic national debt (the major part of which is war-related), has reduced the politically feasible tax and borrowing potential remaining to be exploited by state and local governments. Beyond this, much of the state and local infrastructure activity has institutionally been financed with substantial federal government subsidy. Thus the trade-off, though somewhat indirect, is very real and powerful.

What, then, is the present state of the American stock of infrastructure capital? Has the distractive-sector capital drain produced the expected deterioration?

The sorry state of America's infrastructure was outlined in chapter 1. Choate and Walter's 1981 study *America in Ruins* describes the infrastructural decay in detail. Newspaper and newsmagazine articles of the early 1980s, such as the *New York Times* and *Newsweek* stories cited in chapter 1, have carried the same theme. "Every other day, a bridge falls, sags, or buckles somewhere in the U.S.," reported *Parade* magazine in 1982; at that time, 40 percent of the nation's 524,966 bridges required major repair or replacement, according to the Federal Highway Administration.[29] The roadbed and rolling stock of the railroad system are in poor condition, a large number of America's 43,500 dams are in need of repair, aging water mains are bursting, aging sewer lines are crumbling, and city streets are increasingly pocked with potholes. Even the interstate highway system—the "jewel" of the American transportation network—is decaying. Nearly 20 percent of this system is in need of rebuilding— a particularly striking statistic in light of the fact that much more attention has been paid to the interstates than to, for example, inner-city mass transit.[30]

The stock of infrastructure capital in the United States is thus in a serious state of deterioration. What is required to put it all back together again? According to the Choate and Walter study, total investment in public works by all levels of government declined by more than 21 percent from 1965 to 1977, from \$38.6 to \$30.4 billion per year. Yet the total bill for repair and reconstruction, i.e., the dollar equivalent of the infrastructure component of *mri*, is almost certain to exceed one trillion dollars, and may be as high as several trillion dollars. (It is interesting to note that current plans for federal military expenditures total about \$1.5 trillion for the five fiscal years 1983–87.) Obviously, we are investing at an annual level far below the current *mri*. Consequently, we can predict that the progressive decay of infrastructure will continue, unless sharp changes in societal resource deployment occur.

Clearly, then, whether considering infrastructure capital or production capital, the capital stock of the contributive sector of the American economy is in a grave state of decline. Unless the American people had elected to support the noncontributive sectors entirely out of present consumption—and hence dramatically reduce their immediate standard of living—it could not have been otherwise.

The decay of productive competence. The chief empirical indicator currently available that directly bears on the productive competence of industry is labor productivity. It is a seriously flawed measure, since it does not include quality adjustment and it measures only exchange value of direct output rather than inherent economic value of full output. Yet it can be used as a rough indicator, and that is sufficient for the present purpose.

In chapter 1, evidence was presented for the sharp deterioration of productivity growth since 1950. Table 2 (p. 11) includes data on the five- and ten-year averages of annual rates of productivity growth in both the entire nonfarm business sector and manufacturing alone. Though the decline in productivity growth was not monotonic, the overall pattern is clear enough. In the fifteen years following 1950, productivity in the nonfarm business sector of the United States rose at an average annual rate of 2.6 percent; in the next fifteen years (1965–79), the average annual rate of productivity growth was only 1.6 percent—a reduction in the growth rate of nearly 40 percent. The past five years have seen a further decline to 1.4 percent. Growth in manufacturing productivity shows a similar pattern: the average annual growth rate of productivity in the fifteen years beginning in 1950 was a respectable 3.6 percent; the next fifteen years saw that rate drop to 2.2 percent—again, nearly a 40 percent decline in the growth rate. In the last five years, however, productivity growth in manufacturing has dropped even more sharply, to 0.7 percent—less than a third of the 1965–79 rate and half the productivity growth rate in the total nonfarm business sector.

The decline in productivity growth is so overwhelming as to no longer be a matter of serious dispute. Its cause, however, has been the source of much confusion and consternation. The title of a 1979 *Science* article bears witness to this confusion: "Productivity Problems Trouble Economy—Everybody talks about the lag in the growth of productivity but nobody seems to know enough to do much about it." In the course of the article a number of possible causes for the productivity problem are cited: "a shift to a 'service' economy";

"the recent rise in energy costs"; "the increase in government regulation"; "changing attitudes among workers"; "a new devotion to leisure and relaxation" (a euphemistic way of stating the "lazy worker" hypothesis). Sexist and racist explanations have also been given some credence: "The labor force has become increasingly inexperienced because of an influx of women"; "The transformation of the U.S. economy is proceeding in the direction taken by the British rather than the Japanese. Anglo-Saxon attitudes may produce a less pressured, less competitive way of life." [31]

The argument that the shift to the service sector and away from manufacturing is the critical element behind the pattern of declining productivity in the United States can easily be refuted. The rate of productivity growth of U.S. manufacturing alone (i.e., excluding services) has been undergoing a similar pattern of protracted decline, as discussed above. Furthermore, Victor Fuchs of the National Bureau of Economic Research has estimated that the growth of the service sector contributed only about 0.1 percent to the decline in productivity growth from the 1960s to the 1970s. Fuchs further estimates that the effect on declining productivity of the influx of (less experienced) women into the labor force was also extremely small. [32]

In a detailed, book-length empirical analysis, Edward F. Denison of the Brookings Institute investigates a wide variety of explanations for the decline in productivity growth, including those cited in the *Science* article. He rejects all of these explanations on the grounds that none of them appear able to explain more than a small fraction of the observed productivity pattern. Yet he offers no alternative explanation. Referring to the post-1973 pattern, he states, "What happened is, to be blunt, a mystery." [33] The Denison analysis should be interpreted cautiously. For one thing, he rejects some explanations on the basis of rough judgments. More important, the main focus of his analysis is fairly short-term—seeking an explanation for a sharp change in the post-1973 pattern. He rejects the explanation that the productivity decline is due to the "long-term deterioration of American technology" because "the deterioration set in much too early to explain the recent productivity slowdown." Thus, Denison both focuses on the short term and ignores the possibility of the kinds of threshold effects to which I have several times alluded. Perhaps more significant is that the development of distractive and of contributive technology are intermingled in various data to which he refers (e.g., data on R&D expenditures). Though Denison recognizes that this is a problem, he does not correct for it.

There is really no mystery here. The sustained, long-term operation of the neutral and distractive sectors drains the very sources of societal productive competence. Without the sectoral differentiation and long-term perspective embodied in the theory of resource diversion it is difficult, if not impossible, to explain either the steady erosion of productive competence or its sharp acceleration as various thresholds of deterioration in absolute and relative productive competence are crossed. It is not enough to study the pattern of aggregate research and development or of aggregate capital investment, for these aggregates lump together components whose economic meanings are radically different. Disaggregation is critical to revealing the long-term, structural economic processes that underlie the decline of productive competence and thus the easily visible signs of decay that abound in the present American economy.

Inflation and unemployment. According to the theory of resource diversion, the decline of productive competence inevitably leads to the deterioration of the material standard of living. In a market economy, this falling standard is likely to be transmitted through a general worsening of inflation, unemployment, and the trade-off between the two. The mechanism by which these worsening conditions are propagated is the shifting of the modal cost behavior of firms from offsetting costs (with more efficient production techniques) to transmitting (passing along) costs to customers by raising product prices.

Since the turning point for the growth of U.S. manufacturing productivity came in the mid-1960s, that should also have been the time for a shift in the cost behavior of U.S. manufacturing industry. A first empirical investigation of the possibility of this shift in modal cost behavior was performed by Byung Hong at Columbia University.[34] Hong developed a simple multiple regression model consisting of the following price equation (1) and wage equation (2), which he fit to quarterly data for U.S. manufacturing for the two periods 1948 (second quarter) to 1964 (fourth quarter) and 1965 (first quarter) to 1975 (second quarter):

(1) $\Delta P_t = a_1 + a_2 \Delta W_t + a_3 \Delta M_t + a_4 \Delta(Q/L)_t + a_5(Q/K)_t + a_6 R_t + e_t$

(2) $\Delta W_t = b_1 + b_2 \Delta(Q/L)_{t-m} + b_3 R_{t-n} + b_4 \Delta C_{t-p} + b_5 U_t + f_t$

Where: ΔP_t = change in wholesale price (percent)
ΔW_t = change in wage rate (percent)
ΔM_t = change in raw materials cost (percent)
$\Delta(Q/L)$ = change in labor productivity (percent)
Q/K = capacity utilization
R = rate of profit (on stockholders' equity)
ΔC = change in consumer price index (percent)
U = unemployment rate (percent of total civilian labor force)
e, f = stochastic error terms
$_t$ = time period (quarter-years in this application)
$_{m, n, p}$ = time lags (measured in same units as t)

In the price equation, the percent change in wholesale prices depends on the percent changes in wages and raw material costs moderated by changes in productivity, as well as on the level of capacity utilization (as a measure of demand pressure), and profit rate. Under conditions of cost-offsetting behavior, the change in productivity would be expected to have a strong negative effect, as pressure was applied to improve productive efficiency in response to rising input costs; under cost pass-along, productivity growth would not be expected to have any significant impact on price increase. On the other hand, profit rate would have little effect on price under cost offsetting, but a clear positive effect under cost pass-along, since profits are maintained or increased mainly by productivity expansion under cost offsetting and mainly by price increases under cost pass-along. Furthermore, high capacity utilization would tend to lead to higher prices under cost offsetting (demand pull) but *lower* prices under cost pass-along (because of lowered fixed cost per unit). Essentially all of the expectations for cost offsetting are statistically supported in the earlier time period, and nearly all the expectations for cost pass-along in the later time span (table 5).

Table 5   Wholesale Price Regression Coefficients and Statistics

Variable or Statistic	1948 (2d quarter) to 1964 (4th quarter)	1965 (1st quarter) to 1975 (2d quarter)
Constant	0.59	14.76*
	(0.082)	(2.49)
Wage Rate	0.39*	0.82*
	(2.72)	(4.52)
Raw Materials Price	0.25*	0.084*
	(8.54)	(5.58)
Productivity Growth	−0.29*	−0.16
	(−5.40)	(−1.95)
Capacity Utilization	−0.079	−0.51*
	(−0.69)	(−6.73)
Profit Rate	0.63	2.39*
	(1.54)	(9.61)
R^2	0.95*	0.98*
Durbin-Watson Statistic	1.63^n	1.63^n

Where ( ) = t-statistic
        * = significant at 1% level
        n = no autocorrelation, at 1% level

Source: B. Y. Hong, *Inflation under Cost Pass-Along Management* (New York: Praeger, 1979), p. 53.

In the wage equation, productivity change represents wage demand justification, past profits are wage demand targets, past consumer price inflation rates represent pressure for higher wages, and the unemployment rate is a kind of bargaining power variable. Under traditional cost-offsetting behavior the unemployment rate would be expected to have a significantly negative effect on wages, reflecting a trade-off of the Phillips curve type, while no particular effect on wage increase would be expected under cost pass-along (since the source of inflation has nothing to do with the demand-pull pressures reflected in the unemployment rate). Because the rate of inflation and the price-change expectations it generates are both high and rising, the consumer price variable would be stronger under cost pass-along than under cost offsetting. All other factors being held constant, a given increment in productivity growth might well have a larger effect on wage increase in a cost pass-along environment than in a cost offsetting one, because productivity growth would be so much weaker in such a period (in essence, there might be the equivalent of decreasing marginal returns to productivity growth in terms of generating wage increases). In any case, again nearly all of the expectations for cost-offsetting behavior are statistically observed in the earlier period (table 6), and nearly all of the expectations for cost pass-along behavior are observed in the later period—a reinforcement of the results obtained for the price equation.

It would appear then that there is at least some evidence that during the mid-1960s one of the theoretically expected thresholds was crossed in the United States. The long-term decline in productive competence had finally reached the point at which a shift in microeconomic cost behavior began to occur. Furthermore, as the manage-

Table 6   Wage Regression Coefficients and Statistics

Variable or Statistic	1948 (2d quarter) to 1964 (4th quarter)	1965 (1st quarter) to 1975 (2d quarter)
Constant	0.23	−1.37
	(0.096)	(−0.53)
Unemployment Rate	−0.82*	0.092
	(−3.39)	(0.34)
Productivity Growth	0.14*	0.21*
	(3.34)	(2.74)
Consumer Prices	0.23*	0.83*
(lagged one quarter)	(2.64)	(6.27)
Profit Rate	0.64*	0.23
(lagged one quarter)	(4.43)	(1.21)
R^2	0.89*	0.94*
Durbin-Watson Statistic	1.69[n]	2.03[n]

Where   ( ) = *t*-statistic
          *   = significant at 1% level
          n = no autocorrelation, at 1% level

Source: B. Y. Hong, *Inflation under Cost Pass-Along Management* (New York: Praeger, 1979), p. 54.

ments of U.S. industrial firms learned that cost pass-along was a viable behavior, the incentives for the internal vigilance necessary for cost minimization were diminished. The decline of productivity growth was thus further aggravated, reinforcing the shift to cost pass-along. Within a few years the macroeconomic cost-push inflationary implications of these shifts became clear. And as predicted (in the theoretical discussion of the implications of long-term resource diversion in an open economy), the same mechanism also began to generate substantial contributive unemployment.

As the prices of U.S.-produced contributive goods rose higher and higher, the nation's industry became less and less competitive vis-à-vis foreign competition. Overseas markets were lost and the U.S. export position weakened; domestic markets were lost to foreign production and the U.S. import position worsened. The progressive loss of markets induced cutbacks in U.S. production, and high unemployment rates resulted. This problem was worsened by the flight of U.S.-owned production facilities to cheap labor havens abroad—a predictable response to the inability to offset higher costs in the United States because of the failure of productive competence.

In chapter 1 it was pointed out that over the long term, inflation, unemployment, and the trade-off between them have in fact become considerably worse in the United States. Table 1 (p. 10) presents five- and ten-year averages of annual rates of inflation and unemployment since 1950. As with the productivity data, the pattern is not monotonic—but it is nevertheless clear. Over the fifteen-year period 1950–64, inflation averaged 1.7 percent, while unemployment averaged 4.9 percent. Over the next fifteen years, 1965–79, the average inflation rate more than tripled to 5.9 percent; unemployment also increased, to 5.4 percent—an increase of more than 10 percent. The first five years of the 1980s saw a further worsening of both inflation and unemployment. Inflation rose to an average annual rate of 7.5 percent during that period (up 27 percent), while unemployment rose even more sharply, to 8.3 percent (up 54 percent).

The loss of competitiveness. The decline in relative productive competence has undermined the ability of American industry to offset whatever input cost increases it may face. The cost-push inflation this has inflicted on the domestic economy, along with some decrease in relative product quality, has led to loss of markets and thus to increasing unemployment. The decline in American productive competence caused by chronic, substantial resource diversion has led to no less than a deterioration of the competitiveness of U.S. industry. All of this is perfectly consistent with the implications of the theory of resource diversion.

It is also predictable that the long-term economic decline that inevitably results from sustained, large-scale noncontributive activity would be relatively unnoticed until the threshold of major market loss had been crossed. As the balance-of-trade data in chapter 1 clearly indicate, the U.S. economy has crossed this threshold with a vengeance in recent years. At last, this loss of competitiveness has begun to receive serious attention.

Testifying before Congress in early 1985, Pat Choate, director of policy analysis at TRW, Inc., summarized and compared seventeen separate studies on long-term U.S. competitiveness, all of which had been issued since 1982.[35] These studies were performed by a variety of groups ranging from presidential commissions to governmental agencies to business associations to labor unions. Though they do not represent a full spectrum of relevant organizations, they do offer considerable variety. Of the more than 100 major recommendations for action identified among the group of studies and summarized, not a single one appears to seriously address the fundamental problems of resource diversion and noncontributive activity. However, it is interesting that, according to Choate, "there was widespread agreement that increasing U.S. competitiveness is essential to meeting our nation's many objectives," and that "these studies also point out that while thoughtful, well-coordinated fiscal and monetary policies are essential to any larger national effort to strengthen long-term competitiveness, other actions will also be required."[36] With these two conclusions, I wholeheartedly agree. It is also notable that more than a quarter of the 104 recommendations summarized had some connection with attempts to stimulate research, development, and technological progress.

Among recent, wide-ranging studies of failing U.S. competitiveness, one of the most interesting is that of the President's Commission on Industrial Competitiveness, chaired by John A. Young, president of Hewlett-Packard. The Young Commission report, *Global Competition: The New Reality*, was issued in January 1985. It is a hard-hitting report, notable for the clarity with which it demonstrates the seriousness of the decline of American competitiveness and the vigor with which it attacks the various "there's nothing to worry about" explanations of the present U.S. economic situation.

The Young Commission's very definition of competitiveness indicates an encouraging breadth of focus:

> Competitiveness is the degree to which a nation can, under free and fair market conditions, produce goods and services that meet the test of international markets *while simultaneously maintaining or expanding the real incomes of its citizens*. [emphasis added]

The report continues,

> It is not our goal to compete by decreasing the real incomes of our people. Other nations may compete by having low wage levels, but that is not an option America would choose. . . . Competitiveness is not a winner-take-all game . . . the goal . . . is not to create disadvantages for our trading partners, but to strengthen and better deploy the advantages America has at her command. . . . Competitiveness does not require American leadership in all economic sectors.[37]

And finally,

> During the past year, thirty leaders from American business, labor, government, and academia have come to remarkable consensus. . . . Are we meeting the competitive challenge? Not well enough. Our ability to compete in world markets is eroding. . . . This report contains compelling evidence of a relative decline in our competitive performance.[38]

There is no doubt that American industrial competitiveness is deteriorating. The strongest and richest economy in the world is showing unmistakable signs of the deterioration that naturally follows decades of economic self-parasitization. Alone among the major industrial nations of the world, the United States emerged from the disaster of World War II with its economy vigorous, its society intact. Yet during that very period of unchallenged economic leadership, America strapped on the heavy burden of noncontributive activity that would ultimately cause it to falter. Like a runner far ahead of the pack, sure of continued leadership, we did not believe the extra weight would really matter. But it greatly slowed our pace just as others were gradually beginning to run faster; the loss of our lead became just a matter of time.

What lies ahead?   The economic prognosis for this decade is not good. It would not be good even if the size of the noncontributive sectors remained stable. But since 1980 there has been a huge acceleration in distractive government spending (chiefly on the military)—an extremely dangerous trend. If the United States continues on its present path, the rates of inflation and unemployment from which we suffered at the end of the 1970s—rates that were viewed as horrific at the beginning of that decade—will look like economic good times compared to what will be commonplace by the early 1990s, not to mention the turn of the century. Productivity growth will continue to deteriorate; real income, and thus material standard of living, will begin an accelerated decline. There is no pleasure in making such a forecast. For there will be a great deal of human suffering, of shattered hopes, behind these numbers. Yet this is the clear implication of the theory of resource diversion developed here, a theory whose predictions correspond depressingly well to the empirical realities of economic life in the last third of the twentieth century.

Of course, there is nothing inevitable about this gloomy forecast. If the theory is correct, there is a clear and powerful set of policies available to reverse this distressing pattern and rebuild a healthy and vital American economy. And this reversal begins with a commitment to the substantial redirection of productive resources away from the noncontributive sectors and back into the contributive economy. It is irrelevant whether or not these conclusions are ideologically appealing. Such a shift of resources is prerequisite to any successful attempt to reverse the present economic decay.

Applicability to Socialist Economies

Throughout this work, the macroeconomic problem has been subdivided into two essential parts—the problem of economic coordination and the problem of resource deployment. It has been argued that monetarist and Keynesian theories address only the former problem, and so are incomplete. I have tried to set forth a theoretical framework for addressing the latter problem, or at least for highlighting the macroeconomic importance of paying separate attention to this question. This same dichotomy provides an interesting point of comparison between socialist and market-oriented econo-mies. Insofar as we confine ourselves to macroeconomic issues, the main distinction between these alternative economic systems is the way in which they deal with the problem of economic coordination. Whereas socialist economies rely on direct planning and explicit co-ordination by government bodies, market-oriented economies rely on the operation of the impersonal market mechanism, supple-mented to a greater or lesser extent by various forms of government intervention. Theories, mechanisms, and policies regarding effective economic coordination in one system are hence likely to have little if any applicability to economies operating under the other system.

But the other half of the macroeconomic problem is remarkably consistent across both these systems in its implications for macro-economic well-being. The division of the economy into contributive, neutral, and distractive sectors depends on the nature of the outputs of those sectors, and the impact thereof on the material standard of living. It has nothing to do with whether the production system for any or all goods and services is collectivized on market-oriented, privately or governmentally owned. Consequently, the theory of re-source diversion speaks as much to the policies and priorities of so-cialist societies as it does to those of societies whose economies op-erate under essentially capitalist principles. If that is so, much of the analysis contained here should be applicable to the present economic situation of socialist countries. In particular, the kind of economic deterioration that results from persistent, large-scale support of non-contributive activity should be as visible in socialist economies as I have just argued it is within the United States.

The extensive planning and production bureaucracy in the USSR is replete with examples of neutral activity—a fact that in recent years has been increasingly acknowledged by Soviet analysts and officials. For example, according to the *New York Times*, a thirty-page memo-randum prepared by a group of economists associated with the Acad-emy of Sciences in Novosibirsk argued that "the main task in reviv-ing the economy lay in reducing the array of intermediate-level bodies, from central ministries to regional administrations, that were said to have mushroomed in the last decade." [39] But though the neu-tral sector has apparently constituted a serious drag on the Soviet economy, it has been dwarfed by the distractive sector. The USSR has, of course, been the main protagonist of the United States in the post–World War II arms race. Accordingly, the military component of the distractive sector has been maintained at a high level in the Soviet Union for about the same period as in the United States. The theory of resource diversion would therefore predict structural consequences similar in kind to those that have occurred in the United States. Has this been the case?

The Soviet economy is one of officially established priorities, and these priorities are most serious in terms of supply considerations. Supply is widely understood as the central problem for both national central planners and managers of individual enterprises in the USSR; there has been very little evidence of insufficient demand. The priorities used in allocating productive resources are critical to the effective functioning of the economy. Every industry has a priority or ranking that in effect determines where it stands in the line of industries waiting for needed productive resources of all sorts (engineers and scientists, production workers, materials, fuels, equipment, and so forth). Military industries, and the portions of other industries that support them, are at the head of every line.

As I have argued earlier, giving high priority to the distractive sector shrinks the resource base of the contributive economy. Because of their top priority in the Soviet system of direct resource allocation, distractive producers receive ample quantities of the highest-quality inputs available. Contributive producers are thus left to vie for the remaining resources. The preemption of productive resources by the Soviet distractive sector thus operates quite directly, without the illusion of equal sectoral competition for resources that characterizes the indirect resource diversion of the distractive sector in the United States.

There is some evidence that the impact of the distractive sector on the Soviet Union's contributive economy goes beyond the direct diversion of resources. There may be a "contingency diversion" that also hampers efficiency. Contributive production facilities and even contributive products have sometimes been designed to allow ready convertibility to military-oriented production—for example, tractors with caterpillar treads rather than wheels to facilitate the switching of production to tank-type vehicles. If practices of this sort persist, they can easily result in inefficient contributive production, adding to the distractive distortion of the contributive economy.

Another somewhat tangential but interesting point about the operation of distractive industry in the USSR is that the head of a large Soviet military enterprise typically will also be both a ranking official in the Communist party and a high-ranking uniformed military officer. Such an individual holds a position of simultaneously high economic, political, and military authority and power. He or she will accordingly be a major force not only in the economy but in the broader society as well, particularly in the region where the enterprise is located. This is especially true if the enterprise is located in a small or remote city.

Partly because the economy is younger and not as large, and partly because the resource base is itself smaller, the burden of maintaining an overlarge distractive sector has fallen more heavily on the Soviet than on the American economy. The drain of technologists and of production and infrastructure capital (and perhaps of other resources as well) is apparently on a scale comparable to that in the United States, a result of the Soviet society's struggle to compete with America in distractive-sector output. The proportionate resource drain on the Soviet economy is thus almost certain to be higher. The distractive sector of the United States grew dramatically following World War II. This distractive growth occurred alongside an advanced, well-developed, and booming contributive economy. The Soviet distractive economy, on the other hand, developed alongside a contributive economy and society horrendously damaged by the war and struggling hard to develop. Thus the Soviet civilian economy was never able to work on breaking its chronic supply problems with a major, systematic, sustained effort. On the contrary, shortages were continually made more severe by the demands of the distractive sector as the arms race between the superpowers escalated.

Though the data are very difficult to come by, it is clear that despite considerable economic growth in the Soviet Union the nation's productive competence remains at a low level. The Soviet economy's chronic shortages of producer—and especially consumer—goods are widely recognized. Furthermore, the shortages are not merely quantitative. The quality of consumer goods, in particular, is recognized to be of a rather low order. Reporting on a Moscow meeting of party officials and economic managers addressed by the Soviet leader, Mikhail Gorbachev, the *New York Times* stated that "the press agency TASS quoted speakers as having said that goods were of poor quality and new machinery was obsolete." [40] Interestingly, the article—"Gorbachev Faults Economic Record"—also reported that "TASS said the meeting also included 'a serious discussion of how to accelerate scientific and technical progress.'"

Although it was not systematic, rigorous, or scientific, my casual personal observation disclosed an impressive array of imported goods during a brief visit to Moscow in June 1984. Telephones manufactured in Poland, railroad locomotives from Czechoslovakia, Hungarian buses and translating equipment, cash registers made in Japan—if this is any real indication of the present situation in the USSR, it bears a striking resemblance to the flood of imports inundating the United States. In the Soviet Union, the burden of sacrificing the contributive output to maintain and expand the distractive sector has apparently fallen more heavily on consumer goods than is the case in the United States. Economic growth has thus been achievable despite a heavy distractive burden, by emphasizing producer goods. What few data are available, however, do indeed indicate a pattern of declining economic growth over the past fifteen to twenty years, mirroring the general deterioration in the U.S. economy that has been detailed here. Excerpts from the text of a Soviet economic memorandum published by the *New York Times* in August 1983 include the following:

> For several decades the economic development of Soviet society was characterized by high rates of growth and stability. . . . But the last . . . years witnessed a tendency to slow down, with the growth in gross national product declining perceptibly. . . . [In] 1966–70 the mean annual growth rate was 7.5 percent, . . . [in] 1971–75 [it was] 5.8 percent, it dropped in . . . 1976–80 to 3.8 percent, and in the opening years of the [next] five-year plan, it was only 2.5 percent.[41]

Furthermore, the emphasis on producer goods has resulted in a Soviet standard of material well-being that is chronically low even relative to the rest of Eastern Europe. And productive competence has certainly not escaped unscathed.

Because of direct government control of work opportunities and prices, the effects of the distractive drain are not as likely to surface in the form of inflation and unemployment as would be expected in a market economy; in fact, they have primarily surfaced in other ways in the USSR. But the continuing shortages of contributive goods and services carry the message rather well. And the end result is remark-

ably similar: a depressed standard of living, relative to what the resource endowment of the society is capable of providing.

It is important to understand, then, that a planned socialist economy is no more or less able to override the negative economic effects
of persistently high noncontributive activity than is a capitalist economy. The impacts of resource diversion are simply superordinate.
The only way to redevelop an economy severely stressed by the burden of an enlarged distractive sector is to rechannel diverted resources back into contributive activity.

Applicability to the Third World

Though the existence of bloated, inefficient (and largely
governmental) bureaucracies in the less developed nations of the
world is often argued, there does not appear to be even a rough quantitative estimate of the size of this largely neutral sector. That is not
surprising, given the difficulties of quantifying neutral activity (discussed earlier), as well as the general lack of reliable data that is one
of the dimensions of underdevelopment. Much more information
is available on distractive activity, particularly military expenditures. Although they are often shrouded in secrecy and distortion,
military expenditures have received sufficient attention to justify
some confidence that the available estimates are at least reasonable
approximations.

Expressed in terms of U.S. currency, from 1960 to 1981 the less
developed countries (LDCs) of the world spent a total of more than
one trillion dollars on their militaries.[42] This staggering sum is nearly
incomprehensible. It would take a continuously operating printing
press, producing a $1000 bill every second, nearly a decade longer to
print this much money than it took the LDCs to spend it! Furthermore, Third World military expenditures have been sharply increasing in relative terms and accelerating in absolute terms. In 1960, the
LDCs accounted for about 10 percent of worldwide military spending; five years later their share was under 12 percent, and by the end
of the 1960s it was still slightly under 13 percent. By 1974, LDC
military spending accounted for more than 19 percent of the world
total; five years later, at the end of the 1970s, their share was more
than 23 percent. As of 1981, the Third World share of the total had
declined slightly to about 22 percent, still more than twice their rela-

tive share in 1960.[43] In absolute terms, military spending in the LDCs rose by a factor of thirteen over this period, from $10 billion in 1960 to $130 billion in 1981.[44] Using any reasonable correction for dollar inflation, this is still a spectacular increase. For example, using the consumer price index for all items to convert these figures to constant 1967 dollars, the figure for 1960 becomes $11.3 billion, rising to $47.7 billion in 1981.[45] Thus, even in real terms, terms of purchasing power, Third World military spending more than quadrupled in only a little more than two decades.

Sustained distractive spending at high levels has caused enormous damage to the economies of *more* developed countries. It has caused substantial economic deterioration in a nation as rich and economically advanced as the United States, playing a major role in ruining the extraordinary economic advantage this nation enjoyed only a few decades ago. It has undermined the capacity of as large and relatively well endowed a socialist nation as the Soviet Union to raise the standard of living of its population even to the level common in Eastern Europe. If distractive spending can do all this, if it can begin to "undevelop" more developed countries, there is little question that its impact on the less developed nations of the world must be even more devastating.

In a developing country desperately trying to build an industrial base and improve agricultural productivity, what is needed is contributive investment: increased education of the labor force, improved health care, an expanded transportation and communication system, and more and better production capital. Present living standards have to be improved. Future capability to produce has to be strengthened to help these nations out of poverty and give them a chance to make development a self-generating and self-sustaining process. It is difficult enough to accomplish these things with all the resources available, but the large-scale diversion of resources to noncontributive activity makes it virtually impossible. It is hard to imagine how economic development can succeed in the face of high levels of distractive spending in light of the enormous economic resource waste that such expenditures imply.

Many of the effects of resource diversion on the Third World are similar in kind, but more severe in impact, than those already discussed. For example, the tax base is generally much smaller in the LDCs and the difficulties of collecting taxes much greater. The diversion of public funds to distractive purposes like military spending therefore undercuts much more seriously the capacity to finance vital public investment in infrastructure. Yet because the poor condition of LDC infrastructure severely handicaps virtually all other development efforts, infrastructure investment is even more crucial in LDCs than in more developed nations.

Production capital is another critical resource that is generally in very short supply. If imported contributive machinery and equipment can fill this void effectively, prospects for development can be greatly enhanced by such imports. But LDCs cannot buy this production capital with their own currencies: they must use so-called hard currencies (e.g., U.S. dollars, Swiss francs, British pounds, German marks, Japanese yen). For most LDCs, access to hard currencies is also very limited. Spending what hard currency they have on importing weapons and other distractive goods further reduces their ability to finance imports of the needed production capital, as well as of other contributive goods.

Certainly, the problem has been less severe in the oil-rich LDCs, especially after the success of the Organization of Petroleum Exporting Countries in sharply raising oil prices in 1973. These countries have a tremendous inflow of foreign currency. It would seem, therefore, that they have more than enough foreign currency to buy both mililtary equipment and supplies of industrial and agricultural equipment. But Iran, for example, despite huge oil revenues, had by 1976 spent so much money on military equipment (it was America's largest arms customer at that time) that it was back in the international money market, borrowing. Trying to do both—to finance contributive and distractive imports—greatly increased the need of the LDCs to borrow money internationally.

Extensive borrowing by the less developed nations has led to a staggering burden of debt. By 1982, Third World debt had climbed to some $626 billion.[46] The International Monetary Fund's conditions for the granting of new loans to these debtor nations, mainly to allow continued repayment of *interest* on the original debt, have amounted to a major infringement of national sovereignty and brought cries of "recolonization." The debt problem is a complex one, and a thorough analysis of its causes and cures is beyond the scope of this analysis. Nevertheless, it is clear that the only way the Third World can permanently emerge from this financial hole and regain a measure of autonomy is if it develops economically. Yet the extraordinary growth in Third World military expenditures over the past decade or two has diverted many of the crucial resources required for that development.

Furthermore, in more directly financial terms, it is interesting to note that over only six years (1977–82), combined military expenditures by the LDCs were cumulatively greater than the total Third World debt outstanding in 1982. If the LDC *share* of world military spending had been the same in those years as it was in the early 1960s, they would have saved enough money from this one source to finance repayment of nearly two-thirds of their outstanding debt.[47]

Another critical resource in very short supply in most LDCs is a highly educated, skilled labor force: technologists, well-trained managers, skilled production workers, and—perhaps even more important—fully literate individuals who can work with blueprints and who have other basic industrial and educational skills. Yet much of this type of labor is diverted into the noncontributive sectors because of the attractive pay and prestige there, making the shortage in the contributive economy much more severe. In the past, this resource diversion mainly involved movement of educated people directly into the military forces, since there was no significant arms production in the less developed countries. But during the worldwide boom in military spending since 1960 (involving all but about a dozen countries), less developed countries have not only been active buyers on the international arms market, but have also increasingly become producers of arms. Israel, India, and Brazil, among a growing number of others, have gone into the business of producing—even exporting—arms. This trend, though perhaps intended to improve conditions by conserving or earning hard currencies, bodes very ill for developing countries. It means that the diversion of both skilled labor and production capital is going to become worse.

The enormity of the worldwide cost of military spending—in terms of the human economic well-being that has been sacrificed—is difficult to comprehend. Perhaps one way to get a general idea is to compare in money terms some rough estimates of the costs of major civilian and military projects. For example, in 1976 Ruth Sivard compiled the following illustrative list of development-oriented programs that could have been financed with a mere 5-percent cutback in world military expenditures (a list that would probably be greatly understated today, given inflation and real growth in military spending): a supplemental protein feeding for two hundred million malnourished children, *plus* a major increase in agricultural investment to increase food production in poor countries on the edge of famine, *plus* an increase in primary schools to accommodate one hundred million children not now attending school, *plus* a permanent large-scale international relief force to assist disaster-stricken countries, *plus* a worldwide fluoridation program, *plus* basic education for twenty-five million illiterate adults, *plus* a worldwide campaign to eradicate malaria, *plus* iron supplements to protect three hundred million women of child-bearing age and children against anemia, *plus* vitamin A supplements to protect one hundred million children in the one-to-five-year age group against blindness caused by vitamin A deficiency.[48] It is a list worth pondering.

Since the end of World War II there have been more than one hundred major wars (wars that each took one thousand or more lives per year). Every year has seen at least four wars—some have seen more than four times that many. All but one of them have been fought in the Third World.[49] Though the causes of these wars have been many and varied, poverty and economic backwardness have without a doubt played a major role in creating the conditions that have fostered so much organized violence. Apart from the moral arguments for making transfers from distractive military to contributive civilian activity, such transfers are a necessity if serious sustained development is ever to become a reality. It is development, not more weaponry or larger armed forces, that is most likely to be effective in reducing the violence, and increasing the security, of the LDCs. And it is development, not military force, that holds the greatest promise for preventing the Third World tinderbox from igniting an all-out nuclear conflagration which could put an end to the human race.

The Value of the Theory

The empirical evidence presented in this chapter is to be taken only as indicative. A great deal more investigation is required to rigorously test the various hypotheses embedded in the theory of resource diversion: that is understood. Nevertheless, it seems quite obvious that, at least in its broad outlines, the theory goes a long way toward explaining the main trends of economic behavior important to the understanding and correction of our present economic woes. If we are to have policies whose effects are cosmetic and short-term, temporarily soothing one pain at the expense of aggravating another, present approaches will suffice. But if we wish to come to grips with and reverse the long-term economic deterioration from which we are suffering, the more structural orientation of the theory developed here will, I think, prove a valuable guide.

In the next chapter, attention is turned to the development and analysis of strategies for reconstructing and reinvigorating economies that have suffered from the debilitating effects of long-term resource diversion.

12

Designing A Program for Economic Revitalization

Any program designed to rebuild an economy that has been subject to a heavy, prolonged noncontributive burden must reach into the economic structure. It cannot rely on generalized policies that average their effects over the economy as a whole. In order to be effective, such a program must be tailored to the specific industrial structure and political economic situation in which it is to be applied. It isn't really possible to provide a broadly (let alone universally) applicable set of blueprints for economic reconstruction. However, the major requirements for successful revitalization can be outlined, along with a set of strategies for achieving them. And some institutional mechanisms that might be useful in smoothing the transition can be suggested.

Analysis of the Present Situation

The first step toward revitalization is a thorough analysis of the existing noncontributive sectors. This should include estimates of overall size and, more important, estimates of just how much of *each* type of capital and labor is involved in each industry. Then, the

geographic pattern of these resources—particularly the labor categories—should be analyzed down to the county level.[1] The purpose of
this step is to provide basic background knowledge about the nature
and extent of the noncontributive resource drain. Though some of
the data gathered here may never be fed into a specific set of calculations, this understanding will provide a proper perspective on the revitalization program—and proper perspective is always critical to
good decision making.

Assessment of Needs

The second step is to estimate the resources required to reverse the deterioration of the public and private contributive sectors.
In the case of contributive activities considered to be the responsibility of the government, this needs assessment can then be used to plan
a program of public works. Decisions must be made as to how the
responsibility for this program is to be distributed among the various
levels of government. The financing requirements of the program,
combined with the distribution of responsibility, imply a distribution
of revenue among governmental levels. If this is different from the
existing pattern, an appropriate pattern of revenue sharing, tax shifting, and government borrowing must be developed.

For example, it might be decided that because of their role in the
reconstruction program, states and localities need more money,
while the federal government can get along with less. The required
shift of funds could be accomplished by grants of federal money to
state and local government. But it could also be done by reducing
federal taxes or by borrowing to make available greater taxing or borrowing potential for the states and localities. All of this is quite separate from the important question of whether the overall tax burden
and levels of government borrowing are too high or too low.

This assessment of public contributive-sector needs is not just a
question of financing. Requirements for productive resources, determined category by category, must be the foundation on which estimates of required revenues are based. The capital and labor requirements are central. Other important issues, such as which part of
public contributive-sector reconstruction should be performed di-

rectly by government and which should be contracted out to private companies, are secondary. Ideally, they should be decided on grounds of efficiency, keeping the *full* output meaning of that term in mind. But most likely, they will also be decided by custom, political expediency, and ideology.

Analyzing how much of which resources are needed to rebuild the private contributive sector is similar to analyzing public-sector needs. The result is applied very differently, however. It is not necessary, not efficient, and not particularly desirable that the capital and labor needs assessment be used to develop a centralized reconstruction plan. This conflicts with the ideology of market-oriented economies and is also inconsistent with their structure and operating principles. The private sector should instead be encouraged to make its own plans, company by company, facility by facility. Information about plans for revitalizing the public contributive sector should be made widely available—particularly the part of these plans that involves work to be contracted out to private firms. Public works programs represent potential markets which private firms, particularly those that will be shifting from government-oriented distractive to contributive activity, may wish to service. Information about the nature and extent of intended cutbacks in public-sector distractive activity is also of great value to private corporate planners, since these markets will be in decline.

Interestingly, it is almost certainly better to decentralize detailed transitional planning of this redeployment of resources—even in socialist economies. There, of course, central planning and coordination has a more important role to play. Nevertheless, the need for tailor-made transitional plans makes some degree of decentralization highly desirable. Transition planning will be discussed in greater detail shortly.

Shrinking the Noncontributive Sectors

No practical, policy-oriented calculus is currently available for finding the best level of noncontributive activity. It is simply not possible to accurately measure the real output of most noncontributive activities; the parts of their output we can measure do not capture the essence of their primary purpose. For example, suppose the central objective of a police force is considered to be protecting the law-abiding public from the activities of lawbreakers. How is that to be measured? Using some measure of intermediate police output, such as arrests, misses the point. A police force might be so effective at discouraging violations of the law that arrests are not necessary; on the other hand, the police may be making scores of arrests while crime runs rampant. It may also be very difficult to precisely trace the relationship between changes in the shape or level of a given distractive activity and the activity's effectiveness in achieving its primary purpose. We are rarely in a position to make statements about that relationship with a high degree of confidence, for example, "Buying five new patrol cars will reduce assaults within the city limits by 6 percent." Yet the lack of precision does *not* mean that we are unable to make reasonable judgments about the appropriate level and structure of distractive activity.

Setting the level of distractive activity.   Since it is known that distractive activities involve serious sacrifice in the present or future material standard of living, or both, it is wise to approach them with a bias toward minimization; this means requiring that any substantial expansion of distractive activity above a minimal level be thoroughly justified. We should be required to justify both whether the basic activity performs a useful function and whether this particular increase adds enough to that useful function to justify its cost. Given the measurement difficulties involved, *any* significant expansion of that activity should be viewed with a degree of suspicion.

For example, a rising crime rate, or a claim that crime rates are likely to rise soon, may bring calls for expanding the size of the police force. Yet before rushing off to hire more police, it would be wise to carefully weigh the evidence behind the claim that the crime rate is or will be rising—and then to consider whether alternative reactions such as toughening legal penalties or speeding the processing of criminal cases in the courts might be more effective than increased numbers of police in slowing or reversing an increase in criminal activity. Similarly, suppose we are told that unless we expand our military might, opponents of our nation may gain control of supplies of foreign resources on which we depend. We should not react to this alleged threat to our national security in a knee-jerk fashion, but should first demand evidence in support of this claim and consider it carefully. Second, assuming we are persuaded that the possibility *is* real, and sufficiently likely to be troublesome, we should then search for *contributive* alternatives. Contributive approaches will generally tend to be more desirable. For one thing, if effective, they provide the same benefit as effective distractive approaches, but without the economic penalties. It may be that our ultimate decision will still be to exercise the military option, but whatever alternative we choose, the decision is more likely to be a wise one.

The first step in evaluating any particular distractive activity is to state the primary purpose of that activity as clearly as possible. This means moving beyond vague phrases to operationally meaningful definitions. For example, saying that the purpose of military forces is to maintain national security sounds impressive and important enough, but it is necessary to look beyond this catchall phrase and ask, what does "national security" mean? Does it only mean preventing the military conquest and continuing control of our nation by those we see as our opponents? Does it also mean preventing the destruction of our country and its people by external military attack? What about assuring continued access to resources on which the nation is economically dependent? Should it also include having other economic and political elements of our national interest taken seriously by the governments and people of other nations?

Once we can at least roughly agree on the primary purpose of the distractive activity, we should evaluate the extent to which (1) contributive activities might replace distractive activities in achieving each part of this purpose, (2) other less resource-intensive means might effectively replace the distractive activity, and (3) a restructuring of the distractive activity might result in achieving the objective more efficiently. Continuing with the example of military activity, suppose it is agreed that reducing the nation's vulnerability to loss of external resources on which it depends is an important part of national security. An example of the first approach would be to achieve this objective by contributive research and development aimed at finding more secure substitutes for the threatened resources, or by contributive exploration activities to locate more secure sources of those resources.

Using economic boycotts or similar sanctions to pressure our opponent—directly or through its allies—to stop threatening the re-source supply would be an example of approach number two. The opposite approach, offering positive economic incentives such as fa-vorable trade status, might also be useful and should not be ignored. Finally, if it is determined that the role of military strength in accom-plishing national security objectives cannot be filled by either of the first two approaches, approach three would be to seek ways of re-structuring military forces to achieve the objectives with a much smaller diversion of resources. For example, consider a different na-tional security objective, the deterrence of nuclear attack. Relying on the existing, relatively invulnerable nuclear missile submarine force to achieve the level of threat required for nuclear deterrence is much less resource-intensive than building new generations of extraor-dinarily expensive and less secure forces of land-based missiles and long-range bombers.

The surest way to guarantee that a distractive activity will be self-perpetuating and will put an excessive and unnecessary burden on the society is to treat it as a sacred cow. Distractive activities of many kinds do have a social purpose, often a critical one. But criticality of basic purpose *need not and should not translate into open-ended commitment*—allowing it to do so is simply foolish. Distractive ac-tivity should always be subject to careful scrutiny with a minimizing bias. In fact, the more crucial the objective, the greater the impor-tance of subjecting that activity to critical scrutiny in order to keep it lean and efficient.

Neutral activity.   The reduction of neutral activity is less complex, but not necessarily less difficult. Since the neutral sector has no output, it generates no societal value of any kind; its optimum level is thus always zero. Cutting back on neutral activity requires a change in the incentive structure that keeps it alive and growing. For example, as long as status and salary are positively correlated with number of subordinates and sheer size of organizational budget, the managerial-administrative neutral sector will persist. If we can find a way to invert the incentive structure, this type of neutral activity will wither away.

The minimum goal.   The assessment of public and private resource requirements for reinvigorating the contributive sector es-tablishes a minimum goal for the quantity of each category of productive resource to be removed from noncontributive activity. The attempt to find viable ways of reducing the noncontributive burden should be carried out with this minimum goal clearly in mind. While *any* level of rechanneling of resources from noncontributive to contributive activity must be considered an economic plus, unless this rechanneling frees enough of the right kind of resources to meet the minimum goal, long-term economic deterioration will continue. It may be slowed, but it will not be halted.

Requirements for Successful Transition

Together, the needs assessment and the definition of the type and size of appropriate reductions in noncontributive activity provide important dimensions of the transition process. Overall, we now know:

1. the number of people whose paid work will be shifted as a result of the revitalization program;
2. the breakdown into the categories we have defined (and perhaps into subdivisions within these categories) of the labor force and physical capital to be shifted;
3. the geographic pattern of the present deployment of this work force and the facilities at which it is employed;
4. the categorical breakdown of the labor force and physical capital needed to rebuild the public and private contributive sectors.

With this information about the endpoints of the transition process, it is possible to develop a rough first estimate of the size and character of the transition task. It is also possible to evaluate how well the resources to be freed from the noncontributive sectors match the resources needed for revitalizing the contributive sector. Crude estimates of the revenue shifts required to finance the transition may also be made.

Contributive and noncontributive contexts. Important, even vital information is still missing, however. Most important is a thorough understanding of how the differences between the worlds of contributive, neutral, and distractive activity might affect the transition process. Since the three sectors are driven differently and operate by different rules, there is a very high probability that resources in the noncontributive sectors (particularly the distractive sector) will become specialized to noncontributive activity. Retraining and reorientation, in the case of labor, and modification, in the case of capital, may thus be crucial to rounding the squared pegs of noncontributive resources to fit the round holes of the contributive sector. If it is to be done effectively, producing a proper fit, this rounding must be done with a full understanding of the nature of both the squaring of the noncontributive pegs and the rounding of the contributive holes.

For example, consider the case of transferring engineers and scientists from distractive-sector activity, say in military-related industry, to the contributive sector. A major part of the problem here stems from the very different requirements for successful military and civilian development and application of technology. Present-day high-technology military products are extremely complex, and are designed with an effort to squeeze every possible ounce of performance out of the product. Whether or not this extra performance capability actually has military significance, the assumption that it is significant clearly underlies the practice of weapons research and development. This has led to the assignment of large teams of technologists to the design of weapons systems—each, in effect, developing and designing a part of a part. Accordingly, the need to become expert in a very narrow range of knowledge has led to extreme specialization of engineers and scientists engaged in military-related work. In addition, the high priority attached to military funding, the common practice of buying weapons on an effectively cost-plus basis, and the pressure for even small increments in weapons capability have led to a de-emphasis of the cost implications of design. In fact, more expensive designs will result in increased sales revenues and perhaps increased profits as well for the firms that generate them.[2]

Successful design for the contributive marketplace, on the other hand, requires great attention to the implications of the specific design for the cost of producing the ultimate product. To successfully minimize costs, designers should be familiar with the overall design of the product, rather than being extremely specialized. This, together with a basic understanding of the cost effects of modifying the design in one way or another, will enable designers to trade off changes in one part of the design against changes in the other. In this way, desired product performance will be achieved at the lowest possible cost. Keeping production cost down enables the price to be kept at a level that will make the product attractive to potential customers. And, of course, attractive product price and quality bring expanded sales and profit to the firm.

Because of these differences, engineers and scientists performing military-oriented work must be retrained and reoriented before they can be successful in contributive research and development. Complete retraining is clearly not necessary, since much of the mathematical, scientific, and engineering knowledge they already have is also required for contributive work. But in order for former distractive-sector engineers and scientists to establish firm connection with the world of contributive-sector design, they must become less specialized and more sensitive to cost considerations.

When military-oriented engineers and scientists are laid off because of the termination of a defense contract, they typically move to another geographic area to follow the contracts, they accept non-technical work, or they simply remain unemployed until the contracts return. This behavior has been read by some as an indication that contributive technology is not starved by the diversion of technological personnel to military areas, since the personnel are not grabbed by contributive research programs when they become unemployed. But the failure of these technologists to be absorbed into the contributive sector is due far more to the inappropriateness of their training and experience than to an overall lack of demand—it is certainly not due to a lack of national or commercial need. This point is periodically illustrated by phenomena such as the development in the early 1970s of a critical shortage of engineers qualified to design new non-nuclear power plants, while at the same time there was a large pool of unemployed military-oriented engineers.

The conversion process must also reach into the educational institutions responsible for training engineers and scientists. In the United States, for example, these institutions have altered their curricula to emphasize specialization, particularly in areas and subareas of interest to the military, and strongly de-emphasize training in cost-related matters. Instruction in mundane contributive areas (power engineering, for example) was curtailed or eliminated, particularly at the "best" schools. All this may have been appropriate given the changing character of the high-paying, prestigious opportunities available to graduates. And yet, these changes meant that engineers and scientists who did go directly into contributive areas were less than optimally trained for the development of contributive technology.

Once the implications of the differing worlds of the noncontributive and contributive sectors are clearly understood, it is possible to work out the degree and type of labor retraining and reorientation, and capital modification, needed for effective transition. This in turn permits assessment of the labor and capital required to *process* the resources being transferred. For example, the number and type of teachers and facilities required for retraining can be estimated. Earlier rough estimates of the shape and size of the transition needed for the economic revitalization program can now be upgraded and refined.

The private sector.   It is easy to see why all of this is necessary for the part of the reconstruction program that directly involves the public sector. But, given that the private sector will be planning its own transition on a highly decentralized basis, why is it necessary to have this information for that part of the program?

In the first place, is it highly likely that much, if not all, of the distractive activity from which resources are being rechanneled will be either directly controlled by the government or oriented to servicing government demand. It therefore seems reasonable that the government bears some responsibility for easing the transition process by providing and coordinating transition support services. Second, though conventional short-term monetary and fiscal policies cannot directly cope with the transition problem, they can provide a climate more conducive to smooth transition, or at least can avoid getting in the way. For example, in a transitional period during which large capital investments are required, policies such as investment tax credits and monetary expansion are very helpful. In order to make appropriate macroeconomic policy decisions, it is vital to know something about the nature and size of capital investment required during transition. This point can easily be extended to other productive resources.

Institutional Transition Mechanisms

Even before a society has made a commitment to the serious reductions in noncontributive activity that are necessary to rebuild its economy, it is both possible and wise to establish institutional mechanisms that are capable of facilitating economic transition. After all, minor but locally important transitions are always occurring. Of course, at the time a program of economic revitalization is instituted, such mechanisms must be in place to ensure smooth transition.

There are many reasonable models for institutional mechanisms that would be useful in implementing a program of economic reconstruction which is based on redirecting diverted resources to contributive activity. To illustrate how such mechanisms may be constructed in a manner sensitive to the special characteristics of this kind of transition, I present in the Appendix draft specifications for federal legislation to set up a mechanism for highly decentralized contingency planning for the conversion of distractive-sector, military-oriented activity to the contributive sector.

To be sure, the institutional mechanisms of this prototype legislation relate to only a portion of the transition process that would accompany a serious program of economic revitalization. But it is intended to illustrate that it is possible to greatly facilitate the deep structural change required to rebuild an economy long burdened by heavy noncontributive activity.

Epilogue

From the time of Malthus, economics has often been labeled "the dismal science." Dismal it has often been, from depressing Malthusian musings on the inevitability of bare subsistence for the majority, to Marx's conviction that market economies must produce progressive impoverishment of the masses, to the belief of present-day dependency theorists that improvement in the economic condition of a part of the human population comes at the expense of increased exploitation and misery of another part. Economics has been dismal not only in many of its conclusions, but also in the mechanistic, calculating, depersonalized view it so often projects of human beings and of their individual and collective behavior.

I do not see any force—economic, political, or otherwise—that compels us either to such depressing conclusions about economic activity or to such a dehumanized view of people as economic actors. We are thinking, feeling, and—if we allow ourselves—caring beings who hold both our economic well-being and the humanity of our society in our own hands. Together we make the choices that make the difference. If we persist in seeing the expansion of economic activity as a goal, rather than as one means to the goal of raising the standard of living for all; if we continue to divide human beings into discrete robotic entities called "consumers" and "producers"; and if we cannot see through the veil of money value to the reality of inherent economic value, then we are condemned to repeat the errors that lead to economic deterioration and anomic, alienated society. We shall continue to divert our capacity for generating real economic development here and abroad and never achieve the improved economic and social conditions that lie well within our grasp.

That would indeed be a great tragedy—greater still because of the pivotal role economic conditions have played in the periodic spasms of mass organized violence and brutality we refer to as war. The technological brilliance we have applied to the improvement of the material well-being of human society over the millennia of our tenure on this planet has given us the technical capacity to assure that no human being need starve, thirst, or lack shelter or any other rudiments of a decent existence. That same technological brilliance, applied to the improvement of the tools of mass destruction, has given us the technical capacity to assure the termination of human society, if not all life on this vital and beautiful Earth that we call home. And as we have followed the path to this destructive capacity, the resources diverted have prevented us from dealing with (and have in some cases created) the economic conditions that may eventually trigger the long chain of events leading to the holocaust this destructive capacity has made possible.

Which of these potentials we will ultimately realize depends more on our wisdom than on our brilliance. It is not a question that will be answered—or that can be answered—technologically, for both poverty and security are human problems, not technical issues. In itself, undoing resource diversion will not even eliminate inflation and unemployment, let alone produce economic utopia. Problems of coordination, distribution, efficiency, and equity remain. But redirecting resources to the contributive sector can eliminate the structural economic deterioration that guarantees a future of declining economic well-being. And it will help to create a world in which the short-term prescriptions of conventional macroeconomic theory have a chance to succeed.

Appendix: Model Specifications for a National Economic Adjustment Act

Title I. Economic Adjustment Coordinating Council

There is hereby established the National Economic Adjustment Coordinating Council (hereinafter referred to as "the Council") composed of:

1. the Secretary of Commerce (Chair),

2. the Secretary of Labor (Vice-Chair),

3. the Secretary of Health and Human Services,

4. the Secretary of Education,

5. the Secretary of Housing and Urban Development,

6. the Secretary of Transportation,

7. the Head of the Council of Economic Advisors,

8. seven representatives of the business management community (chosen from nondefense industries),

9. seven representatives of labor unions.

An Office of Economic Conversion shall be established to provide staff support for the Council. The members of the staff shall include marketing specialists, production engineers, plant layout and enterprise design experts, urban planning specialists, and labor training experts, none of whom can have had a majority of their professional experience working in defense- and space-related agencies or industries. At no time shall the size of the staff (including all secretarial and clerical personnel) exceed fifteen persons.

The Council shall be charged with the responsibility for encouraging and coordinating the process of planning for the conversion of defense-related facilities and the personnel employed therein to efficient civilian-oriented productive activity, and overseeing national concerns related to the implementation of those plans. The Council shall serve as facilitator, coordinator, and advisor for the process of conversion planning and conversion plan implementation, but the ultimate authority and responsibility for planning and implementation of conversion plans for specific facilities shall be with the local Conversion Committees, as defined in Title II of this Act. The Council shall also serve as liaison between the local Conversion Committees and the other offices of the federal government, where necessary.

In order to carry out these functions the Council shall:

1. Encourage the preparation of concrete plans for civilian-oriented public projects addressing vital areas of national concern (such as mass transportation, housing, education, health care, environmental protection, and renewable energy resources) by the various civilian agencies of the federal government, as well as by state and local governments. The Council shall collect and coordinate such plans and encourage the preparation of the plans wherever possible, to the stage at which contract bids can be solicited upon availability of funding. It shall make information concerning the nature and status of such plans readily available to any local Conversion Committee or any firm (whether or not defense-related) requesting such information. The plans shall be reviewed and revised as necessary and appropriate every two years.

2. Oversee the establishment in the Department of Labor of a Job Information Bank intended to coordinate state, local, and federal employment services to serve as a resource for civilian job information for employees released from particular defense-related employment as a result of the shifting and/or reduction of defense-related expenditures.

3. See to the preparation and distribution of a Conversion Guidelines Handbook which shall:

   a. include a discussion of the basic problems involved in the retraining, reorientation and reorganization of personnel (managerial, technical, administrative, and production) and the redirection of physical plant for efficient, civilian-oriented productive activity,

   b. outline the basic requirements of programs for professional retraining of managerial personnel in order to reorient them to the management of civilian, market-oriented enterprise,

   c. outline the basic requirements for a program of professional retraining of technical personnel in order to effectively reorient them to the prevailing conditions of research, product design, and production operations within civilian-oriented facilities,

d. outline the basic requirements for the length and nature of occupational retraining for production workers and junior-level administrative employees,

e. include case studies of successful conversion to efficient civilian-oriented production (hypothetical or actual), or references thereto, for each of the major defense-related industries and types of facilities,

f. provide a checklist of critical points requiring attention at each stage of the conversion process,

g. contain an annotated bibliography of conversion-related works,

h. be less than 300 pages in length.

This handbook shall be revised, as necessary, every two years.

Title II. Economic Adjustment Planning

There shall be established at every defense-related industrial facility with at least twenty-five employees and at least 20 percent of gross revenue derived from sales of defense materials, a local Conversion Committee, as an absolute condition of participating in defense-related contracts. Such a local Conversion Committee shall also be established at every military installation, base, or other military facility employing at least twenty-five persons.

Each local Conversion Committee shall be composed of a minimum of nine persons: one-third designated by management of the facility in question; one-third designated by the nonmanagement employees of that facility; and one-third (not to include any individuals employed in any capacity at the facility) designated by the chief executive officer of the local government.

Each local Conversion Committee is charged with the authority and responsibility for developing detailed plans for the conversion of the facility at which it has been formed to efficient, civilian-oriented productive activity. It shall be provided with funds for the purposes of planning, derived from the military contract or base operating costs at a rate not exceeding $80 per employee per year in the first year and $40 per employee per year in subsequent years; it shall also be provided with office space. It shall have the authority to:

1. Gain access to the facility records necessary for inventorying in detail all on-site plant and equipment with applicability to civilian productive operations and for inventorying the occupations and skills of all civilian personnel.

2. Spend funds allocated to it as it deems necessary, including the hiring of staff personnel as well as any specialists it may wish to consult, without requiring authorization by the facility management, owner, local government, or any other authority.

3. Directly request the advice of and/or otherwise utilize the services of

the national Economic Adjustment Coordinating Council and its staff, and/ or any other persons or organizations, private or public.

Each local Conversion Committee shall:

1. Develop a comprehensive plan or set of plans for the conversion of the facility (at which it has been established) to efficient operation in one or more areas of civilian-oriented productive activity; the plan or plans shall:

   a. be designed so as to maximize the extent to which the personnel required for the *efficient* operation of the converted facility can be drawn from personnel with skill levels and types approximating those possessed by civilian personnel employed at the facility prior to its conversion,

   b. specify the type and duration of retraining appropriate for retained personnel, and a plan for achieving that retraining,

   c. specify the numbers of civilian personnel, by type and level of skill, employed at the facility prior to conversion, whose continued employment is not consistent with efficient operation of the civilian-oriented converted facility,

   d. specify the numbers of positions (by level and type of skill, if any, that will be needed at the converted facility) whose skill requirements are *not* approximated by those of sufficient numbers of personnel employed at the preconverted facility,

   e. indicate in detail what new plant and equipment, and modifications to existing plant and equipment, are required for the converted facility,

   f. include an estimate of financing requirements and a financial plan,

   g. provide for completion of the entire conversion process within a one- to three-year period.

2. Review the entire conversion plan or plans, and revise them where necessary, at least once every two years, until the facility is actually converted to civilian-oriented activity or is permanently closed.

3. Provide occupational retraining and reemployment counseling services for all employees to be displaced by the implementation of a conversion plan or the closing of the facility, beginning eighteen months before the date of commencement of the implementation of that plan or the permanent closing of that facility.

4. Dissolve itself and return all of its assets to the control of the management of the facility immediately upon final completion of the conversion process.

Title III. Occupational Conversion

It being understood that even the most conscientious and imaginative conversion planning efforts will produce plans whose implementation involves some degree of occupational retraining, reorientation, and/or geographic dislocation, and it being further recognized that the prime commitment of any conversion process is to the provision of productive, economically meaningful civilian-oriented work for all employees affected by the process and not merely to the successful conversion of physical facilities, the following program of occupational conversion is established. It may be utilized by any and all employees of defense-related facilities and military bases immediately upon notification of the intention to reduce military-related activity at the facility, but not more than eighteen months before the closing of the facility or before the date at which the implementation of plans for the conversion of that facility to civilian-oriented activity is to commence:

1. Job retraining

a. All managerial and technical employees who have spent more than 25 percent of their professional lifetimes working in defense-related industry or at military bases must participate in or have completed a program of professional retraining, meeting the requirements specified in the Conversion Guidelines Handbook of the National Economic Adjustment Coordinating Council, in order to be eligible for the special financial assistance, relocation aid, and special job information services provided by this Act. All other managerial and technical employees may elect to enter such a program if they so desire.

b. All other employees who require occupational retraining in order to be employable at the converted facility, or in order to facilitate their reabsorption into other civilian productive activity, will also be eligible for the retraining benefits of this Act.

c. Any individual who is required to or who elects to engage in retraining as a part of the conversion process under the provisions of this Act, shall be entitled to a grant of federal monies just sufficient, when added to all other local, state, federal, and private foundation grant funds available to that individual, to cover the full cost of any and all tuition and fees normally charged for a comparable program of training up to a maximum of $6,000 per year for a retraining period not to exceed eighteen months. No individual shall be entitled to such a grant for more than one retraining period. The institutions eligible to give such retraining shall be those listed by the Veteran's Administration.

2. Supplementary income support

a. Federal supplementary income grants, sufficient, when added to all other employer, union, and other governmental payments, to maintain the income of an eligible employee at a level equal to 90 percent of the first $30,000 per year and 50 percent of the next $10,000 per year of that employee's earnings during the last twelve months of employment preceding the first payment of the grant (a maximum reimbursement of $32,000), shall be paid to any eligible employee engaged in full-time retraining or temporarily unemployed as a result of the conversion process.

b. These payments shall continue for the duration of the period of retraining to the point of reemployment at the converted facility (or another civilian-oriented facility), or for three years, whichever is less.

c. All civilian personnel (except those managerial employees who choose not to engage in the retraining specified in this Act as a condition of their eligibility for the benefits of this Act) employed at a defense-related industrial facility or military base scheduled to implement conversion plans or close down within eighteen months are eligible for these grants while unemployed or engaged full time in a retraining program meeting the requirements specified in the Conversion Guidelines Handbook.

3. Relocation allowances

a. Any employee who finds it necessary to relocate in order to become reemployed at a civilian-oriented job which minimizes or eliminates any job downgrading or unemployment that employee would otherwise have to endure, shall be provided with a special allowance to cover the necessary and usual costs of relocation, up to a maximum of $3,000.

b. No individual shall be eligible for such allowance unless the new job location is at least fifty miles from the previous job site.

c. No individual shall be eligible for more than one conversion-related relocation allowance.

4. Maintenance of other benefits

During the period of retraining and/or unemployment related to the conversion process, up to a maximum of three years, any employee eligible for Supplementary Income Support shall also receive the following benefits:

a. vested pension credit under any applicable pension plan maintained by the facility from which that employee was displaced

b. maintenance of any hospital, surgical, medical, disability, or life (and other survivor) insurance coverage which that individual (including members of his or her family) had by reason of employment at that defense-related facility or military base.

5. Employment services

In addition to the normally available state and local employment services, all displaced employees shall have access to the special services of the Job Information Bank at the Department of Labor through the local Conversion Committee. Counseling on occupational retraining requirements of various potential job opportunities shall also be made available to all employees who become displaced as a result of the conversion process, through the offices of the local Conversion Committee or by arrangement with the state employment service.

6. Reemployment facilitation

In order to facilitate reemployment of displaced personnel and minimize the economic disruption of the process of economic adjustment, any civilian employer that signs a contractual commitment to employ a worker displaced by the conversion process, contingent upon the successful completion of a mutually agreed program of retraining, shall be entitled to a federal tax credit equal to ten percent of the employee's annual wages at the end of the first year of that individual's continuous reemployment.

All of the benefits to individual employees included under this Title shall be administered through the Employment Services of the states in which those employees reside. The National Economic Adjustment Coordinating Council shall contract with the Employment Services of the states for their performance of these administrative functions.

Title IV. Economic Adjustment Fund

There is hereby established in the Treasury of the United States a trust fund to be known as the Workers Economic Adjustment Reserve Trust Fund (referred to in this Act as "the Fund").

Every contractor producing defense material under contract to the United States government, or any other party to which the federal government permits sale of such defense materials, shall be required as an absolute condition of the contract (and/or the grant of permission) to deposit 1.25 percent per annum of the value of the gross revenue on such sales into the Fund. The same deposit requirement in the same percentage per annum of gross revenue on defense-related sales shall also apply to all contractors providing repair, maintenance, consulting, or other services to any Defense agency of the United States and/or to any party to which the federal government permits sale of such services.

The monies accumulated in the Fund shall be used for funding the various employee benefits, such as retraining scholarships, income support, and relocation allowances, provided under this Act. No part of the monies in the Fund shall be used for any other purpose.

The total amount of money in the Fund shall be available for payment of employee benefits provided under this Act for any eligible employees. In the event that the total monies in the Fund have been exhausted at any time, whatever additional money is required for provision of worker benefits under the provisions of this Act shall be drawn from the budget allocation for the Department of Defense, if not provided for by special budget appropriation to the Fund from general federal tax revenues.

Title V. Special Investment Tax Credit

A special conversion investment tax credit equal to 10 percent of the purchase price of physical capital acquired for the purposes of converting a defense-related industrial facility to efficient civilian-oriented production shall be granted to the firm implementing the conversion process at that facility. This credit is applicable only to investment in physical capital at the facility undergoing conversion and related to the creation of an efficient civilian-oriented production system at that facility. Furthermore, the amount of conversion-related investment on which the special tax credit is allowable shall be reduced by the full value of the firm's investment in physical capital purchased in the same year for any facility still being used by that firm for production of defense material or defense-related services. The special conversion investment tax credit shall be applicable only in the year of the initial purchase of the capital in question and shall be above and beyond any other investment tax credits that may be applicable to said facilities and equipment.

This tax credit shall be available only during the first twenty-four months immediately following the first payment of conversion benefits to employees at that facility.

No facility shall be eligible for this special investment tax credit for more than one two-year period.

Title VI. Authorization of Appropriations

There are authorized to be appropriated such sums as may be necessary to carry out the provisions of this Act.

Questions and Answers Concerning Key Points of the Prototype Legislation

1. Q: Why is the main planning responsibility and authority placed in the hands of a *local* conversion committee, rather than a central federal agency?

   A: Because of the huge number of major military contractors (20,000 prime contractors plus 100,000 subcontractors) and large bases (400) in the United States, an attempt to plan detailed plant and base conversions, or to evaluate conversion plans, from a centralized office is almost certain to be extremely expensive—as well as ineffective. To be workable, each conversion plan must be tailored to the specifics of the facility for which it is made. This requires the sort of detailed knowledge of labor force and capital equipment, plant site advantages and disadvantages, and even economic characteristics of the surrounding community, that is most effectively obtained by those who know the facility and area best—those who work and live there.

In addition, the employees, local management, and local community people have the greatest vested interest in making sure the conversion plan will work if put into effect. They clearly have far more to lose from its failure (or gain from its success) than any distant planning expert, no matter how well intentioned. Finally, if the local committees feel the need for expert technical assistance in their planning, they have full authority to hire consultants from the planning funds they are given.

2. Q: Why a three-part local committee? Why not leave the planning up to the management?

   A: The purpose of a tripartite structure is to bring together all three interested parties in a setting that prevents any one of them from roadblocking. It is clear that though labor, management, and the community all have a major stake in contributing to the planning process, they each have a different point of view and different particular interests. There is real value in the interactive process that will result from the conversion committee's mandate to produce a single, unified plan.

3. Q: What assurance is there that the plans will be well done and workable?

   A: There is no way to guarantee that the plans will work, but giving the people most affected by the success or failure of the plan the responsibility and authority for drawing it up makes it highly likely that it will be done seriously and well. Self-interest is a powerful motivator. Direct federal oversight, evaluation, and certification of plans is simply unworkable, for reasons discussed earlier under the question of local versus central planning. And it is not clear that such oversight would improve plan quality.

4. Q: Why isn't the Department of Defense at the head of the national council?

   A: The organizational mandate of the Department of Defense is to deal with military problems. Conversion is not a military problem—it is an economic, business, and labor problem, and such problems do not properly fall within the purview of the Defense Department, but rather within that of federal agencies such as the Departments of Commerce and Labor.

5. Q: What if a facility can't be converted?

   A: It will probably be an extremely rare event that no feasible contributive alternative can be found for a given military facility. What is more likely, in fact nearly certain, is that some types of workers employed at any given military facility will not be employed at an efficient contributive version of that facility. This is particularly true of engineers and scientists who are present in military industry firms in concentrations far greater than is consistent with any contributive alternative. But that is precisely why this bill provides for a people-oriented rather than a facility-oriented conversion process. Provisions are made for relocation aid, job placement assistance, retraining, etc., so that all civilian employees of the military facility are assisted in their personal job conversion, whether or not they will be employable at the converted facility. Note, though, that the conversion committees are instructed to develop a plan which minimizes this kind of relocation (within the context of efficient contributive operation).

6. Q: Where will the new markets for the products of converted facilities come from?

   A: The National Council is empowered to direct each civilian department of the federal government to draw up a ranked list of specific projects they would fund if they received additional monies as a result of changed federal budget priorities. These lists are made into a master list of contributive government funding priorities (which could also include tax cuts and funds to be returned to state and local governments) that would be made available to the conversion committees. Because these lists are in order of priority, the committees would have a clear idea of what markets are likely to come into being when money is shifted from the military, and hence could build at least part of their plan around these potential markets.

7. Q: What is to prevent all the conversion committees from planning for the *same* civilian products, unless there is some sort of central plan coordination?

   A. There is no unique product to which the attention of any given facility can be turned. It is nearly always possible to come up with a number of different products, serving different markets, that are viable alternatives. Such diversified planning will be encouraged by the guidelines in the handbook prepared by the National Council. If each conversion committee develops multiple plans, the likelihood that a large number of facilities converting at once would all choose the same product from their planned options is remote. As some facilities convert, they may saturate a particular product area; but since planning is an ongoing process, that would only mean that the committees at unconverted facilities would drop that product from their own plans.

8. Q: Wouldn't such a bill generate a huge new government bureaucracy?

   A: At the federal level, a statutory maximum of fifteen new staff people would be hired. Maximum use is made of existing state agencies to administer worker adjustment benefits, so as to avoid generating bureaucracy. Decentralized planning will also eliminate the need for a large new government apparatus. The bill is strongly oriented to minimizing central government administration.

Notes

1. The Appearance of Progress, the Reality of Decline

1. *Economic Report of the President (February 1985)* (Washington, D.C.: Government Printing Office, 1985), app. B, table B–2, p. 235.

2. Ibid., year-to-year changes in the consumer price index for all items, app. B, table B–56, p. 296.

3. Ibid., app. B, table B–33, p. 271.

4. Ibid., app. B, table B–104, p. 351.

5. R. Pear, "Rate of Poverty Found to Persist in Face of Gains," *New York Times*, 3 Aug. 1984.

6. R. Pear, "U.S. Poverty Rate Dropped to 14.4% in '84, Bureau Says," *New York Times*, 28 Aug. 1985.

7. "Doctors Find Hunger Is Epidemic in U.S.," *New York Times*, 27 Feb. 1985.

8. *Economic Report of the President (February 1985)*, app. B, table B–41, p. 279.

9. From Federal Deposit Insurance Corporation data supplied by S. Welch of the Statistical Division of the Federal Reserve Bank of Dallas (13 Mar. 1985 and 15 Oct. 1985).

10. *Economic Report of the President (February 1985)*, app. B, table B–79, p. 325.

11. A. Malabre, Jr., "Whither the Deficit When Recession Arrives," *Wall Street Journal*, 20 Sept. 1985.

12. R. Pear, "Reagan Has Achieved Many Goals, But Some Stir Opposition," *New York Times*, 20 Aug. 1984.

13. Remarks of E. G. Corrigan, president of the Federal Reserve Bank of New York, before the American Bankers' Association's chief financial officers' forum, 18 Sept. 1985.

14. Ibid.

15. *Economic Report of the President (February 1985)*, app. B. Prime interest rates charged by banks from table B–66, p. 310; year-to-year changes in the consumer price index for all items from table B–56, p. 296. The real interest rate is calculated by subtracting the latter from the former.

16. B. Franklin, "Foreclosures on Homes Rise as Inflation Falls," *New York Times*, 18 Feb. 1985.

17. Ibid.

18. "The Outlook: Despite Tax Breaks Americans Won't Save," *Wall Street Journal*, 8 Oct. 1984.

19. *Economic Report of the President (February 1985)*, app. B. Data on foreign holdings of U.S. Treasury securities are from table B–102, p. 349; data on total U.S. Treasury securities outstanding are from table B–79, p. 325.

20. L. Silk, "Foreign Funds Help on Deficit," *New York Times*, 14 Sept. 1984.

21. F. Bleakley, "The Eurodollar Bond 'Mess': Many Issues Go Begging," *New York Times*, 14 Feb. 1985.

22. Ibid.

23. *Economic Report of the President (February 1985)*, app. B, calculated from table B–102, p. 349.

24. P. Kilborn, "U.S. Nears Status of Debtor Nation," *New York Times*, 20 Feb. 1984.

25. J. D. Robinson, "Superdollars and Superdebt," *New York Times*, 16 May 1985.

26. *Economic Report of the President (February 1985)*, app. B, table B–101, p. 348.

27. P. Samuelson and R. Solow, "Analytical Aspects of Anti-inflation Policy," *American Economic Review* (May 1960), pp. 177–94.

28. *Economic Report of the President (February 1985)*. The unemployment rate (from table B–33, p. 271) used here is for all civilian workers; inflation rate (from table B–56, p. 296) is the year-to-year change in the consumer price index for all items.

29. For example, labor productivity typically rises during the expansionary phase of the business cycle as output grows faster than employment. Businesses ordinarily do not hire additional workers until they become convinced that rising demand for their products will continue. The opposite occurs during periods of contraction. None of this, however, reflects any real or necessary change in the fundamental efficiency with which these businesses are capable of producing.

30. There are a variety of specific ways of calculating the trade balance, and they do not yield precisely the same results. Nevertheless, the basic pat-

terns described are not greatly affected (though many detailed, particular comparisons would be). The source of data for continually positive balance of trade from 1894 to 1970 is Department of Commerce, Bureau of the Census, *Historical Statistics of the United States: Colonial Times to 1970* (Washington, D.C.: Government Printing Office, 1975), Series U–187–200, pp. 884–85. The source of data for the period 1971–84 is *Economic Report of the President (February 1985)*, app. B, table B–101, p. 348. In the latter source, the trade balance definition used was "exports-imports, c.i.f." (cost, insurance, and freight), since only the data given under that definition were consistently presented for the entire 1971–84 period.

31. Ibid.

32. S. Melman, *Profits Without Production* (New York: Knopf, 1983), p. 38.

33. Ibid.

34. Department of Labor, Bureau of Labor Statistics, unpublished data prepared April 1982; cited in Melman, *Profits Without Production*, p. 309.

35. P. Choate and S. Walter, *America in Ruins: Beyond the Public Pork Barrel* (Washington, D.C.: Council of State Planning Agencies, 1981), p. 1.

36. J. Herbers, "Alarm Rises over Decay in U.S. Public Works," *New York Times*, 18 July 1982.

37. "The Decaying of America: Our Bridges, Roads, and Water Systems Are Rapidly Falling Apart," *Newsweek*, 2 Aug. 1982, pp. 12–18.

38. J. Wilson, "America's High-Tech Crisis: Why Silicon Valley Is Losing Its Edge," *Business Week*, 11 Mar. 1985, pp. 56–67.

39. Ibid.

40. See, for example, B. Bluestone and B. Harrison, *The Deindustrialization of America: Plant Closings, Community Abandonment, and the Dismantling of Basic Industry* (New York: Basic Books, 1982).

41. Wilson, "America's High-Tech Crisis," p. 59.

42. Ibid., p. 60.

43. J. Holusha, "Toyota Calls Tune in Its GM Venture," *New York Times*, 30 Jan. 1985.

44. D. Cuff, "Tennessee's Pitch to Japan," *New York Times*, 27 Feb. 1985.

45. M. McAdam, "The Growing Role of the Service Sector in the U.S. Economy," in *1985 U.S. Industrial Outlook* (Washington, D.C.: Department of Commerce, 1985), pp. 38–41.

46. Department of Commerce, Bureau of the Census, *Statistical Abstract of the United States, 1985* (Washington, D.C.: Government Printing Office, 1984), table 694, p. 417.

47. K. Young and A. Lawson, "Where Did All the New Jobs Come From?" in *1985 U.S. Industrial Outlook*, p. 32.

48. M. McAdam, "The Growing Role."

2. The Macroeconomic Problem

1. The natural rate of unemployment is defined as the rate that would prevail in free, competitive labor markets—labor markets without government intervention and without other restrictions, such as those imposed by labor unions.

2. For a more detailed discussion of the new classical economics, comparing it to Keynesian and mainstream monetarist approaches, see J. L. Stein, *Monetarist, Keynesian, and New Classical Economics* (New York: New York University Press, 1984).

3. For a far more detailed discussion of the Keynesian-monetarist controversy see F. C. Wykoff, *Macroeconomics: Theory, Evidence, and Policy* (Englewood Cliffs: Prentice-Hall, 1976), chaps. 15, 16, 17. See also J. Prager, ed., *Monetary Economics* (New York: Random House, 1971), part 5; and H. J. Sherman and G. R. Evans, *Macroeconomics: Keynesian, Monetarist, and Marxist Views* (New York: Harper & Row, 1984).

4. M. Friedman, *A Program for Monetary Stability* (New York: Fordham University Press, 1960).

5. "Rational" behavior is here defined as that which moves us toward the objectives that motivate us, and "irrational" behavior as that which moves us away from our goals.

3. Rethinking Basic Economic Concepts

1. Some of the most creative and interesting work in this area is being done by Robert A. Karasek. His works include "Job Socialization: A Longitudinal Study of Work, Political, and Leisure Activity in Sweden" (paper presented at the Ninth World Congress of Sociology, Uppsala, Sweden, 15 Aug. 1978); "Job Demands, Job Decision Latitude, and Mental Strain: Implications for Job Redesign," *Administrative Science Quarterly* 24 (June 1979), pp. 285–308; and (with coauthors K. P. Triantis and S. Chaudhry) "Coworker and Supervisor Support as Moderators of Associations Between Task Characteristics and Mental Strain," *Journal of Occupational Behavior* 3 (1982), pp. 1–20.

2. For an interesting analysis concerning the nature of the work process and its effects on the worker see J. Yudkin, "The Viability of Craft in Advanced Industrial Society" (Ph.D. diss., Stanford University, 1986).

3. As anthropologist Marshall Sahlins of the University of Michigan has pointed out, "By common understanding an affluent society is one in which all the peoples' wants are easily satisfied. . . . [W]ants are 'easily satisfied' either by producing much or desiring little, and there are accordingly two roads to affluence" ("Notes on the Original Affluent Society," in R. Lee and

I. Devore, eds., *Man the Hunter* [New York: Aldine Publishing Company, 1968], p. 85).

4. While this is true in general, it is not true that the nature of the process by which the worker creates a product never has any effect on the value of the finished good. We are often willing to pay more for craft products, and we often prize them more highly, because of the skill that the worker incorporates into the good. This is true even if the good, viewed more objectively, has similar characteristics to one produced by a less personal process. See Yudkin, "The Viability of Craft."

5. There is a serious point behind this seemingly less than serious remark. Economists typically view the structure of utility patterns as exogenous—another example of the tendency to treat people as less than full human beings. Every aspect of the behavior of human beings, economic and otherwise, importantly influences and is influenced by all other major aspects of their behavior and experience. While some compartmentalization is useful in understanding human behavior, excessive compartmentalizing can produce a tunnel vision that is counterproductive (and sometimes even dangerous) in the making of social policy. When trying to solve real human problems, we should never be bound by the confines of any one traditional discipline. After all, people are neither merely economic beings, nor biological, nor sociological, nor psychological, nor political—but complex beings that combine all of these aspects and more. That's what makes us so intriguing.

6. C. W. Mills, *The Causes of World War Three* (New York: Ballantine Books, 1960), pp. 93–94.

7. An interesting analysis of the relationship (or lack of relationship) between material goods and human satisfaction is contained in economist Tibor Scitovsky's *The Joyless Economy: An Inquiry into Human Satisfaction and Consumer Dissatisfaction* (New York: Oxford University Press, 1976).

8. In fact, chapter 1 of the first book of Adam Smith's epic work *The Wealth of Nations*, originally published in 1776, is titled "Of the Division of Labour."

9. The late-nineteenth-century and early-twentieth-century studies along these lines by Frederick W. Taylor and Frank B. Gilbreth were fundamental to the development of the field of industrial engineering in general and to time and motion study in particular. Time and motion study slowly gave rise to the modern field of human factors engineering.

10. The importance of—and possibilities for—incorporating at least some of these effects into more realistic aggregate measures of output has not been entirely ignored. See W. Nordhaus and J. Tobin, "Is Growth Obsolete?" in *National Bureau of Economic Research, Fiftieth Anniversary Colloquium V* (New York: Columbia University Press, 1972), discussed

briefly in P. Samuelson, *Economics* (New York: McGraw-Hill, 1980), 11th ed., pp. 183–85. See also P. Barkley and D. Seckler, *Economic Growth and Environmental Decay* (New York: Harcourt Brace Jovanovich, 1972), pp. 36–47. On the other hand, these and other similar discussions have yet to have a noticeable effect on major collectors and publishers of aggregate economic data, or on the way such data are used by economists, business people, and politicians.

11. This is not meant to imply that all changes in workplace design that increase physical output efficiency have negative effects on the work force: that is certainly not true. In fact, much of what makes work more interesting, creative, and enjoyable may also raise the physical output per worker as well, both through its direct effects and through its indirect impact on worker morale and loyalty. Similarly, procedures that reduce environmental pollution may also increase production efficiency—for example, burning fuel more efficiently tends to reduce both the costs of production and the levels of pollution generated. So does finding uses for previously discarded wastes.

4. Contributive, Neutral, and Distractive Activity: The Fundamentals of Resource Use

1. In other words, an activity cannot be contributive unless it has a positive marginal product. This leads quite naturally to the proposition that the magnitude of the marginal product of an activity may be at least a rough measure of its contributiveness (assuming that the process it is a part of is contributive).

2. These concepts are discussed in R. Nurkse, *Problems of Capital Formation in Underdeveloped Countries* (Oxford: Oxford University Press, 1953); and J. Viner, "Some Reflections on the Concept of 'Disguised Unemployment'" in *Contribuicões a Analise do Desenvolvimento Economico* (Rio de Janeiro: Livraria Agin Editora, 1957).

3. Calculated from data appearing in R. L. Sivard, *World Military and Social Expenditures, 1983* (Washington, D.C.: World Priorities, 1983), pp. 6, 32.

4. Ibid., 1983 and earlier annuals.

5. Beginning with Seymour Melman's *Dynamic Factors in Industrial Productivity* (New York: John Wiley, 1956), and continuing with a series of Ph.D. dissertations completed at the Department of Industrial and Management Engineering, Columbia University, considerable empirical analysis casts serious doubt on the existence of a direct relationship between production-related administrative activity and productivity enhancement. The works in the Columbia series include A. Dogramaci, *Administrative Overhead and Industrial Performance under State Managerialism* (1975); N. M. Fraiman,

Growth of Administrative Employment and Output in the U.S. Steel Industry (1977); and T. O. Boucher, *Productivity and Industry Structure* (1978).

6. A. Smith, *The Wealth of Nations* (New York: Random House, 1937), p. 314.

7. Ibid., p. 315.

8. Ibid., pp. 325–26.

9. Ibid., pp. 315, 325.

10. It is by no means a foregone conclusion that defense against either external military attack or internal coup d'état cannot be achieved—perhaps more effectively achieved—by nonviolent means. For that matter, deterrence may also be achievable by nonviolent methods. It is an idea worth pondering. See G. Sharp, *Social Power and Political Freedom* (Boston: Porter Sargent, 1980).

11. T. C. Smith, "Arms Race Instability and War," *Journal of Conflict Resolution* 24 (June 1980), pp. 253–84. Analysis of twenty-four international arms races that had ended revealed that only one ended in a lasting peace without war (Norway vs. Sweden, 1895–1905).

12. H. H. Gerth and C. W. Mills, eds., *From Max Weber: Essays in Sociology* (New York: Oxford University Press, 1946).

13. The reduction in unit cost will, of course, be absolute only if all input costs do not escalate compensatingly; but it will in any case be relative to what unit costs would have been in the absence of productivity growth.

14. C. N. Parkinson, *Parkinson's Law, or the Pursuit of Progress* (London: John Murray, 1958).

15. Cf. note 5.

16. Quoted in I. Robertson, *Sociology* (New York: Worth Publishers, 1981), p. 474, legend of fig. 18.3.

17. Ibid., p. 474.

18. The time and effort expended in search is inversely dependent on the frequency of purchase of a good, since marketplace knowledge obsolesces. It is directly dependent on the size of the expenditure involved, since the marginal benefit of search, in terms of possible savings, is typically greater for expensive than for inexpensive goods, at any level of search, while the marginal cost will be similar. Reducing the frequency of purchase of expensive consumer durables is thus especially beneficial in terms of reducing the costs of search.

5. Breaking Down Capital and Labor

1. See, for example, P. Blumberg, *Industrial Democracy* (New York: Schocken Books, 1969); Organization for Economic Co-Operation and Development, *Worker Participation* (Paris: OECD, 1976); D. Zwerdling,

Workplace Democracy (New York: Harper & Row, 1978); J. Simmons and W. Mares, *Working Together: Employee Participation in Action* (New York: New York University Press, 1985).

2. Cf. M. H. Halperin, *Bureaucratic Politics and Foreign Policy* (Washington, D.C.: Brookings Institute, 1974), pp. 235–79.

3. J. Thomson, "How Could Vietnam Happen?" *Atlantic Monthly* 221 (Apr. 1968), pp. 47–53; D. Halberstam, *The Best and the Brightest* (New York: Random House, 1972).

4. A. Schlesinger, *The Imperial Presidency* (Boston: Houghton-Mifflin, 1973).

5. C. Argyris, "Single Loop and Double Loop Models in Research on Decision Making," *Administrative Science Quarterly* 21 (Sept. 1976), p. 366.

6. Technicians are individuals with skills useful in the technological development process but with much less concomitant understanding of and training in the scientific and engineering disciplines (e.g., lab technicians).

7. For an interesting study of the sources of nineteenth- and twentieth-century invention, including the role of the single inventor, see J. Jewkes, D. Sawers, and R. Stillerman, *The Sources of Invention* (New York: Norton, 1969).

8. For example, much of the early technology for artificially induced, sustainable chain reactions was a product of the Manhattan Project. This enormous government program resulted directly in the development of the atomic bomb and indirectly provided much basic knowledge of nuclear physics and its applications—thereby giving birth to the nuclear power industry.

6. The Impact of Noncontributive Activity on Productive Competence

1. Jewkes, *The Sources of Invention*, makes this clear.

2. The usual assumption that the transformation curve is concave to the origin is sufficient to guarantee that the opportunity costs of shifting production from one category of goods to another will increase at the margin the greater the magnitude of the shift. Using only contributive goods as arguments in the transformation function and allowing noncontributive activity to enter the function as a shift parameter thus shows heightened resource diversion by an inward shift of the transformation curve.

3. For example, Edward F. Denison's recent work *Accounting for Slower Economic Growth* (Washington: Brookings Institute, 1979) includes an estimate that nearly 54 percent of the increase between 1948 and 1973 in adjusted national income per person employed in the United States was due to the advance of knowledge.

4. D. D. Dudley, *Holography: A Survey* (Washington, D.C.: Government Printing Office, 1973), pp. 3–4.

5. In other words, the critical diversion threshold with respect to the question of reversibility is more likely to be an interactive function of both the magnitude and duration of the diversion than a function of the duration alone. Yet this function may not be continuous in both variables. Instead, the function itself may be subject to an internal switching effect in which the duration variable may be irrelevant until the magnitude variable exceeds a primary threshold.

7. Productive Competence, Unemployment, and Inflation

1. There were, of course, a number of wars fought by the United States during this period, including the Korean War and the war that was undoubtedly the country's most divisive conflict in this century: Vietnam. But neither these conflicts nor any of the other American military involvements of this period were the result of an official Congressional declaration of war, as required by the U.S. Constitution. It is in this sense that the period was one of official peacetime.

2. It is important to note that the United States had also managed to virtually avoid any significant domestic war damage. Aside from the tragedy of the death of about 400,000 American soldiers and the serious debilitation of thousands more, very little of the resource base of the U.S. economy had been destroyed. In contrast, nearly half of the 52,000,000 people killed during World War II in other affected countries were civilians, killed as their countries became theaters of combat. Every major industrial economy in the world except the U.S. economy suffered serious damage, if not devastation, in that war.

3. "Attention" is one of the critical resources whose scarcity is often overlooked by economists. Yet it is certainly true that people—whether managers, entrepreneurs, or simply individuals making personal decisions—cannot pay attention to all relevant factors at once. Furthermore, uncertainty and lack of information make it unrealistic to assume that people will always pay attention to the subset of relevant factors that has the greatest significance to the decision they are making.

4. The United Nations, for example, has compiled a list of development indicators, with twelve major list categories and seventy-three separate indicators (D. V. McGranahan et al., *Contents and Measurement of Socioeconomic Development: An Empirical Enquiry*, United Nations Research Institute for Social Development Report no. 70.10 [Geneva: UN, 1970]). See also United Nations Conference on Trade and Development Secretariat, *The Measurement of Development Effort* (New York: UN, 1970).

8. The Economics of Transition

1. President's Economic Adjustment Committee, Office of Economic Adjustment, *1961–1981, 20 Years of Civilian Reuse: Summary of Completed Military Base Economic Adjustment Projects* (Washington, D.C.: The Pentagon, 1981).

2. J. Herbers, "Cities Find Conversion of Old Military Bases a Boon to Economies," *New York Times*, 26 Apr. 1979.

3. D. Gelman with B. Gangelhoff, "Teenage Suicide in the Sun Belt," *Newsweek*, 15 Aug. 1983, p. 72.

4. The term *social-emotional unit* is meant to be broader than the term *family*, and may be more appropriate for the problem at hand. A social-emotional unit is a group of two or more people with close social and emotional ties to one another. It therefore may include not only traditional nuclear and extended families, but also live-together families of various composition, as well as people who do not live together and are not genetically related but who are close friends.

5. Scitovsky's *The Joyless Economy* argues against the neoclassical microeconomic assumption that the level of consumer utility is tied to the level of real income alone. Rather, the level of utility is sensitive to increases in real income to the extent that material goods providing "comfort" are our point of focus.

6. There are a number of cases for which this has been true, for example, the problem of energy use, particularly in the United States, as I discussed in my earlier book *The Conservation Response: Strategies for the Design and Operation of Energy Using Systems* (Lexington, Mass.: D. C. Heath, 1976).

7. A. Toffler, *Future Shock* (New York: Random House, 1970).

8. For interesting analyses of participatory decision making applied to the workplace, see J. Witte, *Democracy, Authority, and Alienation in Work: Worker's Participation in an American Corporation* (Chicago: University of Chicago Press, 1980), and J. Simmon and W. Mares, *Working Together*.

9. This hypothesis was substantiated by a brief and simple analysis I performed of a small sample of labor management conflicts selected from the rather bloody history of the early labor movement in the United States, "Civil Violence in U.S. Labor Disputes, 1885–1940" (unpublished).

9. The Theory of Resource Diversion

1. This raises the issue of how labor and capital resources are allocated to particular subcategories in the first place. One general theoretical view would be that "raw labor" is processed through a "skilling function" and distributed among the various labor subcategories in accordance with parameters assumed to be exogenously determined. These parameters could poten-

tially be constrained so as to allow for the uneven distribution of various types of manual and intellectual capabilities, as well as varying predispositions and predilections for various types of labor. An essentially similar theoretical view could be taken with respect to capital. However, it is perhaps as easy, and somewhat more realistic, to treat each subcategory of capital like any other contributive good.

2. The question arises of whether the externalities generated by the neutral and distractive sectors should also be included in SMP. This is a complicated issue that will not be addressed here. These externalities have been excluded because the SMP concept is intended to focus attention on measuring the output of activity directed toward the enhancement of the material standard of living. It is judged that including these other externalities would only muddy the waters.

3. If distractive-sector investment demand were sufficiently high prior to the stimulation to bottle up much of the capacity of key capital goods industries, attempts at stimulating contributive-sector demand would largely be frustrated on the supply side in the short run. Given the long gestation period for such capital, previously signed contracts could not be adjusted quickly; capital goods prices for orders in the queue thus could not be driven up. Consequently, it might be impossible in the short run to stimulate a sufficient dollar volume of increased contributive investment—even considering all multiplier effects—to raise aggregate contributive demand enough to get rid of contributive-sector unemployment. This could well be true despite the existence of current levels of contributive investment demand that are inadequate in both the short- and long-term senses.

4. It is actually irrelevant whether their assessment of the need for such distractive expenditure is correct or not—it is sufficient that they perceive such a need and are able to persuade enough additional people to adopt their view.

5. In a series of papers, I have argued that the arms race in general and the nuclear arms race in particular have long since entered this stage. On military and technical grounds (setting aside economic, moral, political, and other considerations), beyond some point, more armaments lead to reduced national security. See "National Insecurity in the Nuclear Age," *Bulletin of the Atomic Scientists* 32 (May 1976), pp. 24–35; "Human Fallibility and Weapons," *Bulletin of the Atomic Scientists* 36 (Nov. 1980), pp. 15–20; and "Armament, Disarmament, and National Security: A Theoretical Duopoly Model of the Arms Race," *Journal of Economic Studies* 6 (May 1979), pp. 1–38.

6. At least, this is the case if we wish to avoid moving toward the dehumanized horror of the "efficient" society caricatured in Aldous Huxley's *Brave New World* (New York: Harper, 1939).

7. J. H. Holloman and A. E. Harger, "America's Technical Dilemma,"

Technology Review 74 (July-Aug. 1971), pp. 32–41; also H. Folk, *The Shortage of Scientists and Engineers* (Lexington, Mass.: D. C. Heath, 1970).

8. Whether or not this is appropriate is a different question, which is put aside here.

9. For example, some years ago medical researchers were able to isolate a substance known in lay terms as "the clotting factor" for the effective treatment of people afflicted by hemophilia, the "bleeders' disease." To date, no one has discovered a way to produce this substance at a sufficiently low cost for the treatment to be economically feasible for most hemophiliacs. The treatment of those afflicted by this dangerous genetic disease has largely been restricted to people rich enough to be able to afford it, and the majority of hemophiliacs remain without access to this life-saving substance.

10. This closely parallels the argument made earlier with respect to technologists and the possible distortion of the institutions that produce them.

11. In the past decade or so, much has been said about the outward shift of the Phillips curve in the United States, as though that were an explanation of the stagflation phenomenon. But unless a coherent elaboration of the causal mechanism underlying this shift is given, the statement that the Phillips curve is shifting outward is merely a description and not an explanation. The long-term effect of resource diversion on productive competence is one plausible candidate for the missing causal linkage.

12. For example, in the 1982 Falklands-Malvinas War between Britain and Argentina, U.S., French, and British weapons were used by the Argentinians.

10. The Theory of Resource Diversion: A More Technical Look

1. Distributional issues are set aside. This should not be interpreted as a judgment that they are unimportant; it reflects only the understanding that questions of distribution can be separated in concept from the issue of maximizing the gross material standard of living generated by the economy as a whole.

2. Advance in technology is not inconsistent with maintenance of productive competence, since improvements in technical knowledge could easily be of a sort that would allow maintenance of productive competence with a lower *mri* than would exist in the absence of technological progress.

3. One way *mpc*s could plausibly differ is if incomes in one of the sectors were systematically higher than in the other. If, for example, distractive salaries were higher (say owing to more lavish spending policies in general by distractive firms), it is reasonable to expect that the *mpc*s associated with income derived from that sector would be lower. If so, an increase in non-

deficit spending on distractive goods would result in a lowered demand for contributive goods.

4. See P. Cagan, "The Monetary Dynamics of Hyperinflations," in M. Friedman, ed., *Studies in the Quantity Theory of Money* (Chicago: University of Chicago Press, 1956).

5. For example, the Nazi party's ascent to power in Germany was undoubtedly aided by the economic chaos created by the post–World War I hyperinflation in that country.

11. Applying the Theory of Resource Diversion

1. See n. 5, chap. 4.

2. Department of Commerce, Bureau of the Census, *Statistical Abstract of the United States, 1985* (Washington, D.C.: Government Printing Office, 1984), and various earlier issues.

3. National Science Foundation, *Federal Funds for Research and Development* (Washington, D.C.: Government Printing Office, 1981), p. 11, plus data drawn from table 3, this text (p. 210).

4. National Science Foundation, Surveys of Science Resources Series, *Characteristics of the National Sample of Scientists and Engineers: 1974* (Washington, D.C.: Government Printing Office, 1976), part 2, table B–16, pp. 128–42.

5. Ibid., table B–15, pp. 113–27.

6. Department of Defense, *Defense Economic Impact Modeling System, Occupation of Industry Model*, table 3, Estimates of Industrial Employment by Occupation (Engineers and Scientists) December 23, 1981.

7. Telephone conversation with David Blond, Senior Economist, Office of the Secretary of Defense, 10 Feb. 1983.

8. L. J. Dumas, "University Research, Industrial Innovation, and the Pentagon," in J. Tirman, ed., *The Militarization of High Technology* (Cambridge, Mass.: Ballinger Publishing, 1984), table 7–5, p. 142.

9. National Science Foundation, *National Patterns of Science and Technology Resources, 1981* (Washington, D.C.: Government Printing Office, 1981), p. 14.

10. Hollomon and Harger, "America's Technological Dilemma," p. 36; see also Folk, *Shortage of Scientists*.

11. Calculated from unpublished National Science Foundation data cited in President's Commission on Industrial Competitiveness, *Global Competition: The New Reality* (Washington, D.C.: Government Printing Office, 1985), vol. 1, p. 21.

12. Ibid., p. 20.

13. S. Ramo, *America's Technology Slip* (New York: Wiley & Sons, 1980), p. 251.

14. National Academy of Engineering, Committee on Technology Transfer and Utilization, *Technology Transfer and Utilization, Recommendations for Reducing the Emphasis and Correcting the Imbalance* (Washington, D.C.: National Academy, 1974), p. i.

15. National Science Foundation, National Science Board, *Science Indicators, 1974* (Washington, D.C.: Government Printing Office, 1975), p. 17.

16. Ibid., p. 19.

17. National Science Foundation, *Report of the National Science Board: 1979; Science Indicators, 1978* (Washington, D.C.: Government Printing Office, 1979), pp. 20, 21.

18. Ibid., pp. 19, 20.

19. Ibid., pp. 146, 174.

20. *Business Week*, "The Breakdown of U.S. Innovation," 16 Feb. 1976, pp. 56–68, and "Vanishing Innovation," 3 July 1978, pp. 46–54.

21. President's Commission, *Global Competition*, p. 19.

22. Ramo, *America's Technology Slip*, p. 251.

23. Department of Defense, Directorate for Information, Operations, and Reports, Washington Headquarters Services, *Department of Defense Real and Personal Property* (Washington, D.C.: DOD, 1983), p. 7.

24. Department of Commerce, *Statistical Abstract of the United States, 1985*, table 1350, p. 758.

25. Department of Commerce, *Statistical Abstract of the United States, 1985*, table 1350, p. 758.

26. *American Machinist*, Oct. 1973, p. 143.

27. "13th American Machinist Inventory of Metal Working Equipment," *American Machinist*, Nov. 1983, pp. 113, 115, 117.

28. National Machine Tool Builders Association, *Economic Handbook of the Machine Tool Industry, 1980–81*, p. 250.

29. J. Pollack, "Our Unsafe Bridges," *Parade*, 28 Feb. 1982, p. 4.

30. Choate and Walter, *America in Ruins*, p. 1.

31. Cited in J. Walsh, "Productivity Problems Trouble Economy," *Science*, 19 Oct. 1979, pp. 310–11.

32. Ibid.

33. E. F. Denison, *Accounting for Slower Economic Growth* (Washington, D.C.: Brookings Institution, 1979), p. 4.

34. B. Y. Hong, *Inflation under Cost Pass-Along Management* (New York: Praeger, 1979).

35. P. Choate, *Statement of Pat Choate, Director of Policy Analysis, TRW, Inc., Before the Subcommittee on Economic Stabilization of the Committee on Banking, Finance, and Urban Affairs.* 99th Cong., 1st sess., 1985. Committee Print.

36. Ibid., p. 2.

37. President's Commission, *Global Competition*, pp. 6–7.

38. Ibid., pp. 1, 5.

39. J. Burns, "Soviet Study Urges Relaxing of Controls to Revive Economy," *New York Times*, 5 Aug. 1983.

40. S. Mydans, "Gorbachev Faults Economic Record," *New York Times*, 9 Apr. 1985.

41. "Excerpts from Soviet Study on the Need for an Overhaul of the Economy," *New York Times*, 5 Aug. 1983.

42. Calculated from data in Sivard, *World Expenditures 1983*, p. 32.

43. Ibid.

44. Ibid.

45. The consumer price index (all items) is from *Economic Report of the President (February 1985)*, app. B, table B–52, p. 291.

46. Sivard, *World Expenditures 1983*, p. 24.

47. This is true for the Third World as a whole. But whether each nation could have financed the repayment of its own debt from this source depends on the distribution of military spending relative to the distribution of debt.

48. Sivard, *World Expenditures 1976*, p. 19.

49. Sivard, *World Expenditures 1983*, pp. 19–20.

12. Designing a Program for Economic Revitalization

1. Little would be gained by carrying out these analyses beyond the level of detail of the four-digit Standard Industrial Classification industry category or, geographically, beyond the county level. It is not even crucial that this group of analyses be carried out to that degree of detail.

2. For an analysis of why incentive formulas designed into military contracts rarely are effective in reducing cost escalation, see L. J. Dumas, "Payment Functions and the Production Efficiency of Military-Industrial Firms," *Journal of Economic Issues* 10 (June 1976), 454–74.

Index